"In clinical, forensic, and correctional contexts, conscious and unconscious attempts at deception plague the psychologist's professional services. With an abundance of research-based citations pertaining to detecting deception, the authors provide a scholarly analysis and description of behavioral cues, interviewing strategies, tests (e.g., the MMPI-2), other available measures, neurocognitive dysfunction, hypnosis, polygraphy, malingering and dissimulation (e.g., with children and adolescents), and psychopathy. This book provides the practitioner with important insights, and is an excellent text for courses relevant to assessment and diagnosis; treatment, forensic, and correctional planning; and legal aspects of psychology. Rather than blindly accept information offered by clients, modern practitioners must assiduously seek to unmask what is reported and obtain reliable and valid empirically-based information."

Robert H. Woody, PhD, ScD, JD, ABPP (Clinical and Forensic),
Professor of Psychology, University of Nebraska at Omaha

"*Detection of Deception* is a valuable resource for any mental-health professional, especially those who conduct clinical or forensic evaluations."

Gregory DeClue, PhD, ABPP (Forensic), Private Practice,
Sarasota, Florida; Author of *Interrogations and Disputed Confessions: A Manual for Forensic Psychological Practice*

D1209093

DETECTION OF DECEPTION

Amy R. Boyd

Alix M. McLearen

Robert G. Meyer

Robert L. Denney

Professional Resource Press
Sarasota, Florida

Published by
Professional Resource Press
(An imprint of Professional Resource Exchange, Inc.)
Post Office Box 15560
Sarasota, FL 34277-1560

This publication is sold with the understanding that the publisher is not engaged in rendering professional services. If legal, psychological, medical, accounting, or other expert advice or assistance is sought or required, the reader should seek the services of a competent professional.

The copy editor for this book was Vicki Kennedy, the managing editor was Debbie Fink, the production coordinator was Laurie Girsch, the text designer was Richard Sullivan, and the cover designer was Stacey Sanders.

Opinions expressed in this work are those of the authors and do not necessarily represent opinions of the Federal Bureau of Prisons, Department of Justice, or other institution with which the authors are affiliated.

Library of Congress Cataloging-in-Publication Data

Detection of deception / Amy R. Boyd . . . [et al.].
    p. cm.
    Includes bibliographical references and index.
    ISBN: 1-56887-099-X
    1. Deception--Psychological aspects. 2. Truthfulness and falsehood--Psychological aspects. I. Boyd, Amy R., date.

BF637.D42D48 2007
155.9'2--dc22

2006044761

ISBN-13: 978-1-56887-099-1
ISBN-10: 1-56887-099-X

DEDICATION

*For Jackson and Landon, may you always seek the truth.
And for Ben, who always helps me find it.*

— ARB

*For Bernice and Milton, and for my husband, parents,
and brother.*

— AMM

*For Sean, Chris, Eli, Evan, Eric, Niklas, Anna, Sophie,
Susanna, Joseph, Katherine, Will, Ben, Adam, Grace,
Sophia, Nathan, Julia, Josh — Each One Grand.*

— RGM

*For Suzie, Sara, Tyler, Mitchell, and Landon, the ones
who sacrifice most for my projects.*

— RLD

ACKNOWLEDGMENTS

For their significant contribution to this book in the chapter "The Detection of Malingering and Dissimulation in Children and Adolescents," the authors wish to give great thanks to Naomi Sevin Goldstein, Constance Mesiarik, Oluseyi Olubadewo, Douglas Osman, and Marcelle Thomson. We would also like to thank Richard Frederick, David Mrad, Richart DeMier, and Heath Patterson for their support and knowledge.

TABLE OF CONTENTS

Dedication iii

Acknowledgments v

Introduction: Basics of Deception and Its Detection 1

Section I:
General Assessment Techniques

Chapter 1: Behavioral Cues and Interviewing Strategies
to Detect Deception 21

Chapter 2: General Psychological Tests in the Detection
of Deception 41

Chapter 3: Use of the MMPI-2 to Detect Deceptive
Responding 59

Section II:
Measures Intended for the Detection of Deception

Chapter 4: Measures Specifically Designed to Detect
Deception 87

Chapter 5: Exaggeration and Feigning of Neurocognitive
Dysfunction 107

Chapter 6: Hypnosis and the Polygraph 135

Section III:
Special Populations

Chapter 7: The Detection of Malingering and Dissimulation in
            Children and Adolescents   161

Chapter 8: The Assessment of Psychopathy and Its Relationship to
            Deception Detection   183

Conclusions: Putting It All Together   203

References   223

Subject Index   257

DETECTION OF DECEPTION

Introduction

BASICS OF DECEPTION
AND ITS DETECTION

This book is intended to assist the clinician in the detection of various types of deception. Whether working in forensic or correctional settings, where deception is prevalent, or in a private practice or other treatment setting, where deception is arguably less often a problem, it is important to be able to recognize, assess, and deal with deceptive examinees or patients appropriately. Because deception is typically more of a problem in forensic or correctional settings, these topics will be the main focus of this volume. However, the intention is to provide a broad look at how individuals can be deceptive in various settings, including forensic and correctional, as well as employment settings and general clinical practice.

This book will review pertinent literature on the subject of various types of deception and its detection. However, it is not intended to be a comprehensive literature review. Rather, the purpose of this book is to be a handbook for the practicing psychologist, highlighting the relevant literature, as well as experience, to guide practical suggestions. We will discuss test selection, administration, and interpretation, as well as the synthesis of multiple sources of information in making decisions about the truthfulness of a subject. In this introductory chapter, we will begin with a discussion of the different types and theories of deception.

NEGATIVE RESPONSE BIAS

A negative response bias can be the result of many different motivations. Basically it involves responding in a way that suggests one is more impaired, sick, or disabled than one actually is. In this type of deception, one may fabricate symptoms entirely or exaggerate genuine symptoms. The motivation may be some external gain, as in malingering, or something else, like enjoyment of playing the sick role, as in Factitious Disorder. A patient or examinee could be making a cry for help, exaggerating symptoms as a way of letting the clinician know that he or she is distressed and in need of attention. The following will describe several types of negative response biases. In each the respondent is presenting in an overly pathological way. The difference is in the motivation for such responding.

First, we will look at what is known about malingering. This is by far the most researched and written about of the various types of negative response bias, so a disproportionate amount of the following review will focus on this clinical condition. We will begin with a thorough discussion of malingering and its prevalence, followed by an exploration of conditions and demographics associated with malingering, and then the presentation of some models of malingering. We will then discuss various other types of negative response bias, including Factitious Disorder; somatoform disorders, which are the unintentional production of symptoms with no physical cause and can at times be mistaken for malingering; the cry for help; and the idea that some individuals will exaggerate symptoms, distress, or other dramatic conditions or situations simply because they can.

Malingering

In a variety of settings, predominantly medicolegal environments, feigning psychiatric symptomatology is common due to its beneficial effects on the actors. For example, an individual accused of a crime may exaggerate or manufacture signs of mental illness in an attempt to reduce the penalty for the criminal act. This process, known as malingering, is not a disorder, but rather a condition that may be a focus of clinical attention. The American Psychiatric Association (APA) defined the phenomenon of malingering as, "the intentional production of false or grossly exaggerated physical or psychological symptoms, motivated by external incentives" (APA, 1994, p. 683).

There are several important components to this definition of malingering. Malingering is clearly differentiated from Factitious Disorder (discussed below) by the locus of the motivation. Persons diagnosable with Factitious Disorder engage in symptom production for purposes of maintaining the sick role in the absence of any external incentive, while persons diagnosable with malingering illness are inspired by identifiable external gain such as financial compensation, the avoidance of work or military duty, or the evasion of criminal prosecution (APA, 1994).

Additionally, malingering may be used by correctional detainees or those seen in other types of treatment settings to obtain prescription medication, to eschew true psychological concerns, or to continue a pattern of entitlement to special services and avoid acceptance of responsibility (Haskett, 1995).

As noted, malingering is not a disorder in and of itself, but rather a condition or pattern of behaviors engaged in purposefully by individuals with some particular goal in mind. Therefore, a standard pattern of signs and symptoms is not required for a pronouncement of malingering; instead, any attempts at falsely producing symptoms will qualify an individual for this taxon. For example, persons who mimic sleep problems and persons who feign hallucinations could both be described as malingering. Additionally, symptoms do not have to be from a single illness or a cluster of related disorders. Rather, malingerers, especially unsophisticated fakers, may choose to feign a variety of symptoms associated with anxious, psychotic, and general medical conditions. In fact, Cohn (1995) found that persons instructed to malinger incompetence typically did not possess knowledge related to psychopathology. Applied definitions of malingering tend to focus on the dissimulation of more severe syndromes, such as those associated with psychosis, but those causing less dysfunction also constitute malingering if, in fact, they are exaggerated or falsified for the purpose of some external gain.

Malingering can range in severity from mild to severe (Rogers, 1997a). However, this continuum tends to occur in a strictly definitional or technical context, as applied measures of malingering tend to view the phenomenon as the presence or absence of a sum of reported psychotic or cognitive difficulties. Additionally, this continuum can be, but often is not, conceptualized in two different ways. First, and more commonly, mild malingering refers to the reporting of a few symptoms that are thought to be falsified or exaggerated, while severe malingering may refer to the more obvious endorsement of a high number of inconsistent symptoms. This "totaling" is the basis of many instruments.

There is a tendency to ignore the second way of viewing this range of expressing malingering. That is, the continuum could be seen as a range from the exaggeration of less severe symptoms, such as anxiety or mild physical complaints, to an upper end of more severe symptoms, such as thought disorder and major cognitive impairment. The true conceptualization of malingering is adhered to by this second definition: Malingering is not viewed as the falsification of any specific set of signs and symptoms; rather, the endorsement of any dissimulated experiences constitutes some level of malingering. In keeping with this line of thinking, what should be the threshold for malingering? Based on the APA's (1994) definition, no specific threshold is set. In fact, by this framework, any attempt at symptom exaggeration is diagnosable as malingering. However, in reality, the cut off score for suspicion of malingering varies by instrument or detection technique.

Although the information provided above suggests that the range of malingering be conceptualized in two ways, current detection strategies often exclude the second definitional aspect. G. P. Smith (1997) identified eight intraitem characteristics such as inconsistent combinations, rare symptoms, and vague complaints that could incorporate lower level malingering concerns. However, items on more common measures of malingering detection (e.g., Structured Interview of Reported Symptoms [SIRS; Rogers, 1992]), typically do not inquire about the experience of stress or minor physical complaints.

A last component of the malingering definition, mentioned briefly above, is the necessity of an external incentive for the behavior. The differentiation between malingering and Factitious Disorder has already been discussed, but the context in which malingering is likely to occur is also part of the definition. As a subset of the malingering definition, the *DSM-IV* (APA, 1994, p. 683) identifies "military duty, avoiding work, obtaining financial compensation, evading criminal prosecution, or obtaining drugs" as common precursors to such behavior. Further, it is noted that malingering should be strongly suspected if any of the following are present: medicolegal context, discrepant findings between reported and observed distress, lack of cooperation during evaluation or in treatment compliance, or the presence of an antisocial personality disorder (APA, 1994). Few studies have sought to differentiate malingering across these different contexts, but several have examined the overall prevalence of malingering and attempted to identify factors most closely linked to the presence of dissimulation. It is these investigations to which we now turn.

Prevalence

Malingering can occur in any setting, but forensic venues are most commonly associated with this phenomenon. Although prevalence rates vary, it has been demonstrated that malingering should be suspected and commonly occurs in correctional settings such as jails and prisons where external incentives (e.g., psychotropic medication, special/segregated housing, reduced sentences, or insanity pleas) are numerous (APA, 1994; Norris & May, 1998; G. D. Walters, T. W. White, & Greene, 1988). The

American Psychiatric Association (1994) also suggested that malingering should be investigated when self-reports differ markedly from objective findings, the examinee is noncompliant during testing or treatment, or a diagnosis of Antisocial Personality Disorder has been made. However, it is important to note that malingering can occur in any context or setting. Thus, even the private practitioner must be prepared to identify persons feigning or exaggerating symptoms. For example, exaggeration of problems may occur during couple's therapy where one partner seeks to gain sympathy from the therapist by feigning distress.

The few studies that have attempted to identify the frequency with which malingering occurs vary widely, but have found malingering in a large proportion of the cases examined. Civil cases often involve the malingering of cognitive deficits, such as memory loss and/or other neurological distress. Rogers, Harrell, and Liff (1993) demonstrated that nearly half of personal injury claimants may have been exaggerating or faking their cognitive impairments. Other studies have found that 20% to 40% of cases in litigation are compromised by malingering (Greiffenstein, Baker, & Gola, 1994; Griffin et al., 1996).

In the criminal arena where cognitive, medical, and psychological conditions are commonly and indiscriminately feigned, it has been acknowledged that no clear epidemiological evidence exists to provide a base rate of the occurrence of malingering (Lees-Haley, 1991). Possibly, this knowledge gap could result from disinterest on the part of clinicians regarding incidence of such behavior. It can be noted, however, that as new detection methods have been developed over the past few years, the publication of such studies has increased.

Of the few pure prevalence investigations, much variation between samples has been found. G. D. Walters et al. (1988) found that 46% of inmates reporting psychological distress were exaggerating their degree of impairment, while Haskett (1995) found a much lower rate of 16% of prison inmates to be malingering. Other studies using pretrial (jail) inmates as subjects have found the prevalence of malingering to range from 8% (Hawk & Cornell, 1989) to 20.8% (Rogers, 1997a) to a high of 37% (Wasyliw & Grossman, 1988). Rogers' (1997a) review of malingering literature indicated that this pattern of behavior occurred in 15% to 17.4% of cases in forensic settings.

In addition to examining the rate at which malingering occurs, some investigations have attempted to link dissimulation to demographic and other factors, including personality. Not only does such information act as an aid in the identification of deliberately faked behavior, it can be used to

differentiate those most likely to be successful from those more likely to
fail in feigning psychopathology or other symptoms.

Race, Age, and Associated Factors

As noted, the exact prevalence rate of malingering remains to be
identified, although recent reviews of the literature suggest that nearly
one fifth of correctional detainees are likely to exaggerate their level of
psychological distress or other impairment (Rogers, 1997a). In isolating
this behavior, certain comorbid conditions are often found. Additionally,
demographic variables such as age and race are more often associated
with true mental illness and recidivism/dangerousness and may affect the
dissimulation of such states.

As noted, certain clinical syndromes often predicate malingered
reporting of symptoms. Most notable, patients with a history of substance
abuse and dependence have been found to blame others or lie to obtain
medication (Rogers, 1997a) and are more likely to malinger when
compared to persons with various psychiatric and medical difficulties
(Sierles, 1984). These individuals comprise as much as two thirds of jail
populations (Wilson, 2000). Further, eating disorders are often
accompanied by deception, which occurs, like malingering, on a deliberate
level. A final diagnostic category often associated with malingering is the
personality disorder taxon. The APA (1994) noted in defining malingering
that a diagnosis of Antisocial Personality Disorder should lead to an
investigation of possible dissimulation, and other disorders in this cluster
may be related to malingering as well. Ford, King, and Hollender (1988)
noted that Cluster B ("Dramatic") personality disorders include behaviors
such as deliberate lying and misrepresentation of the truth. In addition,
these conditions often overlap. For example, Lacy (1993) found a large
proportion of bulimics to engage in such impulsive behaviors as stealing
and substance abuse, while personality disorders often contain elements
of impulsivity and abuse of others as well.

Race and age may also be related to malingering, given their
relationship to the prevalence of mental illness and recidivism. For example,
disorders such as schizophrenia occur most often in young males, and
both psychotic and depressive disorders tend to be more prevalent among
Caucasians than among people of color in correctional settings (APA,
1994; Teplin, 1994). Severe mental illness occurs at a rate of 6% to 15%
in jail populations (Lamb & Weinberger, 1998). Violence, dangerousness,
and recidivism are also affected by demographic factors. For example,
Minor, Hartmann, and Terry (1997) found that African-American male
youth were most likely to reoffend in a sample comprised by different

ages, races, and genders. Sierles (1984) also found that race and age had small but significant relations to deceptive behavior. Haskett (1995) found that African-Americans were more likely than other male prisoners to feign impairment. These variables could be used in the identification of malingering.

A condition or trait with possible relation to malingering is psychopathy. There is a large literature base on psychopathic behavior and common sense suggests that many of the same factors that lead to an individual being labeled psychopathic would lead an individual to be more likely to malinger. This issue will be explored in detail in Chapter 8 of this volume.

Aside from demographics and psychiatric conditions, other factors have demonstrated relationships to deceptive behavior. The effects of personality variables such as knowledge of mental illnesses and general intellect have been investigated with regard to malingering. Conflicting results have been found in attempts to assess the influence of disorder-specific knowledge on dissimulation. Franzen and Marten (1996) found that psychology graduate students and faculty were able to successfully feign cognitive dysfunction when identification was based on probability theory, but were detected as malingering when standardized tests were used. Schwartz et al. (1998) also examined the ability of knowledgeable subjects to feign intellectual difficulty. Results suggested that not only could individuals given injury-related knowledge dissimulate head trauma, but there was a relationship between education and ability to successfully malinger on intelligence and memory tasks. However, in a sample of adults selected from respondents to advertisements, Wetter et al. (1994) found that disorder-specific information did not increase the ability of instructed malingerers to evade detection on the MMPI-2. Further support for the role of intelligence in successful malingering can be found in Hayes, Hale, and Gouvier's (1998) study of mentally retarded individuals attempting to feign psychological distress. In this investigation, 89% of malingerers were correctly classified, suggesting that persons with diminished intellectual skills did not have a high success rate when attempting to feign or exaggerate psychopathology.

Criminal defendant status may also be related to malingering. Resnick (1984) postulated that pretrial individuals commonly fake auditory hallucinations. Further, he suggested that these persons also try to mimic organic conditions. C. R. Clark (1997) has held that confusion, disorientation, and concentration difficulties are also commonly seen in criminal defendants malingering psychopathology or cognitive impairment.

A final factor related to malingering of psychopathology is known as response style. Guy and colleagues (2000) identified strategies thought to differentiate successful and unsuccessful malingerers. Four approaches to test-taking were found to be most related to "beating" the inventories: avoidance of bizarre items, avoidance of attempts to appear "crazy" by endorsing extreme levels of psychopathology, avoidance of attempts to mimic emotional deficits, and basis of answers in personal experiences. This information may mean that malingerers are likely to endorse items regarding lower threshold conditions such as anxiety.

The Importance of Detecting Malingering

Based on the accumulation of dissimulation knowledge, malingering detection is being continually refined. However, this process can be enhanced further. Certainly, detecting false claims of insanity or disability are necessary for proper functioning of our legal system and society. In a review of court proceedings and associated studies, Melton et al. (1997) noted that the insanity defense is raised in only 1% of criminal prosecutions nationwide, although the proportion of cases involving malingering is unknown. Further, the insanity defense is successful in approximately 25% of the cases in which it is raised. Again, malingering may be a factor in many of the unsuccessful cases (Melton et al., 1997). Added to this figure is the exceedingly high number of individuals thought to be exaggerating the degree of injury or impairment in civil cases (Rogers, Harrell, & Liff, 1993).

The knowledge that a significant proportion of criminal and civil litigation proceedings may be compromised by deception makes the development of strategies for malingering detection compelling. Further uses of dissimulation detection methods occur outside the courtroom, both prior to and following trial and/or sentencing. Although clinically indicated, application of malingering assessment to jail and prison settings has been largely ignored. In such settings, where malingering is widespread, detection of malingering may serve to relieve strain on an underfinanced and overworked mental health system. Inmates in need of immediate services may be delayed in receiving treatments when resources are devoted to those feigning psychopathology. Further, Haskett (1995) stated, that in such settings, "malingering breeds contempt for mental health as a system" (p. 48). Detainees who malinger are not lacking in their need to obtain mental health treatment. Instead, failure to address such behavior is tantamount to condoning criminal patterns by allowing the abuse of medication and services, and supporting a continued sense of privilege.

Explanatory and Theoretical Models

Conceptualizing malingering involves understanding the theoretical origins of the behavior. Three explanatory models have been developed to assist clinicians in detecting deceptive behavior and identifying its probable roots. Two of these theories, the pathogenic and criminological models, have been largely disregarded following a lack of empirical support. The adaptational model, on the other hand, explains malingering as the byproduct of a survival instinct, and is gaining acceptance through confirmatory data and a relation to the technical definition of the phenomenon (Rogers, 1997a).

Early in the development of malingering conceptualization, psychodynamic theory was a dominant perspective in psychology. Given this fact, the first explanatory model of malingering incorporated Freudian terminology such as projection and denial into a formulation suggesting that malingering results from an attempt to control emerging symptoms (Rogers, 1997a). Also referred to as the "coping model," this theory posits "malingering is an ineffectual way of coping with the early stages of mental disorder that ultimately develop into a full-blown disorder" (Heinze, 1999, p. 391). Limited support for this model has been generated. For example, Heinze (1999) noted anecdotal information suggesting that upon recovery from major psychiatric illness, some individuals have reported exaggerating or faking symptoms to deny the fact of their psychopathology. Additionally, in a sample of sex offenders, Ward, Hudson, and Marshall (1995) found that denial was a factor in recidivism and that persons guilty of deception often came to believe in their own dissimulation. Other studies (e.g., Rogers, Sewell, & Goldstein, 1994) have supported different models and failed to confirm the utility of viewing malingering in this way.

The pathogenic model's failure to adequately address most aspects of the phenomenon of malingering led researchers to seek alternate explanations. Drawing from the increase in legal cases involving the report of psychiatric symptomatology by defendants, practitioners became concerned that successful portrayal of mental disorder may equate to freedom from prosecution (Rogers, 1997a). This led to the development of a second explanatory model: the criminological model.

Also known as the interpersonal management model, the criminological framework appears to have developed based on diagnostic criteria articulated in the *DSM-IV* (APA, 1994; Heinze, 1999). Specifically, malingering is to be suspected when individuals warrant a diagnosis of antisocial personality disorder or are evaluated for forensic purposes (APA, 1994). According to Rogers (1997a), the basic premise of this model is that malingerers are bad. They engage in dissimulation for the purpose of being uncooperative and manipulative. Persons with personality disorders are often conceptualized as engaging in malingering behavior simply to be deceitful. In addition to lacking in empirical support, this model suffers from conceptual inconsistency. For example, Rogers (1997a) cited numerous examples of times when individuals may be uncooperative for reasons other than the desire to deceive. For example, psychotic individuals often refuse to cooperate to avoid being given medication, and persons with substance abuse disorders often show limited investment in evaluation and treatment procedures. Further, the assumption that criminal accusations are associated with badness as a character trait are unwarranted and may lead to faulty conclusions.

For some time, depictions of malingering as a tool of survival, rather than one of illness or manipulation, have existed. For example, early reports of malingering involved soldiers attempting to be relieved of field duty by feigning illness. According to Waud (1942) the phenomenon was rare in times of peace, but increased in prevalence during wartime. This functional use of dissimulation is often referred to as the adaptational model of malingering. By this proposition, persons are likely to malinger when placed in negative or adversarial circumstances in which they feel exaggerating or feigning mental illness is likely to lead to a beneficial outcome. This process certainly applies to the various stages of criminal prosecution. According to Rogers (1997a), under the adaptational model, "would-be malingerers engage in a cost-benefit analysis when confronted with an assessment they perceive as indifferent, if not inimical, to their needs" (p. 8). Further, by this tenet, malingering would occur more commonly in situations involving high personal stakes and an adversarial context where no other options appear to be feasible (Rogers, 1997a).

The adaptational model appears to be supported both conceptually and empirically. The American Psychiatric Association (1994) noted, in defining malingering, "under some circumstances, malingering may represent adaptive behavior" (p. 683). Under this designation, malingering may still be manipulative, but it derives from self-preservation, rather than simply criminal, motivation. Perhaps the single largest piece of supporting evidence for this framework came from G. D. Walters and colleagues' (1988) investigation of malingering in postsentence federal detainees. Results demonstrated that dissimulation was not common under neutral circumstances, but more frequent when used to attain some important object or other advantage. This study replicated earlier data using a sample of hospitalized psychiatric patients (B. M. Braginsky & D. D. Braginsky, 1967). According to Rogers (1997a), descriptive findings also support this model, as prevalence rates of malingering are considerably higher in adversarial settings such as jails, prisons, and the courtroom.

As noted previously, the customary conceptualization of malingering involves the generation of psychotic symptoms to gain highly desirable outcomes such as release from incarceration. However, consistent with the adaptational model, malingering may occur on a smaller scale as a response to unpleasant surroundings. For example, persons in jails may feign psychiatric or medical impairment to avoid or delay prosecution. Individuals not desirous of avoiding a trial, on the other hand, may still utilize dissimulation as a method of obtaining goals perceived as necessary. Attention from staff, access to single cell accommodations, and receipt of psychoactive medications are certainly desirable, and may be viewed as crucial to optimal functioning for correctional detainees. Thus, inmates may engage in lower-threshold symptom exaggeration to acquire such benefits. In fact, the jail environment often encourages malingering by rewarding complaints of sleeplessness or uncorroborated psychosis with medication (Haskett, 1995).

Factitious Disorder

Factitious Disorder (FD) represents another way that individuals may intentionally feign or exaggerate symptoms. In this condition, however, individuals are not attempting to gain some external reward such as escape from prosecution or medication. In fact, the definition of this disorder specifies that external gain must not be present in order for this diagnosis to be made (APA, 1994). The motivation in this type of deception is the sick role itself. Otherwise known as Munchausen's syndrome, this condition can easily be confused with malingering if the clinician does not pay careful attention to motivation. The symptoms that are intentionally feigned can be physical, psychological, or both. These can be presented in the form of exaggerated self-report of subjective symptoms or the infliction of wounds or other illness upon oneself.

Very little is known about the prevalence of FD. Often this condition may not be recognized, and therefore it is likely underreported. However, there is also a possibility that chronic cases are overreported, in that they go from one doctor to another, sometimes using pseudonyms, and may be repeatedly diagnosed with the syndrome (APA, 1994). By exploring the records of 93 patients diagnosed with FD over 21 years, Krahn, Li, and O'Connor (2003) attempted to provide some descriptive data about the condition. They found that the group was composed primarily of women ($N = 67$, 72%). The mean age of patients with FD was 30.7 years ($SD = 8.0$)

for the women in the sample and 40.0 years ($SD = 13.3$) for the men. The average age at which the disorder began was 25.0 years ($SD = 7.4$). The women in the group were more likely than the men to have jobs or training in the health care field, with the percentages equaling 65.7% and 11.5%, respectively.

Research on the psychological benefits of the sick role has been done by Hamilton, Deemer, and Janata (2003). These authors found support for the idea that taking on the sick role provides an increase in or maintenance of the patient's self-esteem. More specifically, they found that subjects rated medical patients more favorably on interpersonal characteristics if the patients had a unique medical condition and when the patients displayed knowledge of medical facts. This suggests that patients may play the sick role in order to gain a sense of importance or esteem, to gain and display medical wisdom, or to gain a sense of being unique and special.

As with malingering, a common presentation of FD with primarily psychological symptoms includes giving answers to questions that are very nearly but not quite correct, as if feigning cognitive impairment or memory loss of some sort. The individual with FD may also ingest some substance to produce symptoms of a psychological or physical nature. This extreme behavior is probably less likely in malingering. Some factors that have been proposed as possibly predisposing one to FD include the presence of a genuine medical or psychological illness that led to significant treatment and time spent in hospitals as a child or adolescent, a high level of dislike for physicians or the medical field in general, employment or training in the health field, a severe Axis II diagnosis, or a history of having a significant relationship with a medical doctor (APA, 1994).

FD should be explored as a possibility if a patient presents with an extensive history of major medical procedures and surgeries, a significant background of travel, few visits during the stay in the hospital, a high level of medical knowledge, arguing with medical professionals, refusing to comply with treatment recommendations, a highly unusual presentation of or combination of symptoms, lack of symptoms when the patient does not know he or she is being observed, hidden substance use, and a presentation that rapidly changes, including development of sudden complications, new symptoms, or relapses (APA, 1994). Many of the above are also present in malingering. When attempting to distinguish FD from malingering, carefully look for possible motives for the feigned symptoms. Look beyond the motives that are typically thought of, such as eluding prosecution, being awarded money, or obtaining medication. Malingering may occur in order to obtain a place to sleep for the night or to avoid work. Any external motivation can mean that the feigned symptoms are the result of malingering rather than FD. If the individual is malingering, the behavior is often adaptive and the production of symptoms usually stops after the goal is obtained or the faking is discovered. In contrast, the course of FD is usually chronic (APA, 1994).

Other Types of Negative Response Bias

An individual may exaggerate symptoms as a way of reaching out for help. This type of feigning symptoms is different from FD in that the sick role is not the motivation. Rather, the goal is to obtain help for actual distress, though the distress may not be as extreme as it is presented to be. (Somatoform disorders, such as Somatization Disorder, Conversion Disorder, and Pain Disorder, may at times be confused with malingering or other intentional negative response bias. It is important to consider these diagnoses and recognize that, though they involve the report of symptoms with no medical cause, these symptoms are not intentionally feigned.)

Other types of biased responding are carelessness and random responding. Some individuals may not pay careful attention to the content of test items and will produce a careless response set. This type of responding results from lack of effort. On the other hand, random responding is a more intentional type of responding. The individual may make a decision to not even read the item content and to just respond without any regard for what the items might be measuring. This type of responding may occur in hostile or uncooperative subjects. Neither of these response sets necessarily qualify as deceptive responding, but they are certainly not straightforward and cooperative and can create problems in an attempt to assess an individual accurately. It is also important to note that some individuals report feigned symptoms for no particular reason other than the fact that they can.

SOCIALLY DESIRABLE RESPONDING

In addition to assessing whether or not an individual is exaggerating or feigning symptoms that are not present, it is often critical to determine whether or not an individual is exaggerating positive traits or claiming virtue that is not realistic. In many types of situations, including employment settings, parole hearings, or child custody evaluations, individuals will present themselves in an overly positive light. A subject may engage in denial of negative traits, or enhancement of positive traits, or both types of deception. Research on socially desirable responding has shown that there are two primary types of this "fake-good" responding. These are Impression Management and Self-Deceptive Enhancement (Paulhus, 1984). We will examine each of these response sets below.

Impression Management

Impression management is similar to malingering but with exaggeration or fabrication of positive qualities instead of symptoms of some illness or condition. Impression management involves the intentional fabrication of positive qualities for the purpose of impressing some intended audience (Paulhus, 1998). In the examples mentioned previously, the individual would be attempting to impress a potential boss, a parole board, or a psychologist or social worker involved in a child custody evaluation, respectively. This type of responding can be part of an individual's character style, like in someone with antisocial or psychopathic traits. Or it may be a response to a stressful situation like being evaluated for one's fitness to have custody of one's children.

Self-Deceptive Enhancement

In self-deceptive enhancement, the individual actually believes that he or she has the positive qualities that are being reported. There is no attempt to intentionally deceive or impress someone. This is a significant lack of insight similar to narcissism (Paulhus, 1998), and would be likely to be present across settings. These two types of socially desirable responding have a very low correlation with each other (Paulhus, 1998). Therefore, the presence of one does not necessarily indicate the presence of the other and distinguishing between them can be important. The assessment of these two types of responding will be explored further in Chapters 3 and 4.

OVERVIEW OF THIS MANUAL

There are three main sections in this book. The first includes a discussion of the use of general assessment techniques and their use in the detection of deception. The second explores techniques, specially designed for the detection of various types of deceptive responding. The third discusses additional considerations with special populations. The final chapter attempts to put it all together and present a comprehensive way of synthesizing information and making decisions about deception.

Each chapter will present as much practical information as is possible. There are hundreds of tests used in psychological assessment. Obviously, we could not cover all of them. We chose to include those that we think are the best and those that we think are popular, but not necessarily the best for assessing deception, such as the Rorschach. Each of the chapters concludes with a summary of key points for quick reference. The following is a brief overview of each of the chapters.

Section I: General Assessment Techniques

Chapter 1: Behavioral Cues and Interviewing
Strategies to Detect Deception

A great deal of published research addresses how to detect deception based on behavioral cues, including facial expressions, body language, and tone of voice. There are also ways that deception can be revealed through a subject's answers during a clinical or other type of interview. Many of the behaviors that are typically thought of as being suggestive of deception are not. Chapter 1 focuses on helping the clinician to become more tuned in to the behaviors that can be suggestive of deception. Learning these strategies can be useful in any type of setting. Since the first contact with a subject is often in an interview of some sort, these techniques often provide the first information about a subject's reliability.

Chapter 2: General Psychological Tests
In the Detection of Deception

Many psychological tests have validity scales built into them. This chapter reviews several of these assessment measures and compares their strengths and weaknesses. Chapter 2 could be particularly helpful for the clinician in general practice who may not have reason to always suspect deception, and therefore a lengthy assessment specific to the detection of deception is not warranted as a general rule. This chapter will provide useful information to help understand the validity scales in the cases in which some level of deception is indicated.

Chapter 3: Use of the MMPI-2 to
Detect Deceptive Responding

The research on the use of the MMPI-2 in the detection of deception is massive. Additionally, the number of validity scales and indices included in the MMPI-2 to detect many different types of deception made it necessary for this measure to warrant its own chapter. Chapter 3 attempts to present the different validity measures in the MMPI-2, their purpose and usefulness, and a way of synthesizing the enormous amount of information obtained in an MMPI-2 profile into a meaningful interpretation regarding validity.

Section II: Measures Intended for the Detection of Deception
Chapter 4: Measures Specifically
Designed to Detect Deception

Many psychological tests have been specifically designed to detect various types of deceptive responding. These include tests intended to detect malingering and those meant to assess socially desirable responding. Tests of both types will be presented in Chapter 4 to give the reader an understanding of how to choose and use such a test in the case where detection is clearly suspected.

Chapter 5: Exaggeration and Feigning
Of Neurocognitive Dysfunction

Many psychological tests have been developed that are specifically designed for the detection of neurocognitive malingering. Several of these tests focus on feigned memory impairment. Additionally, many general neuropsychological measures and batteries have malingering scales and indices. Chapter 5 helps the reader to develop an understanding of the strategies used in many neurocognitive assessments of malingering, such as forced-choice responding. It also provides a comprehensive review of many of the specific tests or indices and the strengths and weaknesses of each.

Chapter 6: Hypnosis and the Polygraph

It is popular belief that hypnosis and/or the polygraph are surefire ways of uncovering deceptive responding. The polygraph is even commonly called a "lie detector test." The purpose of Chapter 6 is to present the realistic information that is known in our field about these techniques and how they might be and should not be used in an attempt to detect deception.

Section III: Special Populations
Chapter 7: The Detection of Malingering and
Dissimulation in Children and Adolescents

As is the case with most types of assessment and treatment, there are special issues that need to be considered when assessing deception in children and adolescents. Special tests have been designed for and normed on these age groups, but there are also particular challenges and ethical dilemmas that arise when attempting to determine if a child or adolescent is lying about something. Chapter 7 presents each of these concerns as well as strategies for attempting to deal with them effectively and professionally.

Chapter 8: The Assessment of Psychopathy and Its Relationship to Deception Detection

Psychopathic individuals are typically believed to be especially good liars. In fact, two of the major characteristics of the condition involve conning and manipulation, and pathological lying. Chapter 8 explores how to best assess psychopathy and when it might be a good idea to do so. It also reviews what the research shows about the relationship between psychopathy and various types of deception and whether or not psychopaths are actually better at different types of deception than nonpsychopaths.

Conclusions: Putting It All Together

The final chapter of the book attempts to present a practical way of pulling together the information gathered in an assessment of deception so that an informed decision can be made about the validity of a subject's report. This chapter will present specific examples, including test selection, scoring, and interpretation for different types of assessments where deception could become an issue.

Throughout this book, and particularly in the final chapter, the point will be stressed that a comprehensive assessment of deception must consist of multiple data sources. No one instrument presented in the chapters that follow should be solely relied upon for making a determination about whether an evaluee is truthful or not and in what way someone might be engaging in deception. Assessment instruments cannot distinguish between malingering and FD, for example. Information about treatment history, background, level of sophistication, reading ability, motivation, attitude, and other variables can often alter the way a test's results are interpreted.

The clinician is tasked for using the information in this book responsibly. We have attempted to put together a very user-friendly guide, but this book cannot substitute for receiving adequate training in test interpretation and reading the manual for a particular test before it is used. In fact, for some tests the reader will have to refer to the manual in order to interpret the results because cut off scores were not published here for test security purposes. This is particularly true for the neuropsychological measures presented in Chapter 5.

Section I

GENERAL
ASSESSMENT TECHNIQUES

Chapter 1

BEHAVIORAL CUES AND INTERVIEWING STRATEGIES TO DETECT DECEPTION

In this chapter, we will examine ways in which deception might be detected by looking at or speaking with a subject. This is often the first opportunity a clinician will have to generate hypotheses about a subject. There is no automatic giveaway that someone is being untruthful. Of course, one's nose does not grow. Nor does the deceiver perform some act that will always betray an untruth. There are some behaviors that can provide cues, however, that an individual is not being truthful. These behaviors will include things that can be observed in body language, tone of voice, and facial expressions, as well as things an individual might say in an interview or general conversation.

Two areas of research will be reviewed here. First is the research on behavioral cues to deception. This includes many well-controlled studies on how people judge when someone is lying, as well as what people actually do when they lie. It has been reported that many of the traditional cues people think of when judging whether someone is being truthful or not (e.g., fidgeting, lack of eye-contact) may not be the best indicators of truthfulness (Ekman, 1992; Mann, Vrij, & Bull, 2004). The second area that will be explored includes information about how spoken words can reveal deception. This will include an exploration of the differences in how symptoms are described by individuals who are truly suffering from mental illness and those who are exaggerating or fabricating symptoms, as well as tips for conducting interviews that are sensitive to detecting deception. These two areas will cover the two reasons, proposed by Ekman (1989), for why lies fail, (a) because the liar's emotions expose the deceit in some way, and (b) because the liar has not anticipated questions about the lie or has not prepared his or her story adequately.

We will review ways in which the findings from such research can be used in practice. Some of these techniques can be quite difficult to use. Some are more obvious. The cues that will be presented are not likely to provide irrefutable evidence that a subject is lying. However, as part of a comprehensive assessment, these strategies can be used to supplement the use of other techniques used to detect deception. They also may provide the initial clue that an individual is attempting to deceive, prompting further investigation into the truthfulness of the person's statements.

PRECAUTIONARY STATEMENTS

Prior to the discussion of ways in which behaviors and speech can reveal deception, it is important to point out that there are many mistakes that can be made when making these types of judgments. Most obvious, is the possibility that one may be wrong in a judgment about an individual's truthfulness. It is important to weigh the consequences of this possibility. An individual who is being truthful could be disbelieved. For example, it could have very devastating consequences if an individual is judged to be malingering when in fact he or she is suffering from a serious mental illness. There could also be severe consequences if an individual is believed when he or she is actually engaging in deception. Practicing in the field of psychology long enough guarantees that one will make a few of these mistakes. A PhD does not render one immune. However, utilizing caution may decrease this possibility, and at least considering the consequences of a mistake will make one less likely to jump to conclusions.

Additionally, it is important to remember when judging truthfulness based on behavioral cues that all individuals are different. A particular behavior, for example, fidgeting, might suggest deceit in a general sense (this is just an example, as research discussed below shows that fidgeting is actually not a reliable indicator of deception). However, some people might be natural fidgeters. Even when not engaging in deceptive communication, some people have a greater tendency to fidget. This is where knowledge of a subject's typical behaviors may become important. If you are aware of how someone typically behaves when truthful, then to note a change in his or her behavior, even more fidgeting than usual, for example, could provide important information. In other words, remember that what may suggest deception in general, may be a natural behavior for any particular individual (Ekman, 1992). Therefore, focusing on behavioral change can lead to more accurate assessments.

Investigators should consider that some of the behavioral cues to deception may be shown in an individual who is being truthful but is afraid of being disbelieved. A display of emotion might simply indicate an individual is concerned that he or she might not be believed, instead of revealing actual deception (Ekman, 1992). So, obviously, the presence of behaviors that might indicate deception does not necessarily mean that an individual is being deceptive. Further, the absence of behaviors suggesting deception does not mean that an individual is being truthful (Ekman, 1992). Some individuals find lying to be a perfectly natural behavior, and they are good at it. Refer to Chapter 8 for a discussion of one such group of people, psychopathic individuals. This point again reiterates the importance of recognizing individual differences in how people typically appear and noting changes in behavior from the norm for any particular individual.

BEHAVIORAL CUES TO DECEPTION

One's behaviors can reveal deception in several different ways. The content of a lie can lead to its surfacing. For example, if an individual does not carefully rehearse what he or she is going to say, and then contradicts himself or herself, this can reveal a lie. These types of errors, called cognitive cues or content errors, will be reviewed in greater detail below. Another problem that can arise for a liar is that of emotion. Most of the cues to deception that come from behaviors arise from emotion. These emotional cues will be explored here. There can be problems with trying to conceal an emotion, such as telling someone one is not angry, when in fact that is the exact feeling that is present. Deception can also be revealed when one attempts to produce an emotion that is not felt. These two types of deception can occur simultaneously. People in this society engage in both of these types of deception fairly frequently. Rather than admitting that one had an awful time at a party, one would be more likely to simply conceal his or her feelings of boredom, produce a smile, and thank the host for a lovely evening. This type of deception is often socially acceptable and considered polite. This deception could also be very important to detect. Consider the case of a patient who is extremely angry with his spouse and is in treatment for anger management related to domestic violence. This individual might be motivated to conceal feelings of anger and produce a calm appearance, all the while intending to go home and abuse the target of his anger.

One's emotions about the act of lying can also reveal the lie. For example, someone may feel fear about being caught, guilt about lying, or what Ekman (1992) calls "duping delight" (p. 65). Duping delight is a term used by Ekman to describe the positive feelings that sometimes accompany successful deception. Some individuals see lying as a challenge or a game and get pleasure out of successfully fooling someone. These emotions can sometimes be strong enough to leak information revealing the lie. For example, the pleasure may be revealed on one's face, or sometimes the individual will reveal it just to be able to share the accomplishment of pulling off the deceit.

People typically pay the most attention to an individual's words and facial expressions. These are often the least reliable sources of information to determine if someone is lying. This is because liars expect that the people they are trying to fool will pay close attention to their words and facial expressions. Therefore, one who is trying to deceive will carefully attempt to control his or her words and facial expressions. Words are easier to control than facial expressions. We will examine clues to deception in the voice, body, face, and finally, the words that are spoken.

The Voice

Pauses in speech are the most common sign of deception arising from vocal cues. If pauses are too long or too frequent, this may suggest deception. When a question is asked of a subject, if he or she pauses at the start of the response, this could also suggest lying. Other types of pauses in speech that could suggest deception include frequent short pauses, errors or non-words such as "Um" and "Uh," repetitions such as "I, I, well I, I mean . . . ," and insertion of partial words like, "I rea- really want that." These types of errors or pauses typically occur when the individual being deceptive did not plan the lie carefully enough and/or is experiencing a great deal of worry about telling the lie (Ekman, 1992).

The sound of the voice, or its pitch, is the best documented sign of emotion. In approximately 70% of people studied, voice pitch becomes higher when the individual is upset, most often when feeling fear or anger. Fear of being caught in a lie can also increase pitch. Increase in vocal pitch is a sign of fear or excitement, not necessarily deceit (Ekman, 1992). Also, when someone is upset, the volume of speech may become louder, and the rate may be faster. This is even more likely when the purpose of the lie is to conceal strong emotions such as fear or anger. The opposite pattern of vocal changes may occur when one is attempting to conceal sadness.

The Body

In an experiment where people saw just the body of a subject, or heard just the words or the tone of voice, those viewing just the body performed the best at selecting who was being deceptive and who was being truthful (Ekman, 1992). Often, body language is overlooked in attempts to determine if someone is being untruthful. Emotions can leak out in gestures and body movements that are unintentional.

Emblems

One way emotions can leak is through the use of "emblems" (Ekman, 1992, p. 101). Emblems are gestures that have a precise meaning within a culture, such as the middle finger or a shrug. These types of gestures can be used instead of words and have meaning on their own, whereas other gestures depend on the words they accompany to give them clear meaning. Sometimes, when an individual is attempting to deceive, emblems may slip out and reveal information the individual is trying to conceal. This can occur in two major ways.

First, when an emblem is not intentional, it may be performed only partially. For example, instead of a full shrug of the shoulders with the accompanying arms bent at the elbows and palms turned upward, which says, "I don't know," a person who is attempting to conceal this lack of knowledge might nonetheless let it slip with only a very slight shrug of one shoulder. The second way this emblem might be slipped is if it is performed out of the range where emblems are typically performed. Most emblems are performed in front of the person, between the neck and the waist. If the emblem is slipped, it might be performed below the waist, for example. Using the example of the shrug emblem mentioned above, if it is slipped and done out of its typical position, perhaps the hands would turn so the palms would face up as in the full gesture, but with the arms hanging straight down so they are not in the usual position.

If an emblem is performed only partially or out of position, it often goes unnoticed. These slipped emblems are typically leaking information the deceiver is trying to hide. Not all individuals who are trying to deceive will display these partial or out of place emblems. However, Ekman (1992) suggested that, when these slips do occur, they are quite reliable indicators of deception.

Illustrators

Illustrators do just that, they illustrate speech as it is spoken. These gestures are less specific than emblems. They do not have meaning without the words they accompany. Typically, illustrators are made with the hands, and commonly are referred to as "talking with one's hands." The extent to which these movements occur differs with different cultures and from one person to another. With illustrators, it is very important to understand the context in which one is viewing them, including their typical use in any given person. The number of illustrators, not the type, can provide information about deception, again, with the caution that there are individual differences in the extent to which people typically use illustrators. These should obviously be taken into account.

When someone uses illustrators significantly less than what is typical for that person, it could suggest that the individual is being deceptive (Ekman, 1992). However, it has also been suggested that, when lying, individuals may increase the number of illustrators they use (Ekman, 1989). The more involved someone is with what is being said, the more illustrators are typically used. A lack of emotional investment in what is being said could decrease illustrators. This can be shown when someone lies about feeling enthusiasm or concern and the common gestures accompanying these emotions are not there. Also, trying to conceal emotions can decrease illustrators.

In instances when someone is thinking very carefully about what to say, illustrators typically decrease. For example, when someone is thinking carefully or being cautious because he or she is being untruthful and perhaps is not prepared, illustrators will likely decrease. Mann and colleagues (2004) conducted an experiment in which they had police officers watch videotapes of suspects and determine whether they were being truthful or not. The officers who were good at detecting lies were more likely to associate a decrease in illustrators with deception than the officers who were no good at detecting lies. Of course, there are many instances when someone might be thinking about what to say when being truthful. It is important to know the person who is speaking and his or her typical use of illustrators before making any judgments about truthfulness based on illustrators. Even then, judgments based on a decrease in these gestures should be made very tentatively.

Manipulators

The movements discussed here might be more commonly referred to as "fidgeting." Manipulators are movements involving the manipulation of one part of the body with another part, that is, massaging, rubbing, twisting, pinching, and so forth (Ekman, 1992). Often, people who engage in these behaviors are mistakenly judged as lying. Mann and colleagues (2004) found that the more police officers reported using stereotypic cues to detect deception, such as manipulators, fidgeting, unnatural posture changes, increased head nodding, or placement of the hand over the mouth or eyes when speaking, the worse they were at differentiating between suspects telling the truth and those who were lying.

We typically associate fidgeting with nervousness, and associate nervousness with having something to hide. These types of movements may show that someone is upset, as manipulators may increase with a person's level of discomfort. However, manipulators may also increase when individuals feel comfortable. This would be the result of decreased monitoring of one's behaviors when in a situation where one feels at ease. Therefore, manipulators are not reliable behavioral indicators of deception.

Another reason these behaviors are not reliable is that they are relatively easy to suppress, and they are commonly viewed as suggestive of deception. If an individual is trying to deceive, and he or she knows that fidgeting behavior is suggestive of deception, he or she will choose not to engage in these behaviors. Body movements are easier to control than facial expressions. Some body movements are not associated with deception, like emblems, and therefore are not typically inhibited. However, people are motivated to suppress manipulators they think will be seen as suggestive of lying, particularly in high stakes lies.

Autonomic Nervous System Cues

Measurement of autonomic nervous system responses is used in polygraph examination and will be discussed further in that context in Chapter 6. However, some responses can be viewed without the use of complicated machinery. If a liar is feeling guilty, fearful, upset, excited, angry, or ashamed, he or she might show rapid breathing, swallowing frequently, heaving chest, or sweating. Blushing may occur if the liar is embarrassed or ashamed about lying or what he or she is lying about. The face may also turn red with anger. Blanching may occur in fear or anger (Ekman, 1992). These behaviors would likely be easily observed. The problem with forming opinions about truthfulness based on these cues is that they will provide information about how strong the emotion is being felt, but not necessarily which emotion is being felt.

The Face

People's faces can show expressions that are intentional, and those that are unintentional. Intentional facial expressions are fabricated. Unintentional expressions are natural expressions of some emotion. Think of the difference between a forced smile and one that arises from a true feeling of happiness. The former must be intentionally produced. The latter occurs naturally, without even the need for thought. Intentional and unintentional facial expressions are controlled by different parts of the brain (Ekman, 1992).

People learn very early in life to manage the expression of their emotions. They learn to control facial expressions of emotion and this becomes habit. People can deliberately inhibit emotional expression or produce expression of an emotion they don't feel. In an experiment in which subjects rated the truthfulness of nurses, if the subjects had to base their judgments of truthfulness only on the nurses' facial expressions, they performed worse than chance in their decisions about who was lying (Ekman, 1992). This is because the subjects paid the most attention to the obvious facial expressions that are easy to see. When someone is lying, these obvious expressions are usually the false ones. To detect deception, one must pay closer attention to more subtle cues in the face.

In his book *Emotions Revealed: Recognizing Faces and Feelings to Improve Communication and Emotional Life*, Ekman (2003) has created an excellent source for information about emotions in facial expression, and the subtle facial cues that reveal these emotions. He clearly describes the facial expressions that are characteristic of the major emotions of sadness, anger, fear, surprise, disgust, contempt, and enjoyment. A worthwhile endeavor is to take the test on reading faces that he presents at the end of the book. This test can give a general idea of how accurate you are at reading facial expressions, as well as assist in the development of the ability to be more deliberate when doing so.

Micro-Expressions
Micro-expressions are expressions that involve the full face but last only a very short time. These expressions typically last less than one fourth of a second. Usually these expressions occur so quickly they are not seen by observers. These micro-expressions do not occur frequently (Ekman, 1992).

Squelched Expressions
Squelched expressions occur more frequently than micro-expressions. They last longer, but are not as complete as micro-expressions. As the emotional expression begins to show on a person's face, he or she seems to notice it and stop it, often covering it with another expression. In this case, even if the concealed emotion does not become obvious, the covering of it may be.

There are certain reliable muscles or facial movements that are not easily controlled or produced voluntarily. These include the movement of the forehead in the expression of sadness, grief, distress, or guilt, the movement of the forehead and eyebrow in the expression of fear, worry, apprehension, or terror, and the thinning of the lips in the expression of anger (Ekman, 1992).

Smiles

People often attempt to cover negative emotion with a smile. This type of smile is called a masking smile and can be distinguished from a genuine smile produced by happy feelings (Ekman, Friesen, & O'Sullivan, 1997). True smiles of enjoyment were described as involving two specific muscles of the face: "the zygomatic major pulling the lip corners upwards towards the cheekbone; and the orbicularis oculi which raises the cheek and gathers the skin inwards from around the eye socket" (Ekman & Friesen, 1982, p. 242). Masking smiles often reveal something of the emotion the person is trying to conceal, be it fear, anger, disgust, or sadness. This often occurs with the action of the zygomatic major, as in a truly felt smile, along with some of the facial movements seen in these negative emotions (Ekman et al., 1997). Often, though the corners of the mouth are being pulled upward, they are simultaneously curving downward slightly, revealing the true emotion. Also, the gathering of skin around the eye socket that occurs in felt smiles is typically absent in fake smiles.

The Eyes

The muscles that control the direction one's eyes look typically can be controlled, so they do not provide much information about deception. Avoiding eye contact or averting one's gaze is commonly seen as a sign of deception. Therefore, the liar may purposefully avoid averting his or her gaze in order to be believed, so this is not a reliable indicator of deception. The study by Mann and colleagues (2004) found that gaze aversion was a cue often used to determine truthfulness by police officers who were not good at detecting deception. No clear relationship has been found between lying and lack of eye contact (Vrij, 2000).

Blinking and pupil dilation typically increase when an individual is aroused, but these behaviors do not reveal which emotion is aroused. One clue associated with the eyes that may actually provide useful information about deception is the presence or absence of tears. Tears can be difficult to suppress, so they may reveal emotion that one is trying to conceal. Also, tears can be difficult to manufacture when the accompanying emotion is not felt.

Clues to Suggest a Facial Expression Is False

Asymmetry. When the same actions are present on both sides of the face but at different levels of intensity, this may suggest deception. Differences between the right and left sides of the face should be shown in voluntary, not involuntary, expressions of emotion. This is because the voluntary production of emotion is controlled by cerebral hemispheres and the involuntary emotions are controlled by more primitive brain structures in the limbic system (Ekman, 1992; Hager & Ekman, 1997). This is a very simplified way of discussing facial asymmetry, but nonetheless, asymmetry in facial expressions suggests the emotion is produced rather than spontaneous.

Timing. This clue to the false production of emotional expression includes the length of time the expression lasts, how long it takes to appear, and how long it takes to diminish. Expressions that last long, usually more than 5 seconds and surely more than 10 seconds, are usually not genuine. In extreme emotional states, such as extreme rage or depression, expressions might last this long. More likely, in such states there would be a series of shorter expressions that, combined, would last longer than usual (Ekman, 1992).

In terms of the time of onset and offset of emotional expression, there is only one definitive rule, which applies to the expression of surprise. Genuine surprise always has a very short onset and offset that is usually less than 1 second. For other emotions, the onset and offset times will vary with the situation (Ekman, 1992). Someone who is lying or faking emotion is less likely to be able to adjust the timing of the onset and offset of emotional facial expressions to the particular situation. In these instances, a person's facial expression of emotion might seem awkward or unusual if he or she is faking it.

Look for the timing of the facial expression relative to changes in voice, flow of speech, and movements of the body. If a facial expression comes after the words that express the emotion, the expression is more likely to be false. If there is a gesture that accompanies a facial expression, and it occurs before the expression, the expression is again more likely to be false. Facial expressions should occur at the same time as the gesture, or perhaps even slightly before the gesture (Ekman, 1992).

Points to Remember

It bears repeating that none of the behavioral cues discussed here can stand alone as a smoking gun indicating an individual is being deceptive. Perhaps the most important aid in the use of these cues is knowledge of a subject's typical behaviors. Other important points to consider include the following:

- Look for behavioral changes that occur in more than one way. For example, if a subject shows changes in voice, facial expressions, and body movements, all of which suggest deception, this provides a strong indicator that something important is going on and the individual's truthfulness should be further evaluated. This is not to say that the presence of only one type of cue should be ignored, but the more types of behavioral cues present, the more reliable hypotheses about truthfulness are likely to be.

- It is more reliable to interpret a change in behavior than to make a judgment based on some behavior a subject repeatedly shows.

- Pay attention to the topic being discussed at the point when a subject's behavior changes. If a subject begins displaying behavioral cues to deception at the mention of a particular topic, this may be an important area to explore further.

- Practice reading facial expressions and body language cues accurately and quickly. A resource for practice in the recognition of facial expressions was noted above in the test presented by Ekman (2003). When developing hypotheses about deception based on behavioral cues, be clear in your own mind about just what particular cues are leading you to suspect deception or believe the subject is being truthful.

- It is important to consider alternative explanations for changes in behavior, other than lying. Perhaps something in the topic of discussion has triggered thoughts of a particularly emotional event, and this is the reason for changes in voice pitch or reddening of the subject's face. There are many possibilities for what may cause such behavioral changes, and it is important to consider these when forming hypotheses about truthfulness.

Note the use of the phrase, "forming hypotheses." The behavioral cues discussed previously will not allow one to come to certain conclusions about whether an individual is being deceptive. These behaviors will need to be part of a more comprehensive gathering of information. One such type of information is the words spoken by the subject. We will now turn to a discussion of how a subject's words can reveal deception.

SPOKEN CUES TO DECEPTION

Mann and colleagues (2004) found that police officers who were good at detecting deception reported paying more attention to story cues. In other words, they made judgments about truthfulness based, at least in part, on the words spoken by the suspect. Obviously, when conducting any type of psychological interview, the words said by the interviewee are very important. In this section we will attempt to review the ways in which detection can be assessed, based on the words spoken. M. G. Frank and Ekman (2004) have called the types of errors that follow "cognitive clues" (p. 486). They suggest that the words that are chosen by liars can be signals to deceit, because the liar gets overwhelmed by trying to both produce false information and decide if what is being said is believable.

Quantity of Speech

Some spoken cues to deception come from the quantity of speech produced. Research has shown that individuals who are being deceptive provide less information than those who are telling the truth (Porter & Yuille, 1995). This can be in the form of providing shorter statements or of providing fewer details. Recent research has found that liars are more likely than truthful individuals to incorrectly believe that providing too much detail makes one appear as though they are trying to hide something (Colwell et al., 2002). The same authors cited evidence that individuals who are telling the truth provide more detail, though they may not explicitly be trying to do so.

Quality of Speech

Colwell and colleagues (2002) reported that one difference in the quality of spoken information between liars and honest individuals is in the spontaneity of the information provided. Individuals who are being truthful are more spontaneous in their telling of a story. In fact, they are more likely to add new details during an interview than deceptive individuals are. This is probably because a deceptive person needs to be very cautious about telling a consistent story, and so will present with carefully controlled speech. In fact, Colwell et al. suggest that decreased detail or content and highly controlled speech, in combination, may be the best-spoken indicator of deception. Although liars showed that they were aware of the need for consistency and a believable story (Colwell et al., 2002), Adelson (2004) cited research that showed that liars' stories are actually more vague, less believable, and less logical than individuals who tell the truth.

Content of Speech

In terms of general content, Adelson (2004) described research done using the Linguistic Inquiry and Word Count software developed by James Pennebaker in which written statements of individuals telling the truth and those who were lying were analyzed and showed some differences. The statements by the individuals who were not telling the truth showed fewer first person statements, more emotion words with negative connotations, and fewer words to differentiate what the liars did from what they did not do, such as but, except, and nor.

Symptom Reports

When conducting an interview in a clinical setting, it is often necessary to assess the veracity of the patient's self-report. This is particularly true in forensic or correctional settings, but can occur in noncriminal populations as well. There can be many reasons for malingering mental illness, even when criminal charges are not involved. Specialized assessment techniques to detect deception will be discussed in detail in upcoming chapters. However, usually the first encounter with an examinee or potential patient is in the first clinical interview. In addition to all the cues discussed above, there are some additional cues based on the content of an interviewee's statements that can provide the tip-off that further assessment of deceptive responding is perhaps warranted.

First of all, let us consider behaviors specific to a clinical interview that may be suggestive of malingering or other deceptive reporting. Harris and Resnick (2003) state that individuals who are feigning psychiatric symptoms are much more likely to point out their illness and symptoms. They may talk about how sick they are. This is particularly unlike truly ill patients who are psychotic. These patients are typically much more hesitant about discussing their symptoms. Truly psychotic individuals are also unlikely to accuse the clinician of disbelieving them, while malingerers sometimes do so.

Similar to the statements above suggesting that deceptive individuals typically provide less detail in their stories, individuals who are malingering mental illness are more likely to answer, "I don't know" in response to specific questions about their symptoms (Harris & Resnick, 2003). They feign positive symptoms of psychosis more often than negative symptoms, but are vague in their descriptions of hallucinations or delusions.

In addition to or separate from feigning psychotic symptoms, individuals will sometimes attempt to feign memory or other cognitive impairment. They may claim to be unable to answer the most basic questions that even a significantly cognitively impaired individual would be likely to answer. An individual who is malingering may claim complete memory loss of all life events and other knowledge, not knowing that such complete memory loss is extremely rare. One example is an examinee who claimed to have a seizure and stated that when she woke up she could not even remember how to do even the most basic self-care activities, such as eating or going to the bathroom. Chapter 5 provides detailed information about how to evaluate feigning of memory or other cognitive impairments.

Harris and Resnick (2003) list certain symptom reports that should raise the suspicion of deception. If a patient claims to have auditory hallucinations, describing them as continuous rather than intermittent suggests deception. Also, descriptions of auditory hallucinations that are vague or inaudible are suspect. Other types of auditory hallucinations that suggest possible malingering are those that are described as questions asking for information, those that are not related to reported delusions, and those that are described as voices speaking in unnatural or stiff language. Additionally, if the patient is unable to describe strategies for managing or decreasing the voices or states that all command hallucinations are obeyed, malingering should be suspected.

In cases where the patient is presenting as possibly having schizophrenia, or claims to have this disorder, and reports visual hallucinations, but not auditory hallucinations, or visual hallucinations that change when the individual's eyes are closed, malingering should be suspected. Typically, visual hallucinations are of human figures that are of normal size and are seen in color. Bizarre hallucinations that are giant or tiny figures or are not in color are suspect. A clear exception to this is in alcoholic, toxic, or organic hallucinations, in which Lilliputian figures are often seen. A common, and highly suspicious claim in individuals who malinger is that they see "little green men." If an individual reports visual hallucinations that are unrelated to auditory hallucinations or delusions, this is also suggestive of deception (Harris & Resnick, 2003).

In the case of delusional thinking, one should be suspicious if the patient calls attention to the delusional beliefs. A paranoid person does not know he or she is paranoid. The exception to this might be found in a patient who is knowledgeable about his or her own symptoms and sophisticated in the language used to describe it. Further, if an individual describes delusional thoughts as having an abrupt onset or termination, deception should be considered. Additionally, if the individual's behavior does not correspond to the delusional beliefs, or if there is no evidence of thought disorder but the delusions have bizarre content, investigate malingering. As an example, if an individual is reporting beliefs that are paranoid in nature, but is not acting in any way that suggests that these beliefs are held, the veracity of the symptom report should be investigated further (Harris & Resnick, 2003).

Posttraumatic Stress Disorder (PTSD; American Psychiatric Association, 2000) is a syndrome for which it is very difficult to determine whether the patient is malingering or not (Harris & Resnick, 2003). PTSD involves only subjective reports of symptoms, so patients can often read what the symptoms are in magazine or newspaper articles or online, and then report these from memory. To determine the genuineness of reports of PTSD, first carefully examine the relationship between the reported traumatic event and the symptoms in terms of the likelihood of the stressor causing the PTSD symptoms and the length of time between the stressor and the reported symptoms. Ask for details of the reported symptoms instead of just relying on a listing of them. Often a malingerer will be able to list the symptoms, but not describe them (Harris & Resnick, 2003). Closely observe the patient's behavior for signs of exaggerated startle response, problems with concentration, and irritable mood.

Other cues that can help to differentiate real from malingered PTSD are as follows: the malingerer focuses on reliving the trauma, while the genuinely traumatized patient focuses more on the numbing that is characteristic of the disorder; malingerers often report nightmares that consist of an exact replaying of the traumatic event, night after night, while true PTSD patients typically report that nightmares begin this way, but eventually begin to include themes from the individual's everyday experience; in veterans who are malingering combat-related PTSD, there will be a focus on the feelings associated with the event and how traumatic it was, while a veteran truly suffering from PTSD will be more likely to downplay the emotional impact of the traumatic events; the individual malingering PTSD is unlikely to report avoidance of situations that are similar to the situation in which the trauma occurred, while this is common in individuals with true PTSD (Harris & Resnick, 2003). Essentially, patients who are truly suffering from PTSD tend to minimize or downplay their symptoms, while malingerers present them in an overly dramatic way and call attention to them.

Interview Strategies

There are some strategies that can increase the sensitivity of a clinical interview to faking by the interviewee. First, do not conduct a clinical interview with a series of symptom checklists. Asking a patient, "Do you experience this (insert symptom)? How about this (insert next symptom from *DSM* criteria)?" makes it much easier for a patient to simply endorse the symptoms and appear to have the disorder in question. Of course, sometimes it is necessary to ask such questions in order to get a complete symptom picture. Asking the patient to describe his or her symptoms, followed by such questions about specific symptoms to rule out or confirm certain diagnoses is likely to be more useful. When the patient does report symptoms, ask him or her for specific details about the symptoms and examples of how they affect functioning. A deceptive individual will be much less likely to be able to convincingly fill in the information about symptoms in this way. If you suspect that an individual is malingering, prolonging the interview may be a way to provide support for this hypothesis, since the individual is less likely to be able to keep up the deception for prolonged periods of time (Harris & Resnick, 2003).

If you know details about an individual's life or a story he or she is telling, such as specific details of the patient's life found in records or a report of a crime in a forensic evaluation, a technique that can be helpful when working with individuals suspected of feigning memory of cognitive deficits is to construct a forced-choice test. This is done by constructing a set of questions about the individual's life or situation, to which you are certain of the answer and the patient should know the answer because he or she was involved in the situation. These questions should be answerable with "yes" or "no," or "true" or "false," creating the forced-choice scenario. Tell the patient to answer every question with one answer. Inform the individual that it is important to answer every question, and to guess if the answer is not known. If the individual truly has no recollection of the events in question, the answers provided would all be guesses. Therefore, there would be a 50-50 chance of getting each answer correct, and the percentage of right and wrong answers would be close to 50%. If the individual answered with a significantly higher percentage of right or wrong answers, he or she probably was feigning the cognitive impairment or memory loss.

Of course, this type of assessment should only be used for exploratory purposes, because of the "homemade" nature of it. If the test can be quickly and easily put together (i.e., the individual's historical information is easily accessible), this technique might be worth trying. The forced-choice testing procedure is used in many neuropsychological measures of malingering and is described in detail in Chapter 5. If one of these measures is available, and/or if the case is likely to involve expert witness testimony, it would probably be more practical to use one of the other validated measures described in Chapter 5. However, if a standardized forced-choice measure is not available, the information is available to construct such a test, and the test is not likely to be put to the test of cross-examination in court, this technique can provide helpful information when attempting to assess feigned cognitive impairment.

SUMMARY

There are many cues that can provide information about whether an individual is being truthful or not. These can be seen in facial expressions or body movements, or revealed in the words that are spoken or tone of voice. When individuals are deceptive, they often present inconsistencies. These inconsistencies can be between statements that are made at different times or between statements and actions. Some of the behavioral cues described are very subtle and could be difficult to notice if one is not skilled in their detection. It is important to practice observing the cues described in this chapter so that over time they will become more easily recognizable.

When using these cues to judge deception, remember that there is no single behavior that defines deception or malingering. The more indicators of deception are present, the more likely it is that the individual is being deceptive. The cues discussed in this chapter can provide valuable information about the possibility that an individual is being deceptive. Depending on the setting in which the interaction takes place, one may wish to use some of the techniques discussed in later chapters to provide more evidence about whether an individual is actually being deceptive. If the evaluation is forensic in nature, the inclusion of standardized testing to support a claim of malingering can be very important. However, if one suspects that a new treatment client is malingering in order to gain access to medication or hospitalization (i.e., somewhere to sleep and be fed), the use of additional measures might not be necessary. If the client's behavioral presentation and symptom report are so bizarre or atypical that it is clear that feigning is occurring, it might be sufficient to simply attempt to discuss this with the patient. Informing the patient that his or her symptom presentation does not fit with an actual mental disorder, and then exploring what the motives for the deceptive behavior were, might allow for continued rapport building and provision of some level of assistance to the patient in a more genuine manner. Utilizing the cues described above can help the clinician make decisions about what additional steps might be warranted in a further assessment of deception.

KEY POINTS

- Utilize caution when using behavioral cues to assess deception. No one indicator definitively suggests deception.

Compare the behavior in question with the subject's typical behaviors if possible.

- If you think a subject's behavior suggests deception, be specific about what behaviors are leading you to this conclusion. This will help you to avoid bias or conclusions based on stereotypic cues that have been shown to be unreliable in the research.
- Vocal cues to be alert to are excessive pauses, stammering, repetitions, errors, or non-words. These cues, as well as a higher vocal pitch, can suggest deception.
- Body language is often overlooked in attempts to detect deception. Possible cues to deception are leaked emblems and a decrease in illustrators, below what is normal for the individual. Fidgeting is not a reliable indicator of deception.
- Watch for micro or squelched facial expressions to reveal deceit. Also, asymmetry in facial expressions and poor timing of a facial expression with speech or action can reveal deception. Lack of eye contact is not a reliable indicator of deception.
- A decrease in detail in a story being told or a lack of spontaneity in the telling of the story can suggest deception. Deceptive individuals tend to be more vague, less believable, and less logical in their stories.
- Be wary of patients or examinees who try to point out how ill they are. Truly mentally ill individuals typically do not try to draw attention to their symptoms, nor do they often accuse clinicians of not believing them, while malingerers sometimes do.
- Malingerers are typically more vague in their reports of symptoms. They are more likely to reply with "I don't know" in response to questions about specific symptoms.
- Malingerers sometimes combine reports of psychotic symptoms with reports of cognitive or memory deficits. Often these cognitive symptoms are highly suspect and do not fit with the individual's level of functioning.
- In patients reporting psychosis, reports of auditory and visual hallucination, as well as delusions, should be related. Auditory hallucinations should be described as intermittent rather than continuous, clear rather than vague, and natural in their language and speech. Also, truly ill patients can typically

describe strategies for managing voices and resisting compliance with command hallucinations. If a subject's presentation does not fit with these descriptions, look further at malingering.

- Visual hallucinations are typically of normal sized people and in color, except in hallucinations caused by organic or toxic conditions. In schizophrenic conditions, visual hallucinations are typically accompanied by auditory hallucinations. Consider deception if the subject presents with symptoms significantly different from these.

- Patients do not typically try to draw attention to their delusional beliefs. In fact, often they do not realize their thoughts are unusual. Delusions usually have a gradual onset and reduction and usually match with the behavior of the individual. If not, explore the possibility of malingering.

- In PTSD, be wary of reports that seem to try to draw attention to the symptoms and the trauma. Individuals genuinely suffering from PTSD tend to downplay their symptoms, while malingerers present them in a more dramatic fashion.

- When interviewing, do not ask questions only in a symptom checklist fashion. Ask for examples of symptoms and more detail about how these symptoms affect daily functioning. Prolong the interview to see if the individual can sustain the malingered presentation. If possible and practical, construct a forced-choice questionnaire regarding aspects of a subject's life (especially if the subject's incorporating cognitive or memory deficits into the clinical presentation).

- Remember there is no "smoking gun." Use the information in this chapter to begin to make hypotheses about a subject's level of truthfulness in responding. Combine these with information gathering techniques presented in later chapters for a truly comprehensive assessment of deception.

Chapter 2

GENERAL PSYCHOLOGICAL TESTS IN THE DETECTION OF DECEPTION

Evidence of malingering behavior existed long before the introduction of standardized psychological assessment. As the use of test batteries became common across settings (hiring evaluations, military fitness, general diagnostic assessments), the need for measures of validity in testing became apparent. As early as the 1940s, when psychological testing was still in its infancy, the concern of inaccurate test results was addressed in what is now the most widely used measure of general clinical assessment, the MMPI/MMPI-2 (Meehl & Hathaway, 1946), reviewed in depth in Chapter 3. At that time, invalid test behavior was divided into a general dichotomy of faking "good" or "bad." While more advanced constructs and scales have been developed, test validity indicators continue to rely on these basic dimensions.

This chapter will explore the use of generalized measures of assessment in the detection of malingering, with an emphasis on those instruments categorized as objective measures of personality assessment. While there are a multitude of instruments falling under the general assessment taxon, we focus on the more commonly used tests. As this manual is a guide for the practitioner, our aim is to provide data and test administration information likely to be useful to the clinician rather than the researcher. It is not our intention to provide a comprehensive review of all tests with malingering indices in this chapter; instead, we focus on those tests most likely to be of use in general clinical, forensic, and correctional practice.

REVIEW OF DECEPTIVE RESPONSE STYLES

In exploring deception on psychological assessment tools, it is important to differentiate between deliberate deception and other inaccurate response styles. Lanyon and Goodstein (1997) identified acquiescence as the most thoroughly researched response set. In this scenario, the tendency is to respond in the affirmative to all test items without regard for item content. A commonly employed strategy to eliminate this measure of bias is simply to incorporate comparable "true" and "false" keyed items without affecting overall item content.

A second invalid, but not necessarily deliberate response style involves making atypical, unusual, or deviant responses. Such a style is often seen on rating scales, wherein an individual has the option of selecting a rating along a continuum and opts for the extremes. Although such responding styles are important to test interpretation, they may be less clinically meaningful than deliberately inaccurate patterns.

As noted above, deliberate deception is often divided into faking-good and faking-bad. The response sets of faking-good have come to be known as social desirability or defensiveness, while feigning illness or dysfunction is often researched under the category of malingering. Both styles represent dishonest portrayals of the test-takers, and are problematic for different reasons.

Clearly, individuals have a variety of reasons for portrayal of themselves in less-than-honest fashions. In forensic evaluations, for example, malingering carries with it an obvious secondary gain incentive (possible evasion of prosecution). Social desirability is common in employment-related testing, as individuals attempt to put their best foot forward in attempt to be hired. Reasons for feigning under other pretexts may be less easily defined; regardless, personality assessment interpretations are often tainted by responses that do not represent true characterizations of a subject's personality. While this chapter is designed to identify and discuss validity indices on major personality tests, for the most part, we limit ourselves to the discussion of malingering. Social desirability measures on these tests are noted, and are also discussed with regard to other measures and methods in Chapters 3 and 4.

Elsewhere in this book, we review instruments designed specifically for the detection of malingering and false responding. In this chapter, we attend to instruments more broad in scope, but which contain measures of malingering, generalized response bias, or other indicators of profile validity/invalidity. It is often the case that the two types of instruments are used in conjunction with one another. We now examine this issue in greater detail.

TEST SELECTION ISSUES

It is important to understand the circumstances under which more generalized instruments would be appropriate detectors of feigned presentation. Specifically, if a clinician is interested in the question of malingering, when would it be appropriate to use a general personality measure to arrive at the answer to the question? We take the stand that if malingering is the sole issue, a malingering-specific test should be used (see Chapter 4). However, rarely are we presented with such clearly defined referral questions, particularly outside the forensic setting. Instead, malingering is often a possibility among several possibilities, and must be a conclusion arrived at through a differential diagnosis process. In our discussion of the Structured Interview of Reported Symptoms (SIRS; Chapter 4), we note that the interview schedule is never to be used to diagnose malingering in the absence of other data, including additional interviewing and assessment. Thus, in the majority of situations where malingering is likely to occur, general personality inventories are likely to be part of a larger assessment battery. As such, it is important to understand the properties of these tests that allow them to categorize honest and dishonest respondents.

In addition to scenarios wherein malingering is a likely outcome (e.g., competency/sanity evaluations), clinicians frequently administer personality tests as diagnostic tools. However, malingering can be an issue in settings that are therapeutic rather than evaluative in nature. In such settings, malingering may still occur, and it is certainly important that test results be valid. Thus, the examiner must be mindful of validity measures. We now review some of the more common personality measures and their scales or other methods for ensuring accuracy and identifying dissimulation.

OBJECTIVE MEASURES OF PERSONALITY ASSESSMENT

The MMPI-2 is by far the most thoroughly researched and utilized personality inventory. As such, we have devoted all of Chapter 3 to the instrument. Due to the overwhelming evidence in support of the MMPI-2 as both a general and forensic instrument, we recommend its use in most cases calling for a general personality inventory. However, there are cases when the test is less practical or when multiple personality measures may be useful. In this section we review the validity proprieties of three of the more popular and robust personality inventories, the MCMI-III, PAI, and NEO-PI-R.

MCMI

The Millon Clinical Mulitaxial Inventory (MCMI-III), a 175-item true-false, self-report measure of clinical and personality traits, is currently in its third revision (T. Millon, C. Millon, & Davis, 1994; also see Craig, 1999). The present version was designed to facilitate differential diagnosis based on the *DSM-IV*, with emphasis given to identification of personality syndromes (Lanyon & Goodstein, 1997). In its present form, the test includes 1 validity index, 3 modifying indices, 11 clinical personality pattern scales, 3 severe personality pathology scales, 7 clinical syndrome scales, and 3 severe syndrome scales (Craig, 1999).

The instrument has undergone several revisions in relatively rapid succession (approximately 1 decade), meaning that much of the empirical data currently relied on is based on earlier versions of the instrument. At this writing, the instrument is among the more popular tools for clinical assessment, and has been the subject of more than 400 published research studies (Craig, 1993, 1997). It was originally designed for use with clinical populations, and is not to be used with "normal" or "worried well" individuals seeking temporary mental health assistance (Craig, 1999). Thus, in cases where malingering is suspected and the existence of any true pathology is unlikely, the MCMI-III is not the desired choice. Instead, an instrument such as the MMPI-2 is indicated.

Understanding the MCMI-III's purpose involves looking at its origin. Aside from practical diagnostic purposes, the instrument was developed as a way to operationalize Millon's complex theory of personality and psychopathology (Craig, 1999). Central to this theory is the idea that maladaptive personality traits formed the core of not only personality disorders, but major clinical syndromes as well. The original instrument was validated using Loevinger's (1957) three-stage process involving theoretical-substantive evaluation, internal-structural evaluation, and external validation. After the first two stages were complete, a final pool of 175 items remained. Norms were then created in the final phase of the validation relying on scores obtained from 1,500 psychiatric patients (Craig, 1999). The instrument underwent its first revision so as to be consistent with the *DSM-III-R* and the aforementioned current version was later designed to parallel the diagnostic descriptors in the *DSM-IV* (T. Millon, 1987; T. Millon et al., 1994).

In its current form, the MCMI-III contains two separate measures of validity or response bias. The simplest indicator of test accuracy is referred to as Scale V, although "scale" appears to be a misnomer. Scale V consists of three items that are highly improbable. In test development samples, the items were endorsed by less than .01% of the clinical population (T. Millon et al., 1994). The test manual indicates that endorsement of two or more of these items completely invalidates the profile. However, endorsement of even one of these three items should lead the examiner to question the validity of the profile and use extreme caution in interpreting the instrument (Craig, 1999).

In addition to Scale V, the MCMI-III contains three modifier indices that are used to explore response bias. Each of these scales is used to apply weight to various items on the clinical scales. Scale X (Disclosure) assesses self-disclosure versus defensiveness, while Scale Y (Desirability) explores social desirability or attempts at favorable self-portrayal. A final scale, Scale Z (Debasement) is associated with malingering. This scale, like exaggeration scales on other instruments, is not a guarantee of malingering, but rather represents overreporting of psychological symptomatology. Elevations on this scale are suggestive of response bias, but again, they are not used to invalidate the testing. Instead, high scores on Scale Z are used for weighting of clinical scales. Specifically, a score greater than 74 on this scale is suggestive of symptom exaggeration/ falsification.

Thoughts on MCMI Usage

The MCMI-III manual makes clear that this test is for use with psychiatric patients. Thus, we do not recommend the instrument simply as a measure of response bias. It is best used in clinical practice with patients who are already suspected of being mentally ill or have a documented history of mental illness. Certainly, mental illness does not preclude feigning. Nonetheless, the validity indicators relating to dissimulation on this instrument are weak; Scale V is so obvious as to call into question why a test was needed for such visible exaggeration. Thus, the test may not be sensitive to malingering and should be used with clients for whom symptom exaggeration is not a major concern. In a client thought to be honest, this instrument will allow insight into invalid responding.

PAI

The Personality Assessment Inventory (PAI; Morey, 1991) is a relatively new assessment tool that is quickly gaining popularity among clinicians in both forensic and general settings (Atkins, 1999; Edens, Cruise, & Buffington-Vollum, 2001). The 344-item, self-report instrument eschews the popular true-false, forced-choice item response dichotomy in favor of a response set with four choices. Each item requires the test-taker to determine the rate of agreement with a statement using the options of "False, not at all true," "Slightly True," "Mainly True," and "Very True."

Although designed for use with adults, the PAI has shown some utility in adolescent samples (Chankin, 2003; Hoekstra, 2000). Nonetheless, the test manual notes that the instrument has been standardized for use with individuals 18 or older. Given the existence of instruments specifically created for use with younger populations, we recommend the use of those instruments for questions of dissimulation. Instruments useful with children and adolescents are discussed in Chapter 7. While the instrument may not be designed for use with children, it is specifically made to be useful with adults having poor reading skills. Unlike other comparable generalized assessment inventories, the PAI can be given to adults reading at the fourth grade level (Morey, 1991; Schinka & Borum, 1993). Thus, when achievement testing or other data indicate reading problems, the PAI may be preferable to the MMPI-2. Additionally, the instrument is shorter than the MMPI-2, and generally requires less than 1 hour for administration (Morey, 1991). A final instrument strength is its availability in Spanish. Many other popular tests do not come in a standardized form in any language but English, requiring a translation that may be imprecise. Thus, this tool is strongly recommended for use with Spanish-speaking populations.

The PAI's 344 items comprise 22 scales, which are divided into the following categories: 4 validity scales, 11 clinical scales, 5 treatment consideration scales, and 2 interpersonal scales (Morey, 1991). Upon completion, raw scores are transformed into T-scores with a mean of 50T and standard deviation of 10T, allowing for standardized interpretation and plotting of scale elevations in graphical form. The instrument was validated with clinical and nonclinical samples and it is meant to correspond with diagnostic nomenclature of the *DSM-III-R* (Morey, 1991). PAI development relied on a construct validation framework highlighting both statistical and theoretical test development concerns (Morey, 1993).

Relevant to this discussion are the four validity scales. Prior to examining these scales, the test author notes that a minimum number of items must be answered for the protocol to be interpretable. In situations where greater than 17 items have not been answered, the instrument is considered invalid (Morey, 1991). Assuming the profile meets this basic criterion, examination of the validity scales will explain an individual's approach to test-taking. Generally, scores more than two standard deviations above the mean on these indices reflects serious profile distortion, and the profile is likely uninterpretable (Morey, 1991, 1998). Aside from these general guidelines, specific interpretive information is provided for each of the four validity scales.

Two of the four validity scales look at response patterns not associated with deliberate malingering but rather with carelessness or irrelevancy. The Inconsistency Scale (ICN) is comprised of 10 pairs of items, both positively and negatively keyed, which are highly similar in nature. The purpose of this index is to gain insight into whether an individual is responding in the same manner throughout the test. Scores below 64T indicate consistent responding, while scores between 64T and 72T indicate some level of inconsistency. While impression management is a concern with scores in this range, the profile remains interpretable. ICN scores greater than 72T indicate too high a degree of inconsistency for meaningful profile interpretation. In fact, 73T is the average score on this index for random profiles (Morey, 1996).

The Infrequency Scale (INF), a measure of carelessness or random responding, is the second of the four validity scales. It identifies respondents who provide atypical answers on the 8-item scale (Morey, 1991). Items on this scale do not have a unifying theme nor do they reflect symptomatic content. Instead, items were placed on this scale because both clinical and nonclinical respondents answered them in the same fashion. Scores below 60T suggest an individual has responded to the protocol with appropriate regard for item content. Any score over 60T can be construed as indicative of idiosyncratic responding (Morey, 1991), but additional research has suggested that scores between 68T and 74T are most likely to result from confusion, scoring errors, reading difficulties, or other failures to attend fully to the test (Rogers et al., 1998). Scores greater than 74T indicate inadequate attention to item content and suggest an invalid profile. INF scores for completely random profiles average 86T (Morey, 1991).

Although the two scales discussed thus far do not provide evidence of malingering, they do give information regarding reliability of conclusions drawn from the test, and are important in obtaining a valid profile. The two remaining scales, The Positive Impression Management Scale (PIM), and Negative Impression Management Scale (NIM) are more likely to be associated with deliberately deceptive responding. The PIM Scale explores the effort an individual makes to deny minor flaws or create a favorable impression (Morey, 1991). Consisting of nine items, the scale has several cut offs to indicate various levels of social desirability efforts, and includes higher cut offs that can be used in settings where impression management is likely to occur (Cashel et al., 1995; Morey, 1998).

Most germane to our focus in this chapter is the NIM Scale. This scale consists of nine items representing rare or bizarre symptoms not typical of true disorder or items that generally create an exaggerated, unfavorable impression. While the items on this scale were endorsed more frequently in clinical samples, none were highly endorsed in normal or clinical samples; however, a significantly greater proportion of individuals instructed to simulate mental illness endorsed these items than in any normal, inpatient, or outpatient sample (Gaies, 1993; Morey, 1991; Rogers, Ornduff, & Sewell, 1993). Morey (1996) makes clear that the NIM Scale is NOT a malingering scale, but rather a starting point in explaining negative, deceptive intent. In evaluating the NIM Scale, scores below 73T indicate a very low likelihood that deception was employed or that symptom feigning has occurred (Morey, 1991, 1996). Scores ranging from 73T to 91T show some degree of exaggeration has occurred, although whether this exaggeration is due to deliberate deceit, a "cry for help," or negative self-image is left to the examiner (Morey, 1996; Rogers, Ornduff, & Sewell, 1993). Rogers et al. (1998) recommend a cutting score greater than 77T for use with forensic referrals. Scores greater than 84T indicate feigning or exaggeration in clinical samples (Morey, 1991). Scores equaling or exceeding 110T should be seen as indicative of feigning across samples.

In addition to being interpreted alone, the NIM Scale should be examined in conjunction with other PAI validity measures. Individuals obtaining NIM scores over 91T with normal scores on INF and ICN have most likely produced malingered test results. On the other hand, persons scoring greater than 91T on the NIM but also elevating the INF and/or ICN scores most likely engaged in random or extremely careless response patterns. In fact, random responders average 96T on the NIM Scale (Morey, 1991, 1996).

Research has shown that elevated scores on the NIM Scale correlate with measures of malingering such as the SIRS across settings and that endorsement of items on the index is more likely among simulators than nonclinical individuals or true patients (Gaies, 1993; Morey, 1991, 1996; Rogers, Ornduff, & Sewell, 1993; Wang et al., 1997). Furthermore, this seems to be true regardless of the sophistication level of the malingerer (Rogers, Ornduff, & Sewell, 1993; Rogers, Sewell, Morey, & Ustad, 1996).

Despite its proven ability in detecting dissimulation, clinicians should be cautious in drawing conclusions from the NIM Scale alone. Although malingering can refer to the feigning of any form of illness, the NIM Scale seems to be most sensitive to attempts at faking severe psychiatric distress such as schizophrenia, but is less sensitive to feigned depression (Gaies,

1993; Rogers, Ornduff, & Sewell, 1993). A second concern with this scale relates to its apparent overlap with true clinical presentations. Individuals with genuine pathology tend to receive elevated scores in this scale (Morey, 1996). Thus, the aforementioned cutting scores for detection of exaggeration must be used with caution in cases where true mental illness is suspected. We suggest the use of multiple data sources to avoid incorrect classification under such circumstances.

In addition to the NIM Scale, researchers examining utility issues with the PAI have developed an additional measure of malingering. The Malingering Index is "comprised of eight configural features of the PAI profile that tend to be observed much more frequently in the profiles of respondents simulating mental disorders" (Morey, 1993, 1996, p. 120). Scoring of the Malingering Index is relatively complex and requires some computation. The eight indicators involve scales not related to validity, but to clinical presentation, and are listed below:

$$NIM \geq 110T$$
$$NIM \text{ minus } INF \geq 20T$$
$$INF \text{ minus } ICN \geq 15T$$
$$PAR\text{-}P \text{ minus } PAR\text{-}H \geq 15T$$
$$PAR\text{-}P \text{ minus } PAR\text{-}R \geq 15T$$
$$MAN\text{-}I \text{ minus } MAN\text{-}G \geq 15T$$
$$DEP \geq 85T \text{ AND } RXR \geq 45T$$
$$ANT\text{-}E \text{ minus } ANT\text{-}A \geq 10T$$

Each of the eight indicators is evaluated and given a weight of one. Scores equal or greater than three suggest the possibility of malingering, while scores higher than five tend to provide strong evidence of malingered profiles.

Thoughts on PAI Usage

This instrument is useful for detecting malingering, as it can be used with both normal and clinical samples of adults and is available in two languages. It is shorter than other popular generalized assessment measures such as the MMPI-2, and may be better suited for individuals with attentional concerns. Furthermore, the instrument requires only a fourth grade reading comprehension level, allowing for its use with some intellectually challenged populations.

Basic PAI scoring does provide some information about malingering, but tends to be more general in providing information about valid or invalid response patterns. More advanced scoring following concerns derived from the NIM Scale and Malingering Index can lead to useful malingering information across settings. Thus, we recommend a systematic approach to malingering assessment with the PAI. Specifically, we suggest clinicians begin by examining validity scales on the instrument. Should NIM Scale indicators described in this chapter suggest the likelihood of malingering, we recommend examination of the additional Malingering Index. These indices, though useful, are still questionable and do not have high classification accuracy rates. If there is any question, we recommend the use of additional measures specifically for malingering detection, such as the SIRS or other, shorter form tests appropriate to the situation. As noted elsewhere in this volume, convergence of evidence is the surest way to draw accurate conclusions about honesty.

NEO-PI-R

Despite the availability of general measures with strong psychometric properties and clinical versatility in terms of normed populations (such as the aforementioned MMPI-2 and PAI), there are times when clinicians rely on other general assessment tools for various reasons such as length, familiarity, availability, or referral question. The NEO-PI-R is one such instrument, and it has demonstrated the requisite utility, reliability, and validity to become a relatively popular and empirically validated instrument (Costa & McCrae, 1989, 1992; Costa, McCrae, & Dye, 1991). The 240-item test comes in two forms, S (self-report) and R (observer-report, in male and female versions) and may be administered via computer or in traditional pencil-and-paper fashion. The test is estimated to require 30 to 40 minutes for completion and is considered to be at a sixth grade reading level. While no specific measures of validity are included in the test, the instrument is considered uninterpretable if more than 41 items are not endorsed. When greater than one, but fewer than 41 items are left blank, the clinician should assign the neutral response option to those items. Additionally, one face valid item inquiring as to whether the test-taker was honest is included in the test. This item is known as validity check Item A. While an affirmative answer does not provide meaningful information, an outright admission of dishonest or inaccurate responding should raise questions and lead to additional evaluation or reconsideration of conclusions.

In addition to the question of honesty, the test includes two additional validity check items known as B and C. Item B asks whether all the items have been answered and Item C asks whether the answers are in the correct locations on the answer form. These items provide no information about malingering, and are actually meant as reminders to the test-taker to check the accuracy of his or her work. Their utility in assessing response set is questionable at best.

The manual for the instrument does offer some guidance in examining three possible biased response sets: acquiescence, nay-saying, and random responding. Acquiescence occurs when test-takers agree with statements simply to be agreeable, rather than because the items truly represent their feelings and opinions. The items in the test are balanced so that they do not all key in the same direction. A study involving volunteers found that only 1% of participants endorsed "agree" or "strongly agree" for more than 150 items (Costa et al., 1991). Thus, profiles with greater than 150 items answered in the affirmative should be interpreted with caution.

Much in the same fashion that acquiescence indicates over-endorsement of items, nay-saying occurs when fewer than the expected number of items are answered with "disagree" or "strongly disagree." If fewer than 50 items are responded to with one of these options, the test results may again be biased (Costa & McCrae, 1992; Costa et al., 1991).

As with other instruments, random responding is a possibility on the NEO-PI-R with dishonest or unmotivated clients. The test authors recommend presenting the material "in a way that will engage the respondent" to avoid random responding (Costa & McCrae, 1992, p. 6). To assess for the possibility that responses are not based on test content, the protocol should be inspected visually. Random responding should be suspected if there are:

Greater than 6 consecutive endorsements of strongly disagree
Greater than 9 consecutive endorsements of disagree
Greater than 10 consecutive endorsements of neutral
Greater than 14 consecutive endorsements of agree
Greater than 9 consecutive endorsements of strongly agree

If any of those response patterns occur, the test authors do not recommend continuing with scoring or attempting to interpret the profile.

The NEO-PI-R seems to have been created with deliberate indifference to the literature on test validity. The authors take the view that the inclusion of malingering indices or complex response style indicators detract from the overall psychometric properties of the instrument (McCrae & Costa, 1983). Other researchers, however, have taken steps to explore the use of this tool with potential malingerers and dishonest respondents. Such studies are particularly important with regard to impression management, as the test is often used in the context of pre-employment testing (see Rosse et al., 1998).

Schinka, Kinder, and Kremer (1997) utilized profiles from a sample of 140 working adults to create three 10-item validity scales: Positive Presentation Management (PPM), Negative Presentation Management (NPM), and Inconsistency (INC). The PPM and NPM scales demonstrated an adequate level of accuracy in differentiating between the response sets and standard responding when administered to a sample of undergraduates (Caldwell-Andrews, Baer, & Berry, 2000). A more recent evaluation using both students and psychiatric patients also suggested utility of these scales, particularly with populations where high base rates of faking are likely (Berry et al., 2001). Nonetheless, further study is required before use of these scales is recommended.

Thoughts on NEO-PI-R Usage

A recent study of assessment practices of 183 psychologists engaged in forensic work found not a single reported usage of the NEO-PI-R (Creevy, Hubbard, & Zapf, 2004). This finding summarizes our opinion on the use of the NEO-PI-R as a way of assessing deception. Put simply, we do not find this test to be useful for such purposes, particularly when there are other tests that provide similar personality information and are able to be used with a wide range of populations, but do include solid measures of validity. We find no credibility to the author's argument that inclusion of validity measures would negatively impact the test. While some researchers have taken steps to develop the requisite validity measures to make this test useful in settings such as prisons or other legal settings, the scales are in need of additional psychometric study before they are used to categorize individuals outside of a research setting.

PROJECTIVE MEASURES OF PERSONALITY ASSESSMENT

It is hard to imagine a scenario where a projective measure would be preferable to the easier-to-use and more psychometrically sound objective tests in identifying invalid or malingered responding. However, such cases do exist. In fact, early proponents of projective measures declared the Rorschach immune to dissimulation (Fosberg, 1938). These findings have been questioned, and Perry and Kinder (1990) summarized the incorrect analyses that led to such conclusions. Regardless, projective measures can be of particular use when the reading level is extremely low or when cultural barriers exist. Limited information is available on the use of these instruments as measures of response bias, but because these instruments remain among the most common instruments on which students are trained, we provide a brief review here.

Rorschach

We have yet to find a more controversial instrument than the Rorschach. The measure requires the clinician to present a series of inkblots to the examinee with no prompt other than "What might this be?" Numerous possibilities are hoped for in response to each stimulus, with later queries as to which parts of the inkblot are involved in the perception. Scoring is extremely complex and tricky, and that topic is not given attention in this volume. Most studies, and certainly most modern investigations, rely on Exner's (1974) Comprehensive Scoring System.

Rorschach supporters suggest its use for nearly all situations, whereas its detractors abhor the instrument and characterize it as idiocy. The authors recognize the popularity of the instrument. In one study of clinicians engaging in forensic work, 18.6% reported use of Rorschach, compared with 73.6% using the MMPI-2, 20% using the MCMI-III, 12.9% using the PAI, and 59.3% using the SIRS (Creevy et al., 2004). An earlier sample held that 41% of practitioners sampled used the Rorschach in emotional injury evaluations, although the test was not necessarily used for the purpose of assessing response set (Boccaccini & Brodsky, 1999).

The debate on the Rorschach as a psychological assessment tool could be the subject of a book unto itself, and, in fact, it has become such. Rather than attempt to add to the fray, we do our best to pull out the most salient points of this raging debate as they pertain to the test's measurement of validity and malingering. The question of whether the Rorschach represents psychological science or psychodynamic silliness has been debated since the instrument's inception and certainly since the prominence of cognitive-behavioral and other schools of thought. As noted, early proponents of the instrument held that it could not be faked, although such a lofty claim has most certainly been overturned (Carp & Shavzin, 1950; Cronbach, 1949; Fosberg, 1938, 1941; L. K. Frank, 1939). Schretlen (1988, 1997) summarized the research findings on the Rorschach and malingering to that time. He found that studies of the Rorschach usually looked at feigned psychopathology rather than malingered brain damage or other cognitive dysfunction. While many studies were poorly controlled or conceptualized, common factors associated with faking were seen. Specifically, clinicians assessing deception were advised to look for "reduced number of responses, slow reaction times, frequent inanimate and animal movement responses (such as blood, sexual anatomy, fire, explosions, and bizarre and aggressive percepts), an attitude of pained compliance, frequent card rejections (e.g., failure to give easy, popular responses, while recognizing more difficult ones), and expressions of perplexity or repeated questions about test directions" (Schretlen, 1988, p. 465).

The early 1990s saw an increase in empirical studies of the Rorschach's ability to detect malingered profiles using the scoring symbols derived by Exner (Shapiro, 1993). For example, researchers looked at the accuracy of the instrument in distinguishing honest and malingered responses with regard to specific disorders. Netter and Viglione (1994) did not find the Rorschach to be useful in detecting feigned schizophrenia, as approximately one third of faked profiles were incorrectly classified. A later study also failed to distinguish between honest and feigned responding groups, but noted a higher number of dramatic responses among fakers (Ganellen et al., 1996). It was suggested that when used together with the MMPI-2, the Rorschach could provide useful information about malingering. Specifically, overly dramatic Rorschach responses, elevated MMPI-2 malingering indicators, and variance in the psychosis indicators on the two tests might be indicative of dissimulation (Ganellen et al., 1996).

The instrument fared slightly better in assessing feigned PTSD, as dissimulators tended to give responses that overstated psychotic type perceptions, were too dramatic, and had higher scores on pure form responses and sum of color-determined responses (Frueh & Kinder, 1994). Nonetheless, participants still showed the ability to fake profiles and create response sets similar to those of true PTSD patients. Contrary to previous findings, malingerers in this study provided more rather than fewer responses to each stimulus card (Frueh & Kinder, 1994). Malingering of depression on the Rorschach has been studied as well. Overall, findings suggest that simulators and individuals with depressive presentations could not be differentiated (Caine, Kinder, & Frueh, 1995).

Following Exner's receipt of the award for Distinguished Professional Contributions to Knowledge, the debate over the Rorschach was ignited with new fury (Widiger, 2001). Garb (1999) called for a moratorium on the use of the instrument in both clinical and forensic settings, while the Board of Professional Affairs referred to it as an extremely powerful assessment measure. Despite the instrument's many, many criticisms, it is clear from clinician surveys that it is being used for legal questions, which most certainly include the possibility of malingering. While we caution against the use of this test for such purposes, McCann (1998a) suggests that it does meet admissibility criteria for use in court. Given its questionable ability to detect deception, and the more widely doubted scoring accuracy issues, we concur with Aronow, Reznikoff, and Moreland (1994) who note that the Rorschach appears more useful for treatment, but not in forensic settings. Although the instrument could be argued to meet the Daubert criteria for admissibility in court on a general basis, we would suggest that it clearly does not meet these criteria as a measure of malingering or other deception.

Detecting Dissimulation With Other Projective Tests

In a review of material related to malingering psychosis, Fautek (1995) devoted space to the utility of projective instruments other than the Rorschach. His examination of the literature found almost no empirical data to back the use of such measures in forensic evaluations or in more general determinations of malingering. The Draw-A-Person Test, though commonly used in clinical practice, does not appear to be useful as a measure of response bias. Additionally, the Word Association Test, one of the oldest measures in existence, also appears to have no use as a measure of validity or malingering. Finally, Fautek (1995) did not find references to the Thematic Apperception Test (TAT) regarding it as a measure of response bias or malingering. A single study on this instrument, conducted in 1967, explores the possibility of examiner effects and alludes to response bias, but the line of inquiry appears to have ended there (Hamsher & Farina, 1967). A recent survey of clinicians doing forensic work found 3.6% had used the TAT to assess malingering in the course of their practice (Creevy et al., 2004). Boccaccini and Brodsky (1999) also found that the TAT was used in 3% of emotional injury evaluations sampled, although whether it was used to detect deceptive responding was not specified.

It should be fairly obvious that the authors do not recommend the use of such tests in settings where malingering is likely or under scenarios where malingering is part of the referral question. Further, such tests should be used with caution in settings where validity is important, as these tools do not contain controls for accuracy.

Thoughts on Projective Test Usage

It has been suggested that one should immediately exit the room if the Rorschach is suggested for an assessment (Dawes, 1994). While we do not take such a stringent position, we do not recommend that clinicians use the Rorschach or any other projective instrument as a measure of response bias. While some literature has emerged suggesting certain indices can differentiate malingered and honest protocols, the studies have yet to provide clear convergence as to how such conclusions can be derived.

The fact remains that the Rorschach is popular among general practitioners and forensic examiners. If it is used under circumstances when possible feigning is of interest, we suggest that other measures be used along with the test. Ganellen et al.'s (1996) suggestion to compare the Rorschach and MMPI-2 profiles bears mention. Before drawing any conclusions from the Rorschach, certain qualities including number of rejections and popular responses, dramatic responses, and questions about test purpose must be given attention.

KEY POINTS

- As stated at the beginning of this chapter, it is not possible to review all validity measures for all instruments. Instead, we have focused on the most common objective and projective personality instruments. Of course, situations will arise when other instruments will be more appropriate for use in an evaluation. In selecting and using any test for detecting malingering, we provide the following common sense caveat: Be familiar with the test you are giving.
- The MMPI-2 is the most frequently used and well-studied objective personality measure and therefore will be discussed at length in Chapter 3; however, there are situations where the use of other instruments may be desirable due to reading level, and so on. To ensure multiple data sources, it may behoove the examiner to use instruments such as the PAI along with the MMPI-2.
- The MCMI-III has undergone several revisions in rapid succession, meaning that some changes may not have been adequately studied. The test includes four measures of validity, although one is simplistic and of questionable value. This test is best for use with individuals who have a documented history of true mental illness.
- The PAI is quickly gaining popularity as a measure of response bias. It is versatile due to its readability (4th-grade level), short administration time (1 hour), and translated form (available in Spanish).

- The PAI has many validity indicators aside from simple malingering. Four basic validity scales assess inconsistent responding, endorsement of atypical answers/patterns, positive impression management (faking-good), and negative impression management (faking-bad).
- The PAI is capable of detecting malingering. Malingering should be suspected if the NIM scale is greater than or equal to 110T or greater than 91T with elevated INC or INF scales. Additionally, a second index suggests malingering is likely under the following conditions: NIM $\geq$ 110T; NIM minus INF $\geq$ 20T; INF minus ICN $\geq$ 15T; PAR-P minus PAR-H $\geq$ 15T; PAR-P minus PAR-R $\geq$ 15T; MAN-I minus MAN-G $\geq$ 15T; DEP $\geq$ 85T AND RXR $\geq$ 45T; ANT-E minus ANT-A $\geq$ 10T.
- The NEO-PI-R does not contain adequate validity measures to ensure test accuracy when response bias is a possibility. The test does include measures of random responding. Validity scales have been developed, but are not developed to the point of being useful in clinical settings.
- Extreme controversy surrounds the Rorschach (and other projective tests). We do not recommend these instruments for use in evaluating deception.

Chapter 3

USE OF THE MMPI-2 TO
DETECT DECEPTIVE RESPONDING

The Minnesota Multiphasic Personality Inventory (MMPI; Hathaway & McKinley, 1940) and its revision, the MMPI-2 (Butcher et al., 1989) have been the most commonly used measures of personality worldwide. They are useful in general clinical practice and in forensic settings because of their many well-developed clinical and validity scales and other indicators. The validity scales can add a great deal of information to aid in the detection of deceptive responding, faking-good or faking-bad, although overall they have been more effective in the identification of fake-bad response sets than fake-good (Lim & Butcher, 1996).

The MMPI-2 consists of 567 items. The items comprising the 10 standard clinical scales are all contained within the first 370 items. The clinical scales are:

1 – Hypochondriasis, assessing somatization or a general sense of being sick or hurt
2 – Depression, which really is more of a measure of general distress and sadness
3 – Hysteria, which assesses tendency toward repression or a lack of insight
4 – Psychopathic Deviate, which taps anger that is oppositional, or a sense of "me against the world"
5 – Masculinity-Femininity, that looks at typical stereotypes of what is masculine and what is feminine
6 – Paranoia, which measures a level of poorly formulated and generalized anger, different from that assessed in Scale 4
7 – Psychasthenia, measuring anxiety and worry

8 – Schizophrenia, very generally measuring confusion and odd beliefs and experiences

9 – Hypomania, measuring a general energy level

0 – Social Introversion, which understandably measures introversion

These descriptions of the clinical scales are obviously very simplified. However, the purpose of this book is not to carefully examine the clinical scales of the MMPI-2, but to assist the clinician in making a determination of whether the clinical scales are interpretable. In addition to the standard clinical scales, the MMPI-2 also contains Content Scales and Supplemental Scales, measuring various types of symptoms and syndromes.

Various cut offs on the scales of the MMPI-2 have been suggested for various purposes. These cut offs are sometimes reported using T-scores and sometimes reported using raw scores. Throughout this chapter, we will use both T-scores and raw scores in reporting ranges and suggested cut offs from the literature. Each time a score is reported we will specify whether it is a T-score or raw score.

The MMPI and MMPI-2 have been used frequently in many forensic settings, both criminal and civil, and have generally been accepted by those within the legal system (Lewak & Meloy, 2000). The courts have decided that the MMPI-2 does measure what it is intended to measure and therefore is generally admissible in court. For example, in *People v. Stow* (1989) the California Supreme Court ruled that no Kelly/Frye showing was necessary to allow expert testimony based on the use of the MMPI (Lewak & Meloy, 2000).

This chapter will focus on the use of the MMPI-2 for detection of deception. The MMPI-2 has many scales that can be used to assist with this purpose to detect both "fake-bad" and "fake-good" responding. First, the traditional validity scales and indices and their uses will be described. Then newer scales and supplemental scales will be discussed. Finally, a suggested model for approaching and using the MMPI-2 validity scales to produce meaningful data about the examinee's response style will be presented.

THE TRADITIONAL VALIDITY SCALES

The "Cannot Say" Scale

The scales on the MMPI-2 that are traditionally known as the validity scales are the ?, L, F, and K scales. The ?, or "cannot say" scale is simply the total number of items left unanswered or that were unscorable because both "True" and "False" were marked. In general, if there are more than 30 items left blank from the first 370 items, the profile should be considered invalid because this will significantly affect the clinical scale scores. However, if there are elevated scores on individual scales, these may be interpretable, and if all or most of the items that could not be scored are after item 370, then the clinical scales may be interpretable. The profile could be interpreted with caution if the ? score is between 6 and 29, and will likely be only very slightly affected, if at all, if the number of unscorable items is 5 or fewer (Friedman et al., 2001).

When a client produces a profile with a high ? score, there are several questions to be answered. First of all, does the client have a reading difficulty? Problems with reading and understanding the questions could lead to many questions being omitted. If it can be determined that this is not the problem, then the examiner should consider that there may be a gross impairment in the abilities needed to make decisions. Then, if this type of impairment can be ruled out, the next question involves whether the client is obsessive, paranoid, or flagrantly being avoidant. It is best to try to prevent this problem by establishing rapport with the client prior to the MMPI-2 administration, and by giving instructions to the client that all items should be completed. Another option is to look at the items that have been omitted and try to determine if they have some significance. It might be useful to point out the missed items to the individual being tested and ask him or her to complete them. Be sure to note which items were omitted prior to asking the subject to do this, particularly in forensic settings where an expert witness might be asked if the subject omitted any items and which items they were (Friedman et al., 2001).

The L Scale

The L scale, or "Lie Scale" is made up of 15 items that are scored only if they are answered "false." These items are typically used to aid in the assessment of fake-good responding. By endorsing many items in the "false" direction, such as "I do not always tell the truth," individuals may be trying to deny any common human frailties, although a high score on this scale is usually only obtained by somewhat unsophisticated or naïve individuals because the items are highly face valid.

Some authors have suggested to use a cut off T score of > 65 to indicate that the profile may be invalid (Butcher & Williams, 2000). Others have shown that a cut off of T > 70 has high specificity in identifying individuals who are not faking-good or being defensive, but its sensitivity to identifying those who are distorting responses may not be very useful (Bagby, Rogers, & Buis, 1994). The L scale has not been especially effective overall in detecting fake-good profiles, although Lim and Butcher (1996) found that both L and K (discussed below) were higher in experimental fake-good profiles than in controls. Additionally, Bagby et al. (1997) found that the L scale and the Edwards (1957) Social Desirability scale (SD, discussed below) were the best of the validity scales used to detect dissimulation at differentiating between fake-good and honest responders in a patient sample. The MMPI-2 suggests using a T score cut off of > 80 as a marker of probable invalidity (Butcher et al., 1989). Such high scores are likely to indicate that the client is overly idealistic and perfectionistic in terms of beliefs about himself or herself. Fortunately, elevations on the L scale do not necessarily render the entire profile invalid, because in general, they are not related to elevations on most other scales; however, deception and suppression of other scale scores should, of course be considered (Meyer & Weaver, 2007).

High L scores may be the result of low education or socioeconomic status (SES). These may also be characteristic of individuals who have difficulty understanding the impact of their behavior on other people, are defensive about their problems, are inflexible and rigid in their problem solving and thinking, and often use denial and have difficulty handling stress. Individuals with high L scores are also likely to deny that they have any need for assistance, or are guilty of any bad behavior, and are unlikely to be straightforward about their shortcomings, or to admit to alcohol abuse. Very high scores may be the result of organic or functional confusion or extreme rigidity and lack of knowledge about societal norms. It should also be noted that regardless of educational level, many individuals with occupations that present a strong demand for a positive image, such as members of the clergy, often have somewhat elevated L scale scores (Meyer & Weaver, 2007).

A score on the L scale that falls within the range of 47 to 57 T (3 to 5 raw score) is typically considered the "normal" range of responding. Most people will deny some common faults. If the L score is lower than 47 T (0 to 2 raw score), there are a couple of possible explanations. This could be the result of candid and nondefensive responding. If the F scale or other scales measuring exaggerated endorsement of pathological items is elevated, a very low L score could be part of an attempt to appear dysfunctional (Friedman et al., 2001). Additionally, since all L scale items are keyed in the "False" direction, an extreme score in either direction may suggest indiscriminant "True" or "False" responding.

The F Scale and Fb Scale

The F scale is made up of 60 items identified as being endorsed by fewer than 10% of a normal adult population. These items originally were used to assess whether individuals were responding to the test without reading the items with attention and/or ability. It has been found that high F scale scores can be suggestive of many different problems in responding. High scores are often considered to indicate fake-bad responding, or malingering, random responding, or a cry for help; however, a high score can also suggest that the client is unable to read or understand the items or the directions, is displaying hostility toward the examiner, is seriously confused, or that there are scoring errors (Meyer & Weaver, 2007). For these reasons, we suggest that when working with a population in which reading difficulties are common, or with a particular client for whom these problems are suspected, a standardized audiotaped version of the MMPI-2 should be used to prevent the possibility of an invalid profile.

In terms of the detection of malingering, the F scale has shown some success, as has the Back F, or Fb scale, that was added to the MMPI-2 to assess infrequency responses in the second half of the test. Wetter et al. (1992) found that the F + Fb scale scores were significantly higher for subjects in experimental malingering groups than for controls; however, those scale scores were also significantly elevated for subjects instructed to respond randomly. These findings suggest that these scales can detect deviance in responding but not necessarily which type. Additionally, F and Fb may not be particularly effective in the detection of deception in settings where the base rate of psychopathology is high. Arbisi and Ben-Porath (1995) found that the mean F scale T score in an inpatient sample was more than two standard deviations above the norm, and the Fb T score mean for this sample was more than three standard deviations above. Using a conservative cut off on these scales of $T > 90$, almost one third of this inpatient sample were above the cut off for F, and more than 40% for Fb. Even using a more stringent cut off score of $T > 100$, almost one fifth exceeded the cut off score for F, and one third for Fb. These relatively high rates of scoring above the cut off suggest that F and Fb may not have very useful discriminant validity in inpatient populations. However, J. L. Lewis, Simcox, and Berry (2002) found that Fb had promise as a screen for malingering of psychiatric symptoms in criminal forensic populations.

With inpatients, an F scale T score above 90 may indicate that an individual is psychotic, but organic brain dysfunction should also be ruled out. Meyer and Weaver (2007) cited Gynther and colleagues (1973) who demonstrated that an appropriate term for these individuals may be "confused psychotic" (p. 299). The F scale may have been increased by items it has in common with the schizophrenia scale (Scale 8) if it is high but the K scale is low. A high F scale score, T > 90, in an outpatient or forensic population should cause the clinician to suspect malingering. However, exaggerated endorsement of symptoms, when there is no clear external incentive suggestive of malingering, may indicate a cry for help, or way of reaching out for attention and assistance (Berry et al., 1996). Note that because the F scale and scales 6 and 8 have considerable item overlap and thus are highly correlated, a high F score with a 6-8/8-6 code-type may be interpreted cautiously (Meyer & Weaver, 2007).

A T score on the F scale that falls within the range of 58 to 64 is considered a moderate score and would not be an unusual score for psychotic or severely neurotic individuals. This type of severe pathology should be ruled out before considering other interpretations for scores in this range. A score in this range may also be a cry for help, especially if there are other indicators of anxiety. Marked emotional difficulties expressed as moodiness or agitation, some confusion, and unconventional or perhaps quite deviant religious, political, and social beliefs may be present in individuals with scores in this range (Meyer & Weaver, 2007).

If items on the test are answered in a truly random fashion (i.e., there is a 50-50 chance that either true or false will be answered on any item), the raw F score will be within the range of 23 to 37, and the raw Fb score will fall between 14 and 26 according to Sinnett, Holen, and Albott (1999). These authors applied the binomial procedure to identify the distribution of random answers and suggested that scores within the above ranges should be considered to possibly result from random responding, while scores above these ranges could be the result of true psychopathology, malingering, or a cry for help. However, it should be remembered that all of these could also be possible even within the "random responding range," and that, because it is uncertain how often clients who respond in a random fashion actually do so with "truly" random responses, it is still possible that random responding could yield scores on F and Fb that fall outside the above ranges. So, while the ranges given above could provide useful information regarding the nature of deviant responding, other scores and indices, discussed below, should be considered before making a determination.

Consider the following as guidelines for F (Friedman et al., 2001):

- Raw F = 2 or less (36-44 T) – The individual is probably responding in a candid way and experiencing little if any distress at the time of the assessment. This low of a score could also be the result of fake-good responding, so look at L, K, and other fake-good scales discussed below to rule out this possibility.

- Raw F = 3 to 7 (45-61 T) – This moderate elevation may occur in individuals with some unusual life experiences, creative people, college students, or others whose ideas and values may differ from the majority. Individuals scoring in this range may be experiencing some psychopathology. In mental health populations scores in this range likely suggest the individual has adjusted well to chronic illness and is not in acute distress.

- Raw F = 8 to 16 (61-92 T) – A score in this range could reflect increasing psychological distress or overreporting of symptoms. If the profile is valid, based on other scale scores, the individual may be experiencing significant disturbance and/or may present with highly unusual values and attitudes.

- Raw F = 17 to 25 (Men – 88-113 T; Women – 88-120 T) – There are several possibilities for why the score may be so high. The examinee may be severely mentally ill, particularly if the assessment is completed in an inpatient setting. The individual may be experiencing extreme distress and may be overendorsing symptoms as a way to make a cry for help. He or she might not have understood the items well or might be uncooperative with the testing process. The individual might be experiencing confused, disorganized, or delusional thinking. The examinee could be malingering. Looking at the scores on other scales, in a way that will be described below, will help to determine which of these possible response styles is present.

- Raw F = 23 to 37 – This is the random range. Utilize scores on the Variable Response Inconsistency Scale (VRIN) to assist with determinations of whether the scores are random. If they are, it could be due to inattention, resistance, or inability to understand the questions. If the scores in this range are not random, look at the descriptions of the range above and below this for interpretive suggestions.

- Raw F = 26 or greater (Men – 116 T and up; Women – 120 T and up) – Scores this high are probably invalid. This does not mean that some valuable information cannot be gained from such scores; it just means that interpreting the clinical scales is likely to be uninformative. With scores in this range, it can typically still be determined whether the examinee was responding randomly (see above), was exaggerating to reach out for help, or was intentionally overreporting for some external gain. If there is no evidence of malingering or random responding, it might be useful to look tentatively at the clinical scales to see what the individual endorsed. The responses might not be particularly reflective of the patient's actual symptomatology, but might give some insights into what types of things he or she is distressed by.

The K Scale

The K scale is composed of 30 items that were generated by comparing the responses of individuals with some psychological disturbance who produced normal profiles with those of nondisturbed individuals who also had normal profiles. This scale is now commonly used to try to identify persons who are responding in a fake-good manner, though this should be done carefully, as the K scale has not generally been very effective for this purpose (Lim & Butcher, 1996). K scale items measure defensiveness that is subtler than that measured by the L scale, and these items are well correlated with measures of social-desirability. So, the K scale items may act to suppress the scores on the clinical scales since many of them are contained in both the K scale and one or more of the clinical scales (Meehl & Hathaway, 1946). The amount of K that contributes to the T scores on the clinical scales should be considered, and, of course, in order to score the MMPI-2 in the standardized way, one must use the K correction. The use of this procedure, which adds a proportion of the K score to several of the clinical scales (Hypochondriasis, Psychopathic Deviate, Psychasthenia, Schizophrenia, and Hypomania), is quite controversial and many claim that it is not necessary or even desirable. Archer, Fontaine, and McCrae (1998) found that using the K-correction did not lead to greater relationships with external variables than did scores that were not corrected. Some clinicians do not use the K-correction, but despite all of the criticisms, we advise that when using the MMPI-2 in any type of legal setting, the standard procedure for scoring should be followed, which includes the K-correction. In fact, while it may be very useful to consider both noncorrected and corrected clinical scale scores in generating hypotheses about a client, the final scoring should always be done the way the test was developed, with the correction (Lewak & Meloy, 2000).

Higher K scale scores correlate with higher levels of education (Butcher; as cited in Lim & Butcher, 1996), and SES, although the effects of these variables on K scores are less on the MMPI-2 than they were on the original MMPI. Meyer and Weaver (2007) state, "The only strong relation with education, K, and clinical scales is with scale 5. The postgraduates show only 5-8 T-score points over a low-educated group, and this probably reflects better mental health rather than a validity difference" (p. 300). Scores in the normal to moderately elevated range of 50 to 60 T suggest a good prognosis for change in treatment and a well-balanced approach to test-taking, and there may even be a rise in K as a result of improvement through treatment (Meyer & Weaver, 2007).

Very high K scores with T > 70 suggest that the profile may be invalid. High scores on K, with a T score between 60 and 70 are indicative of individuals trying to deny any vulnerability and psychopathology. These individuals are unlikely to cooperate in treatment, because they will not admit to any deficiencies in psychological or physiological functioning and will probably blame any difficulties they are experiencing on others. There is often very little insight present in persons with scores in this range, and they may be quite intolerant of behavior in others that they consider deviant or disturbed (Meyer & Weaver, 2007). These individuals typically present themselves with a "stiff upper lip" (p. 202) and as maintaining an emotionally controlled lifestyle (Friedman et al., 2001).

A K scale score between 47 and 56 T (raw score 14-18) is considered in the normal range. Individuals with scores in this range display appropriate control of emotions. These individuals are likely to display coping ability, even if some of the clinical scales are elevated (Friedman et al., 2001).

Low K scores may indicate that a client is faking-bad, or may be the result of confusion, and a compliant or critical and suspicious stance. A raw score between 8 and 13 (Men – 35-45 T, Women – 35-46 T) may suggest that the individual is in pain or feeling vulnerable and that he or she has difficulty keeping emotions and behaviors under control (Friedman et al., 2001). Low self-esteem may be a problem for these clients who are likely to be quite harsh and unskilled in their interactions with others. As a result, serious interpersonal difficulties are prevalent in this score range. Low scores are also suggestive of individuals who are exaggerating their difficulties as a way of asking for help (Meyer & Weaver, 2007). Friedman and colleagues (2001) suggest that low scores on K are a sign of someone with a tendency to "wear one's feelings on one's sleeve" (p. 201). This "tell all" stance may become "excessive openness to the point of masochistical confession" (Meyer & Weaver, 2007, p. 300).

Very low scores with a T < 35 may suggest several possibilities. If there are elevated scores on F, Fb, and F(p) the profile may be malingered (Friedman et al., 2001). However, if the rest of the profile is valid, a K score in this range is likely to indicate severe disturbance (Friedman et al., 2001), and possibly even an organic or functional confusion (Meyer & Weaver, 2007).

The Validity Scale Profile

Looking at these validity scales in combination usually reveals more and better information than any one of them alone. For example, if L and K are in the normal range with F being higher, even somewhat elevated, this is generally an indication of the potential for positive treatment outcome, because defensiveness and denial are relatively low and the individual is experiencing enough distress to motivate him or her in treatment. However, if F is very high with L and K below average, an individual may be malingering, crying out for help, trying to communicate a feeling of being overwhelmed, and perhaps unable to carry on. If L and K are above 60, and F is high, there is quite a bit of confusion present, which can originate from functional, organic, or toxic causes. If this pattern is reversed, and L and K are high with a low F, the client is likely engaging in both conscious and unconscious denial, faking-good or blaming others for problems and is probably a poor candidate for treatment (Meyer & Weaver, 2007).

If F and K are both elevated, intentional faking is a good possibility. If L is high, with F and K scores in the normal range, the individual may be responding in a fake-good manner, but may also be naïve and/or unsophisticated. If the K score is high, with L and F in the normal range, consider a more sophisticated defensiveness. The combination of a high K score with a 1-3/3-1 code-type and low scores on scales 2, 7, and 8 suggests an individual who is defensive and unlikely to admit to having any faults. This type of individual has a poor treatment prognosis, because the patient role will be intolerable (Meyer & Weaver, 2007). More information will be presented below about combining these and other scales to make decisions about deception.

The F-K Index

The F-K index (Gough, 1947, 1950) is computed by subtracting the raw score on K from the raw score on F. Gough (1950) suggested that a score of 9 or higher suggested an attempt to fake-bad on the MMPI. The MMPI-2 test materials (Butcher et al., 1989) suggest a cut off of 15 to indicate faking-bad or exaggeration of symptoms, but this high cut off may not be particularly effective in forensic settings or in use with inpatient populations. Lachar (1974) suggested using 12 as the cut off for faking-bad.

Generally, F-K scores between 0 and 11 are considered normal. Scores between 12 and 16 indicate that malingering is likely. The exception to this would be in psychiatric populations, where such high scores would not be unlikely. Scores greater than 17 indicate that the profile is invalid and intentional exaggeration, particularly in light of other scores suggestive of this, is probable (Friedman et al., 2001).

Butcher and Williams (2000) have asserted that the F-K index should not be used to detect faking-good or defensiveness, as it has not typically been found to be useful for this purpose. However Bagby and colleagues (1994) found that a cut off of < -15 had fairly high utility for discriminating experimental defensives from controls and forensic inpatients. If the index is less than -12, the traditional interpretation is that the client is trying to be seen as emotionally healthy and invulnerable. Meyer and Weaver (2007) suggest interpreting negative scores as being increasingly indicative of an individual who is trying to present a good image and deny problems. However, when trying to make a decision about whether an individual is responding in an overly self-favorable way, the F-K index is not the score to rely on. Other scores and indices discussed below and in Chapter 4 can provide much more reliable information about this type of responding.

The above cut off scores for the F-K index work best when F and K are relatively low, and even when this is the case, false positives and negatives are not unusual. For example, clients who are severely distressed or psychotic may legitimately obtain an F score between 65 and 80, and without a corresponding high K score, these individuals may be misidentified as malingering (Meyer & Weaver, 2007). Rogers, Bagby, and Chakraborty (as cited in Bagby et al., 1994) found that F-K may be susceptible to being unable to detect response sets that have been coached.

The F-Fb Index

Another index score that may be used to aid in the detection of malingering is the F-Fb. Pensa et al. (1996) hypothesized that as the MMPI-2 questions progressed, malingerers would become less able to sustain their deviant responding, so Fb would clearly be lower than F. The results of their study, in which they compared a group of diagnosed psychotics with male volunteers who had been given educational information about psychosis and instructions to malinger psychosis, found that the malingerers endorsed fewer deviant items as the test continued, while the subjects with diagnosed psychosis maintained fairly stable levels of deviant responses.

The F-Fb index score is computed by subtracting the raw score on Fb from the raw score on F. If this yields an index score of 10 or higher, the profile may be invalid. Or if Fb is greater than F by 8 or more points and is elevated between 15 and 19, the second portion of the test may be invalid, while the clinical scales might still be interpretable if there are no other signs of deviant responding (Friedman et al., 2001). However, the content of the items on the F and Fb scales is different. The F scale contains a much greater proportion of items containing psychotic content, where the Fb scale contains more items suggestive of depression. So, there may be a legitimate difference between these two scores and the elevations of the other scales should be examined.

The L+K Index

As an attempt to identify individuals who are faking-good, the L+K index (Cofer, Chance, & Judson, 1949) seems to have received little attention in the literature. This index score is reached by summing the raw scores of L and K. Using a cut off score of > 25, Baer et al. (1995) obtained an 80% correct classification rate for this index. Adding the raw scores of the Wiggins' (1959) Social Desirability (Sd) scale and the Superlative Self-assessment (S; Butcher & Han, 1995) scale (Sd and S are discussed in more detail below) to the L and K raw scores, and using a cut off score of 74 has been suggested by these authors as providing the highest level of differentiation among honest responders and those who are faking-good with an overall correct classification rate of 88%. This could be a useful means for detecting fake-good response sets; however, this finding has not been replicated, so this summing procedure should be used with appropriate caution.

Measures of Random or Inconsistent Responding
VRIN

The Variable Response Inconsistency Scale, or VRIN, and True Response Inconsistency Scale, or TRIN, were developed for the MMPI-2 to measure random or inconsistent responding. VRIN is made up of 67 item pairs that produce one or two, out of a possible four, item sets that would be semantically inconsistent. These sets can be true-true, true-false, false-true, or false-false. A high score on this scale suggests that an individual is responding randomly, which can be intentional or the result of a state of confusion. If one responds in a truly random fashion, the VRIN score is 97.

Raw scores on VRIN from 0 to 8 are indicative of consistent responding. However, a raw score of 8 is generally considered to be too low to use as a cut off for random responding (Friedman et al., 2001). Most clinicians will agree that a raw score of 16 or higher on VRIN is clearly indicative of inconsistency and that scores from 9 to 15 are unclear (Meyer & Weaver, 2007). However, this extreme score seems too conservative and is likely to miss many invalid profiles. The MMPI-2 manual recommends a cut off of 13 to suggest random responding (Butcher et al., 1989). Some authors suggest that the optimal cutting score for VRIN to detect random responding is > 14 (Bagby et al., 1994).

VRIN can add useful information to the traditional validity scales in the detection of random responding. The validity scale profile for fully random responding consists of a T score for L of approximately 60, for F approximately 110, and 55 for K. Also, scale 8 will be elevated to approximately 95 T in females and 110 T for males. Scale 6 usually has the lowest score. An MMPI-2 profile that is randomly generated resembles a profile of fake-bad malingered responding in many ways (Meyer & Weaver, 2007). VRIN has been shown to be the most useful validity scale for differentiating between random and fake-bad response sets. Wetter and colleagues (1992) found that F and Fb were significantly elevated in an experimental group instructed to fill out their answer sheets in a random fashion, as well as in two groups instructed to malinger. VRIN scores were elevated for the random response group, but not for the malingering groups. These results suggest that if F and VRIN are both elevated, random responding is likely. If F is elevated and VRIN is within a normal range, malingering is more likely, although it should be remembered that F can be elevated because of genuine psychopathology as well.

In an attempt to examine the relationship between VRIN scores and external criteria, Archer and colleagues (1998) had each of their subjects complete an MMPI-2 and a Symptom Checklist-90-Revised (SCL-90-R; Derogatis, 1994). Each of the subjects was also rated by staff psychologists with the 18-item Brief Psychiatric Rating Scale (BPRS; Overall & Gorham, 1962) and was given a Global Assessment of Functioning (GAF) rating. They found that these external variables were correlated at lower levels with protocols on which the VRIN T score was > 80 than with protocols on which the VRIN score was lower. These findings add to the level of confidence that can be applied to the ability of VRIN scores to identify invalid profiles. However, these authors noted that in psychiatric inpatient populations, some level of random responding seems to be common. In this population, even with VRIN T scores > 80, there was some relationship between MMPI-2 scores and SCL-90-R scores.

TRIN

TRIN consists of 20 pairs of items that are inconsistent if both are answered "true" or both "false." For example, one TRIN pair is "I am happy most of the time" and "Most of the time I feel blue." For 3 pairs responding either true or false to both is inconsistent. For 11 of the pairs, only a true response to both items is considered inconsistent, and for 6 pairs, only 2 false responses. To obtain an index score between 0 and 20, subtract from 9, which is the total possible number of inconsistent false pairs. Graham (1993; as cited in Meyer & Weaver, 2007) suggests a score of 13 is sufficiently high to indicate indiscriminant "true" responding. Indiscriminant "false" responding is indicated with a score that is less than 6 (Meyer & Weaver, 2007).

If all items on the MMPI-2 are answered "true," the score on F will nearly go off the scale; L will be about 35 T, and K will be at 30 T. The clinical peak will be on scale 8 with a T score of approximately 105 for females and 125 for males. A second peak will be on scale 6 with a T score of 90 for males and females. If "true" and "false" responses are alternated, an individual will obtain T scores of approximately 55 on L, 105 on F, and 65 on K, with a score of up to 120 on scale 8. The rest of the clinical scale scores will also be high (Graham, 1993; as cited in Meyer & Weaver, 2007). If a client has responded in one of the above ways it is likely that it will be easily noticed by quickly glancing over the answer sheet, so it is worthwhile to take a moment to do this before taking the time to score the profile or sending it out to be scored and interpreted.

Other Scales Used to Detect Fake-Bad Responding
The F(p) Scale

As was mentioned above, there are many reasons that the F scale may be elevated, including genuine psychopathology. It is difficult to use the F scale to detect malingering in settings in which there is a high base rate of psychopathology, because standard cut off scores used in other settings are not able to discriminate as well between honest and fake-bad responding (Arbisi & Ben-Porath, 1998). The F(p), or Infrequency Psychopathology Scale (Arbisi & Ben-Porath, 1995), was developed to assess infrequent responding in populations with high levels of psychopathology by using a set of 27 items from the MMPI-2 that are rarely endorsed by either psychiatric inpatients or those in the normative sample.

F(p) significantly improves the classification of honest and malingering clients over F used alone with psychiatric inpatients using an F(p) cut off score of $T > 100$ (Arbisi & Ben-Porath, 1995, 1998). The use of both F and F(p) in the detection of exaggeration of symptoms in VA and inpatient populations was supported by research conducted by Strong, Greene, and Schinka (2000). However, Storm and Graham (2000) found that F(p) was better than F at differentiating psychiatric patients from malingerers when the malingerers were coached on the validity scales of the MMPI-2.

If F is elevated, it could be from random responding, faking-bad, or actual psychopathology. Arbisi and Ben-Porath (1995) assert that the first step after finding an F scale elevation in an individual who may be suffering from significant levels of psychopathology should be to check VRIN (T > 80) and then TRIN (T > 100) for random responding, yeah-, or nay-saying. If these scales are in the normal range, the next step is to check the F(p) score. If the F(p) score is elevated, T > 100, consider malingering nonexistent symptoms or exaggerating current pathology. If F(p) is normal, the F elevation may be due to genuine psychopathology. Meyer and Weaver (2007) have suggested that when the F scale raw score is > 16 and F(p) is < 4 raw, it is highly possible that the profile is valid, but when the F(p) raw score is > 8, it suggests invalidity.

The Fake Bad Scale

While F, Fb, F(p), and F-K have all been useful in detecting malingering of psychiatric symptoms, their usefulness in the detection of neuropsychological malingering is questionable. Larrabee (1998) noted that in settings where neuropsychological assessments are done, complaints of somatic symptoms are common. These symptoms are measured on the MMPI-2, primarily on scales 1 and 3, and each of these scales contains only one F scale item. This suggests that the MMPI-2 scales used to measure overreporting of symptoms may not be particularly useful in the detection of somatic symptom exaggeration (Larrabee, 1998). Greiffenstein, Gola, and Baker (1995) found that the F scale and the F-K index were unable to differentiate between groups of individuals referred for neuropsychological assessments who were classified into three groups: a traumatic brain-injury group, a persistent postconcussion group, or a probable malingering group.

The problems with using the F scale and F-K to detect malingering in neuropsychological evaluations were noted by Lees-Haley, English, and Glenn (1991), who developed the Fake Bad Scale, or FBS, as a way to deal with this. The FBS is made up of 43 items. These items were selected because of their content (as opposed to empirically selected), and the desired content was determined based on frequency counts of the responses of malingerers on the MMPI-2 and the observation of malingerers in personal injury cases (Fox, Gerson, & Lees-Haley, 1995). Lees-Haley et al. (1991) found that many malingerers in personal injury cases showed features of both fake-good and fake-bad responding. For this reason, the FBS is composed of items that are keyed when answered "true," and items that are keyed when answered "false." There are 18 true and 25 false items on the scale, and many of these items appear on clinical scales 1 and 3.

The cut off scores recommended by Lees-Haley for the FBS are raw scores of 24 for males and 26 for females. These cut offs yielded sensitivities of 75% for men and 74% for women, and specificities of 96% for men and 92% for women.

FBS and clinical scales 1 and 3 seem to be promising indicators of somatic malingering. There is some overlap between the three scales, but not to the extent that the FBS would incorrectly classify individuals with somatoform disorder, who score high on scales 1 and 3, as malingering. Even if all of the items on scales 1 and 3 are endorsed, the FBS score is only 20, which does not meet the recommended cut offs of 24 for males and 26 for females. It is recommended at this time that if FBS is elevated above the appropriate cut off score, and scales 1 and 3 are elevated with T scores above 80, malingering of somatic symptoms is very likely. If an individual scores above the cut off on FBS and a T score > 80 on only scale 3, somatic malingering is possible and should be investigated further (Larrabee, 1998). The FBS is explored in greater detail in Chapter 5.

The Dissimulation Scale

Gough (1954) developed the Dissimulation Scale (Ds) as a way to detect fake-bad responding on the original MMPI. This 74-item scale was composed of items that discriminated real patients from individuals who were asked to feign psychopathology. This scale was eventually revised, and the resulting Dissimulation Scale-Revised (Ds-R; Gough, 1957) included only the 44 items from the original scale that were best able to discriminate between real and faked responses. On the MMPI-2 only 58 items remain from the original Ds that make up the Ds-2 scale, and 34 items remain from the Ds-R to make up the Ds-R2 scale. The Ds-2 scale has been found to be better at detecting feigned response sets than the shorter Ds-R2 (Friedman et al., 2001). It functions similarly to the F and Fb scales, but the content is subtler. On the Ds scale the pathological or atypical response is not as obvious as it is on F and Fb (Friedman et al., 2001). Using a cut off score of 34 on the Ds-2, G. L. Walters and Clopton (2000) found that it was as successful as F(p) and Fb in identifying malingering, and that these scales generally detected invalid responding better than F, F-K, and O-S.

In a meta-analysis of the MMPI-2 and its ability to detect malingering, F(p) was found to be especially useful and consistent for this purpose. F was shown to be effective, though the usefulness of Fb was questionable. Ds-2 was found to be particularly good in the detection of malingering because it uses a sophisticated strategy for this detection, it yields few false positives, and its cut off scores are consistent (Rogers et al. 2003).

Raw scores of 18 and below on the Ds-2 suggest that psychopathology that is reported is genuine. Even if other scales suggesting overreporting are somewhat elevated, a score in this range on the Ds-2 indicates that malingering is unlikely (Friedman et al., 2001). Of course, if there are greater elevations on other fake-bad scales, F(p) in particular, and VRIN is normal, malingering should still be suspected even if the Ds-2 is this low. Raw scores on Ds-2 between 19 and 27 suggest some level of invalidity. If other scores indicate the profile is exaggerated, this level of score on Ds-2 supports invalidity, especially the closer it gets to 27. However, if the other validity scales are normal, the profile is probably valid with Ds-2 in this range (Friedman et al., 2001). With raw scores on Ds-2 between 28 and 33, the profile is most likely exaggerated, even if other scales do not suggest overreporting. However, severely mentally ill patients could score in this range and not have an invalid profile (Friedman et al., 2001). Raw scores between 34 and 37 almost always indicate the profile is malingered, and scores above 38 suggest this even if the other scales suggest the profile is valid (Friedman et al., 2001).

The Md Scale

The Malingered Depression (Md) scale has recently been developed to assess malingering of depressive symptoms on the MMPI-2 (Steffan, Clopton, & Morgan, 2003). This scale attempts to determine how much subjects know about depression and about how the MMPI-2 validity scales work in addition to trying to determine which individuals try to malinger depression. The scale consists of 32 items. These items were able to differentiate college students who exaggerated depressive symptoms from students who were actually depressed. At this time, more research is needed to determine how useful this scale will be for assessing malingered depression.

The Fptsd Scale

The Infrequency-Post Traumatic Stress Disorder (Fptsd) scale was created from items that were infrequently endorsed by combat veterans receiving treatment for PTSD (Elhai et al., 2002). Early attempts at validating the scale suggested it could differentiate real from feigned PTSD better than F, Fb, or F(p). More recent research suggests that this ability may apply only to PTSD resulting from combat trauma, as F(p) outperformed Fptsd when discriminating genuine from exaggerated PTSD in cases of noncombat related trauma (Elhai et al., 2004). As with the Md scale, this scale needs further research to determine its true usefulness in detecting malingered PTSD.

The O-S Index

Another method for assessing validity is to compare the endorsement of items that were arrived at through Wiener and Harmon's (1946) ratings of items as subtle (S) or obvious (O) in terms of how they related to psychopathology in general. The subtle items have been thought to be helpful in detecting deceptive responding, because individuals engaging in a deceptive response style would not be able to see the relation of these items to psychopathology and would not know how to answer them in the desired direction (Bagby, Nicholson, & Buis, 1998).

The O-S index is controversial, and there are some conflicting reports about its utility. The O-S index score is determined by summing across all T scores on O and subtracting the sum of those on S (Meyer & Weaver, 2007). It has been found to have competitive utility in the classification of experimental malingerers using a cut off score of > 169, and in classifying defensive responding with a cut off of < -24 (Bagby et al., 1994). In general, O scales are more highly correlated with their respective full clinical scales and have higher validity coefficients with criminal history variables than S scales in a male inmate population (Osberg & Harrigan, 1999).

In a meta-analysis of research on the MMPI-2 fake-bad indicators, Rogers, Sewell, and Salekin (1994) found that the O-S index had very strong effect sizes for normal and psychiatric samples that were comparable to those of F and F-K. This suggests that these scales may be the most useful in the detection of malingering, although Woychyshyn (as cited in Meyer & Weaver, 2007) and Hollrah et al. (1995) propose that the Subtle/obvious scales may be more useful in the detection of fake-good profiles than fake-bad.

O-S discriminated between males with diagnosed psychosis and those instructed to malinger psychosis in a study conducted by Pensa et al. (1996). These authors found that using a cut off score of 150 on this index led to correct classification 87.5% of the time. D. Boone (1994) reported that, in all of the clinical scales that include subtle items, the full-scale reliability (including subtle items) was lower than the scale's reliability with only the obvious items. G. L. Walters and Clopton (2000) reported that O-S generally performed significantly more poorly than F, Fb, F(p), F-K, and Ds-2 in detecting malingering.

Scales Used to Detect Fake-Good Responding

The Positive Malingering (Mp; Cofer et al., 1949) scale was developed for the MMPI, but it lost only a few items on the MMPI-2, so it can still be used in conjunction with the K scale to aid in the assessment of defensiveness (Meyer & Weaver, 2007). A cut off score on Mp of T > 14 has been shown to have relatively good utility in differentiating between experimental subjects instructed to respond defensively, controls, and forensic inpatients (Bagby et al., 1994). This same cut off was used by Baer and colleagues (1995) and produced an overall correct classification rate of 82%. The Mp scale should be used in conjunction with other measures of socially desirable responding when making decisions about whether an individual is responding in a fake-good manner. For example, if K and Mp both have T scores greater than 60, then the test taker is probably intentionally responding in an overly positive manner. However, if the T score on K is greater than 60 but the score on Mp is lower, the K scale elevation is likely due to a lack of awareness about the self rather than intentional impression management (Caldwell, 1988).

The Wiggins (1959) Social Desirability (Sd) scale, the Edwards (1957) Social Desirability (SD) scale, and Hanley's (1957) Test-taking Defensiveness (Tt) scale can all still be of some use, although they were all developed for the original MMPI. The Sd scale is made up of items that were found to differentiate student subjects responding in a standard way to those who were instructed to use a socially desirable response set. Using a cut off of > 18 on Sd on the MMPI-2 yielded a correct classification rate of 78% overall in distinguishing between individuals instructed to fake-good and those given standard instructions (Baer et al., 1995). The SD scale consists of items on which judges agreed unanimously on the response considered to be socially desirable. Baer and colleagues obtained an overall correct classification rate of 81% using a cut off score of > 33 on SD. The Tt scale also is made up of items for which the socially desirable response was agreed upon by judges, but only half of a normative group responded to these items in the socially desirable direction. A cut off of >15 was used to yield a correct classification rate of 82% overall (Baer et al., 1995).

The Superlative Self-assessment (S) scale was developed as a way to improve the assessment and detection of fake-good responding by detecting overly positive self-presentation without being easily distorted, as the face valid L scale is, and by evaluating defensiveness more effectively than the K scale (Butcher & Han, 1995). The scale consists of five subscales: Beliefs in Human Goodness, Serenity, Contentment with Life, Patience/Denial of Irritability and Anger, and Denial of Moral Flaws. The S scale and its subscales have demonstrated potential for fake-good profile detection (Lim & Butcher, 1996). The S scale correlates well with K at about .80, although the two scales only share 10 items (Friedman et al., 2001). S has shown some incremental validity over K and seems to be more useful with nonpsychiatric patients (Meyer & Weaver, 2007). In evaluations done in family custody and access cases, Bagby and colleagues (1999) found that the S scale and Wiggins Sd scale identified 74% of the litigants as underreporting, while L and K identified only 52%, suggesting that S and Sd may be more useful for the identification of faking-good in this population. Baer and colleagues (1995) also found that S and Sd demonstrated significant incremental validity over L and K in the differentiation of honest and fake-good profiles. These authors used a cut off score of > 32 on S, which resulted in 83% of subjects being correctly classified into either a fake-good or standard instruction group. Raw scores of 38 or higher suggest exaggeration of positive qualities (Friedman et al., 2001).

The Socioeconomic Status (Ss) scale (Nelson, 1952) has been described by Caldwell (1988) as important in the understanding of K scale elevations. Along with Mp and Sd, the Ss scale has been used to determine how much an elevation on K is due to high SES and how much is due to intentional impression management. For example, if K is elevated with a T score of 65 and Ss is also elevated with a T score of 65, but Mp and Sd are relatively low, it is likely that the K scale elevation is due to SES and not an intentional exaggeration of personal strengths. However, if K, Mp, and Sd are elevated, with Ss being relatively low, it is more likely that the K elevation is due to intentional fake-good responding.

The Other Deception (Od; Nichols & Green; as cited in Baer et al., 1995) scale was developed for the MMPI-2 using items from Sd and Mp. To the degree that Od, S, and Mp scores are high, along with an elevated K, intentional faking-good should be considered (Meyer & Weaver, 2007), particularly if Ss is low (Caldwell, 1988). The Od and S scales were found to be the best, of the scales used for detecting fake-good responding, at discriminating between faking-good and responding honestly in a sample of students. The Wiggins Sd scale was the best at discriminating between students who were responding honestly and patients who were faking-good (Bagby et al., 1997). Using a cut off of > 18 on Od correctly classified 81% of subjects as faking-good or responding honestly (Baer et al., 1995).

The Positive Mental Health (PMH4; Nichols, 1992; as cited in Baer et al., 1995) scale is a general measure of good mental health. It is composed of items that are included on at least 4 of the 28 supplementary scales intended to measure positive characteristics. A cut off score of > 27 classified 82% of subjects correctly (Baer et al., 1995).

There are two types of fake-good responding: impression management, which is a purposeful attempt to present oneself in an overly positive way, and self-deception, a nondeliberate attempt to hide symptoms (Paulhus, 1984). These two types of socially desirable responding were described in more detail in the introduction, and additional methods for assessing these will be examined in Chapter 4. As for the MMPI-2 scales, impression management seems to be measured more by L, Sd, and Mp, and self-deception more with K, S, and SD (Strong et al., 1999).

Mean Elevation

The Mean Elevation (ME) of the clinical scale T scores is another possible indicator of deceptive responding. The ME is typically within the range of 45 to 55 for normal individuals, and between 55 and 65 in psychiatric inpatients. When the ME is greater than 75, consider malingering, especially when there is no documentation or evidence of severe mental illness (Meyer & Weaver, 2007).

Critical Items

Examining the critical items of the MMPI-2 can be another way to gather information about the possibility that an individual is not responding honestly. Different sets of critical items have been proposed (i.e., Koss-Butcher, Lachar-Wrobel). After the MMPI-2 administration the clinician should always check over the critical items, even if dishonesty is not suspected. This is because the client completing the test most likely has some expectation that the clinician will know what he or she endorsed. In particular, the clinician should look for items suggestive of suicidal ideation or other extreme distress, so that these issues can be dealt with appropriately with the client.

The critical items can also be used to structure an interview. Certain items that were endorsed by the client may be of particular interest for further exploration in an interview, and addressing the way that the item was endorsed may be a useful way to approach the topic with the client. Questioning of critical items may also reveal information about the extent to which a client was paying attention when answering the items. When questioned, a client may state that he or she did not intend to answer an item in a certain way. Critical item questioning can be particularly useful when dealing with clients who are functioning at a relatively low level intellectually or who are unsophisticated. Such clients may not fully understand some items or may answer items literally. An example of this is when a client endorses the item "Peculiar odors come to me at times" and upon questioning, reveals that he or she was referring to the smells coming from a dumpster outside the window.

If it is revealed through questioning about the critical items that an individual was not paying attention to his or her responses at times during the test, or that he or she has misunderstood items or answered them literally, this may provide important information to supplement the validity scale scores. For example, if an individual is suspected of malingering because of elevated F and F-K scores, and inquiry reveals that this individual endorsed many psychotic items after interpreting them literally, malingering may not be the problem. However, if malingering is suspected and the critical items are questioned, and the individual cannot answer questions like, "Tell me about a time when this happened," this may provide more evidence to support a decision that the individual is in fact malingering.

SUMMARY

The MMPI-2 consists of numerous scales for determining the validity of test administration. The vast amount of information obtained about validity can make interpretation of an MMPI-2 profile daunting, but it also makes the MMPI-2 one of the best instruments to use in a wide variety of settings, whether deception is likely or not. The MMPI-2 is relatively inexpensive and easy to administer, so it makes sense to use it as an early step in an assessment of deception. Even if deception is not a great concern, as in a treatment setting, this test makes sense because it can provide rich clinical information if the profile is valid, and identify possible areas of concern if it is not. The MMPI-2 is one of the most versatile and widely used, researched, and accepted measures available. The following Key Points will outline a suggested strategy for interpreting the validity of an MMPI-2 profile.

KEY POINTS

- First, look at the overall pattern of responding and the number of responses left blank or scored as both "True" and "False." If it is clear that the profile was scored with all true or all false responses, or if there is some obvious pattern, such as alternating true and false responses throughout the test, the examiner should assess the respondent's understanding of the instructions, reading level, and motivation. After trying to understand the reason for such responding and discussing with the examinee the importance of the testing process, it might be worthwhile to attempt to get the participant to redo the test. If the poor responding was due to a reading difficulty, use the audiotaped version of the MMPI-2. If the problem is that there are too many items left blank, it may be helpful to simply ask the subject to complete the items left blank. If there are more than 30 items out of the first 370 items left blank and the examinee refuses to complete these items, the profile is invalid.

- Second, look at VRIN. The score on VRIN trumps all other validity scale scores if it is elevated. This is because a VRIN score in the random range suggests that the profile is invalid because of random responding. The rest of the scores are not going to reveal useful data. Elevations on the rest of the validity scales will likely be due to random responding. So, if VRIN is ≥ 13, the profile is invalid due to random responding.

- If VRIN is < 13, look next at F. We do not recommend using a specific cut off on F to determine malingering. However, as F increases to a raw score of 8 and higher, overreporting becomes more and more likely. Remember that elevations on F can be due to genuine psychopathology. If the F score is high and suggestive of possible malingering, look at other indicators to provide additional information to aid with understanding the F score, such as Fb, F(p), FBS, and Ds-2.

- Raw scores on Fb below 4 suggest a lack of exaggeration in a profile that is otherwise valid and not elevated on other scores. As with F, such low scores on Fb could go along with an attempt at underreporting, so consult the appropriate scores to determine this (discussed below). However, as Fb increases, particularly as it approaches a raw score of 14, it could contribute to a picture of overreporting. As scores get closer to 19, the probability of malingering increases (Friedman et al., 2001).

- F(p) can provide very important information about intentional overreporting when F and Fb are unclear. When other validity scales clearly suggest invalidity, a raw score on F(p) between 4 and 9 would confirm this, particularly if the test is being given outside of an inpatient setting. If other scores suggest possible invalidity, then a raw score on F(p) of 5 or higher would support a determination of invalid responding due to symptom exaggeration. A raw score on F(p) of 10 or higher would suggest exaggeration even if the other scales do not indicate invalidity (Friedman et al., 2001).

- Raw scores of 18 and below on the Ds-2 scale suggest valid responding. Scores between 19 and 27 suggest possible malingering or other exaggerated responding, especially if other validity scales are elevated. Scores of 28 and higher indicate that fake-bad responding is likely even if other scales are not clearly suggestive of exaggeration (Friedman et al., 2001).

- If FBS and scales 1 and 3 are elevated, consider administering additional measures of neurocognitive symptom feigning. These measures are described in detail in Chapter 5.

- Take into account each of the different scales and indices for assessing exaggeration mentioned above. The more evidence you have that the profile is exaggerated, the more likely it is. Remember, determining malingering cannot be done based on test data alone. These scores can suggest negative response bias, but will not reveal motivation. Combine the findings on these scales with behavioral observations and other tests. The MMPI-2 can be a good screen for malingering, and if it is indicated, using a more sensitive measure like the SIRS would be a good way to confirm negative response bias.

- If F is extremely low with a raw score of 2 or lower, it could mean that the individual is responding candidly, or that he or she is presenting in an overly positive manner. Consult the scores on L and K to explore this possibility further.

- If the L scale and/or the K scale is elevated and faking-good is suspected, there are many scales and indices that can be used to help one make a decision regarding this type of response set. Among these are the L+K index, the O-S index, Mp, Sd, SD, Tt, S, Ss, Od, and PMH4. As suggested by Baer and colleagues (1995), the sum of the L, K, Sd, and S scales may also be a strong index for detecting an overly positive self-presentation. The more these scales and indices are in agreement, the more confident the clinician can be with decisions made about deviant responding.

- Again, before making definitive decisions based on the findings of the MMPI-2 scales, administer additional measures of socially desirable responding such as those described in Chapter 4.

- The MMPI-2 has so many scales that it is tempting to take the combination of these scales and consider them to be irrefutable evidence in support of a finding of deceptive responding. However, even with so many different scales to provide convergent evidence, many of these scales share items, and the bottom line is that they all come from only one measure. We have stressed throughout this book the importance of utilizing multiple data sources, including behavioral observations, collateral information, and other assessment data. The MMPI-2 is often the easiest, cheapest first step in assessing response validity. However, as was mentioned above, it should not be the final step. There are many measures discussed elsewhere in this book that can provide additional data to support MMPI-2 findings. If psychiatric malingering is suggested by elevations on F, Fb, and F(p), administer a SIRS to clarify this issue. If an elevation on FBS suggests possible somatic or neuropsychological malingering, administer some of the tests described in Chapter 5 to more clearly understand the extent and nature of the feigning. And if socially desirable responding is suspected based on elevated scores on L, K, Mp, Sd, and the other scales measuring this, definitely administer additional tests to assess this further, as the MMPI-2 has been found to be better at detecting fake-bad responding than fake-good.
- Even if a profile is found to be invalid, it is usually not necessary to simply discard it and think that no valuable information can be gained from it. Use the information to generate hypotheses about motivations and attitudes so that the remainder of the assessment can be planned accordingly, as described above. In certain settings it might even be useful to inform a client of the response bias suggested by MMPI-2 findings in order to explore reasons for this and encourage more candid responding during the remainder of the testing. The MMPI-2 validity scales can provide more information than simply whether a profile is valid or invalid, if one uses the information in the ways suggested here and in combination with the strategies suggested throughout the rest of this book.

Section II

MEASURES INTENDED FOR
THE DETECTION OF DECEPTION

Chapter 4

MEASURES SPECIFICALLY
DESIGNED TO DETECT DECEPTION

As noted earlier in this tome, there are a number of psychological instruments designed for general purposes that contain validity measures allowing for the detection of dissimulation. The MMPI-2, discussed in detail in Chapter 3, is perhaps the most widely used measure of this kind. General tests, reviewed in Chapter 2, provide the evaluator with diagnostic, characterological, and other information while allowing for an examination of the likelihood that the gleaned data represents truthful information on the part of the respondent. Such comprehensive measures are clearly useful across a variety of settings, including general clinical intervention practice as well as forensic evaluation.

Given the robust nature of commonly used and wide-ranging tools, such as the MMPI-2, PAI, and Wechsler Adult Intelligence Scale–Third Edition (WAIS-III), the novice evaluator may question the purpose of using other, less comprehensive instruments in the assessment of malingering or biased responding. There are instances, however, when the use of such tests may be helpful, and, in fact, preferable. For example, tests designed solely to examine response style are made to answer a specific question without muddying the water with extraneous data. They are quicker, and often less expensive than traditional measures, making them ideal for settings such as jails where time and budget constraints limit options. The issue of test selection is given greater attention at the end of this chapter, as well as in the conclusion.

In addition to being malingering-specific rather than general, many of these instruments have been heavily researched and are themselves robust with regard to psychometric properties. The SIRS, for example, has been the subject of several hundred published studies. Furthermore, some experts have questioned the use of general, broad-based devices in forensic contexts when tests exist that speak directly to the malingering issue (Nicholson & Norwood, 2000).

This chapter will explore the development of malingering-specific tests and the issue of selecting an instrument from the general/malingering-specific dichotomy. The SIRS, arguably the most well-known and robust of these instruments, will be reviewed in detail. The recent spate of screening instruments will also be highlighted, complete with identification of the strengths and weaknesses of some of the more common of these instruments. This chapter will offer suggestions for situations in which malingering-specific tests are likely to offer the greatest benefit.

Most of the research in this area is directed toward measures specifically designed to detect malingering or other negative response bias. However, as was mentioned in the introduction, individuals can intentionally deceive in a manner that attempts to present an overly positive impression of themselves. Assessment of socially desirable responding was explored in Chapter 3, as the MMPI-2 has many scales designed to detect this. There are also shorter scales intended specifically for the detection of socially desirable responding. These will be presented at the end of this chapter.

THE DEVELOPMENT OF MALINGERING-SPECIFIC TESTS

As noted, assessment of dissimulation, and more specifically, malingering, can be done using generalized instruments, although there are downsides to the use of such lengthy and comprehensive measures. In particular, when an evaluation is being conducted and the assessment of malingering is the salient purpose of testing, the examiner may have difficulty justifying the administration of expensive, intrusive broad measures. Although murky, some kind of boundary does seem to exist between tests that are general in nature or are more specific in addressing the question of malingering. Examples of general instruments providing validity information include the aforementioned MMPI-2, PAI, and WAIS-III, as well as the MCMI-III. These instruments provide the examiner with a wealth of information, which can be useful under certain conditions. This same abundance of information can be cumbersome, as well as unjustified, on other occasions.

Prior to 1985, assessment of malingering was done only with general psychological instruments, as no malingering-specific tests were in circulation. At that time, research had been done looking at identifying individuals who attempted to portray themselves poorly, but testing was still done using traditional psychological instruments. In the late 1980s and early 1990s, attention turned towards the detection of malingering, and in particular, the specific detection of feigned psychosis. The M Test, a screening instrument discussed in greater detail later in this chapter, was arguably the first such instrument (Beaber et al., 1985). At the time the M Test was in development, Grisso (1986; see also 2003) published his now popular model delineating the assessment duties of the forensic evaluator, and forensic psychology began to gain notoriety as a specialty field (Committee on Ethical Guidelines for Forensic Psychologists, 1991; Nicholson & Norwood, 2000). The needs of the field may have acted as a guide that led to the development of the malingering-specific instruments. Around the time the M Test was being developed, work began on a full-length, malingering-specific tool, the SIRS. Although several instruments and interview schedules of varying lengths have been developed to target malingering behavior, the SIRS and its neurocognitive counterpart, the Validity Indicator Profile (VIP; Frederick, 2003), appear to be more commonly used than other malingering-specific tools. The VIP is covered in Chapter 5 with other neuropsychological methods. Thus, we now turn our attention to the SIRS and its utility for clinicians.

THE SIRS

As noted, as forensic psychology formalized as a discipline, researchers recognized a need for tests looking at deceptive, rather than legitimate clinical presentations. The SIRS, a multiscale interview schedule, was designed to address malingering and related forms of dishonest responding (Rogers, 1995; Rogers, Bagby, & Dickens, 1992). According to the professional manual, this interview schedule was created, "to assess systematically deliberate distortions in the self-report of symptoms . . . the primary emphasis of the SIRS is on the evaluation of feigning" (Rogers, Bagby, & Dickens, 1992, p. 1). The prominence of feigning as a salient, if not sole purpose of the instrument, set it apart from other generalized assessment devices.

Originally developed in 1985, the SIRS currently includes 172 items divided into three categories, with each category of question occurring twice during administration of the full interview schedule. Detailed Inquiries present the evaluee with the opportunity to endorse a wide range of symptoms, both subtle and obvious. Endorsed symptoms are then attended to with the prescribed follow-up question regarding the severity of the reported experience ("Is it unbearable?"). Repeated Inquiries are as the name implies: restatements of the previously covered Detailed Inquiries. These items require test-takers to recall which symptoms were previously endorsed, which may prove difficult if those symptoms are not valid. By including this measure, test authors cite examples of dissimulating subjects who demonstrated inconsistency in reporting the same symptoms over time (Rogers, 1988). The third type of item, General Inquiries, makes up the largest portion of the instrument. General Inquiries explore reports of specific symptoms and types of symptoms, and are often divided into two-part questions.

Items on the SIRS are organized to comprise eight scales, with alpha reliability coefficients ranging from .77 to .92 (Rogers et al., 1991). Scales correspond to various malingering strategies identified in earlier malingering literature (Rogers, 1984). Items were placed on scales using the judgment of experts, then subjected to statistical procedures resulting in the removal of three items, and finally the aforementioned alpha coefficients. The eight strategies or scales of the SIRS include: Rare Symptoms (real symptoms that are quite uncommon in true patients), Symptom Combinations (comorbidity of rare symptoms that are not likely to co-occur), Improbable or Absurd Symptoms (ludicrous symptoms so outrageous that there is no likelihood they could be true), Blatant Symptoms (overall tally of number of symptoms that are obvious signs of disturbance), Subtle Symptoms (everyday problems, endorsed disproportionately, that are not likely to measure actual mental disorder), Severity of Symptoms (high number of symptoms reported as being extreme), Selectivity of Symptoms (overall tally of endorsement of symptoms), and Reported versus Observed Symptoms (examines consistency between responses and behavior that can be readily observed during the interview). In addition to these eight scales, the instrument includes five supplementary scales, which may be helpful during interpretation of the scored protocol.

In terms of content, the items on the SIRS refer mainly to symptoms or false symptoms of mood and thought disorders, although a few items do highlight neurocognitive dimensions. Malingering behavior can include feigned psychopathology, feigned cognitive dysfunction, both, or neither. The type of feigning behavior may influence test selection. Although some research suggests the SIRS is useful with suspected malingerers of retardation, patients responding "I don't know" and "I can't remember" to questions posed prior to testing may be better evaluated with instruments other than self-report tests like the SIRS (Hayes et al., 1998). Thus, at this juncture, the practitioner is urged to become familiar with malingering tools covered in other sections of this book.

Referred to as a structured interview, the SIRS requires approximately 30 to 45 minutes for administration and is expected to be included as part of a larger clinical evaluation (Rogers, Bagby, & Dickens, 1992). Authors recommend the administration be discontinued as nonstandard if the administration of the first section requires greater than 15 minutes of time. The "structured interview" categorization requires clarification, as the instrument does not allow for any variation from the protocol. Rather, the administration is much like a self-report measure, with the exception that items are read to the test-taker, instead of being read by the individual. Administration guidelines do highlight this practice of reading items to the evaluee, and note the importance of maintaining bland expressions when inquiring about clearly ludicrous symptoms. Inquiries are to be presented verbatim and in a "matter-of-fact tone" (Rogers, Bagby, & Dickens, 1992, p. 12). Although this is the only instrument known to explicitly draw attention to the importance of not providing cues as to which items do not capture legitimate symptoms, we will take this opportunity to apply such a rule to all measures of deception. In the evaluation of malingering, it is necessary for diagnosticians to refrain from "giving away" the answers. One assumption of many dissimulation detection devices is that would-be feigners do not know precisely how to fake a disorder. Humor displayed towards certain items may provide malingerers with cues allowing them to more realistically portray feigned mental illness. With this caveat, administration of the protocol is relatively easy. In fact, Rogers et al. (1991) found interrater reliability to be .96.

Interpretation of the SIRS is somewhat less "cut and dried" than some other instruments, as it employs both threshold and clinical decision and involves models. First, the instrument is scored by totaling the 13 scales. Because this process is somewhat laborious and must be done by hand, we recommend verifying outcomes by retallying scales. The protocol provides a diagram to plot scores, causing each primary scale score to fall in one of four ranges: honest responding, indeterminate, probable feigning, and definite feigning. Due to the ramifications of overdetection of malingering (e.g., denial of services, failure to treat/recognize legitimate disorder), these categories were designed to minimize false positives, despite a slight decrease in overall accuracy (Rogers, 1997b).

Once scored, the protocol can be interpreted. Rogers (1997b) cautions that the test should never be used alone, but interpreted in light of other tests, interviews, and third party data. According to the threshold model delineated by Rogers (1997a), feigning should be suspected when any of the following conditions occur: four or fewer SIRS scales fall in the honest responding range, two or more SIRS scales are in the probable range, or the SIRS total score is greater than 66. The SIRS manual identifies relevant data demonstrating the likelihood an individual is feigning or responding honestly based on the number of scales in honest versus probable ranges. Classification criteria based on the clinical decision model suggests that a diagnosis of malingering warrants consideration when any single scale falls within the definite range, three or more scales fall in the probable range, or the SIRS total score is greater than 76 (Gothard, 1993; Rogers, 1997b; Rogers, Bagby, & Dickens, 1992). We strongly recommend thorough review of the SIRS manual to understand definitions of the methods of interpretation, as well as review of the provided case examples.

Research on the SIRS

Given the space we have devoted to this single instrument, it is to be expected that a significant amount of research has been done on the SIRS. As one of the more widely used instruments, its robust nature and utility have been well documented. Since this guide is for clinical practice, a comprehensive review of all SIRS-related literature is beyond our scope. However, in deciding to use this instrument, practitioners should be aware of its basic psychometric properties.

Summarizing the research on the SIRS, it can be said that the instrument is both reliable and valid in forensic and offender samples and with majority as well as minority populations. The instrument has even demonstrated utility with adolescent samples, a quality that makes it unique among malingering tools (McCann, 1998b; Rogers, Hinds, & Sewell, 1996). Specifically, during validation of the instrument, effect size was large between honest and feigning groups in both simulation and known-groups designs (Rogers, 1997b; Rogers, Bagby, & Dickens, 1992). Aside from the research conducted by Rogers and colleagues, the SIRS has demonstrated excellent psychometric properties in studies completed by other investigators.

In a simulation design with offender and psychotic inpatient participants, the SIRS demonstrated a hit rate of nearly 90% (Connell, 1991). Discriminant function analyses showed that the SIRS, taken together with the MMPI-2, resulted in an overall correct classification rate of over 95%. Kropp (1992; as cited in Rogers, 1997b) explored the ability of the SIRS to detect feigned mental illness among psychopathic offenders receiving treatment. In addition to finding that the instrument made adequate distinctions in this simulation design, the interaction examination showed that psychopathy did not improve malingering ability. Other studies conducted later reported similar findings (Gothard, 1993; Kurtz & Meyer, 1994). The relationship between psychopathy and deception will be explored further in Chapter 8. Of note, Kurtz and Meyer (1994) found the SIRS to show greater classification accuracy than the MMPI-2 in a sample of simulators, offenders, and psychiatric inpatients. Furthermore, in this study, no incremental validity was gained by the addition of the MMPI-2. This finding is particularly important in light of test selection issues such as time constraints and expense of multiple instruments.

An overall examination of the SIRS shows the instrument to have far more strengths than weaknesses. It is psychometrically sound, well documented for use across settings, versatile with regard to various populations, and relatively easy to use once proper training/study has occurred. While scoring is mildly time consuming, clinical formulation can be accomplished quickly, and interpretative guidelines are made quite clear in the test manual. In settings where time constraints and expenses are prominent, such as correctional facilities, the instrument does impose quite a cost and requires more time than may be available. As such, screening instruments may provide greater utility than comprehensive instruments such as the SIRS. We will summarize these selection issues at the end of the chapter, but now we turn our attention to the variety of self-report screening inventories available to clinicians assessing malingering and deception.

SCREENING FOR MALINGERING USING CONSTRUCT SPECIFIC TOOLS

The development of malingering-specific tests for assessment of deception has led to the creation of both longer, comprehensive tools for examining dissimulation as well as a number of shorter, self-report measures. In some cases, the instruments have limited clinical utility, and represent research endeavors not particularly relevant to the practitioner. Other tools were designed with the practitioner in mind and are made to be affordable (or are in the public domain), quick, or otherwise more practical than their longer counterparts.

The classification of the instruments discussed here as screening devices is somewhat loose, with the general concept being that these instruments are not generally designed to be used as diagnostic tools without significant follow-up in the form of additional assessment. Further, there is a great deal of variation between these instruments in terms of scope of coverage and psychometric soundness. The following discussion will excerpt relevant information on these instruments with an eye towards utility concerns such as cost, availability, and ease of administration/ scoring. Additionally, attention will be given to research on the instruments' psychometric properties and research relevant to clinicians in different practice settings, when such studies exist.

M Test

This brief, true-false instrument was the first screening measure for detecting malingering of a specific disorder, and arguably one of the first malingering tests in circulation (Beaber et al., 1985). Designed to identify only those feigning schizophrenia, this test contains 33 true/false items, of which 10 are true symptoms and 15 are false symptoms that may appear true to unsophisticated fakers. The instrument consists of three scales: Confusion, Schizophrenia, and Malingering. The premise of the instrument is that would-be malingerers would be unable to differentiate between genuine and false symptoms of schizophrenia.

For an instrument of this length, and with such a narrow scope, the extent of the validation research is quite remarkable. The original validation study compared responses of inpatients with schizophrenia to control subjects who had been educated on schizophrenia and informed the purpose of the M Test is to detect feigned psychosis. In accuracy analyses, the test correctly classified 87.3% of the true schizophrenics and 78.2% of the malingering control group. A second simulation-design endeavor replicated these findings (Gillis, Rogers, & Bagby, 1991). G. P. Smith and Borum (1992) then attempted cross-validation using suspected malingerers and inpatients, but detected just fewer than 70% of malingerers. A series of additional studies followed, with variable results in terms of accuracy (Hankins, Barnard, & Robbins, 1993; Schretlen, Neal, & Hochman, 1995, as cited in Rogers, 1997b). Alternate scoring procedures were used to improve the classification accuracy of the instrument, with resulting improvements (Rogers, Bagby, & Gillis, 1992; G. P. Smith, Borum, & Schinka, 1993).

Although this instrument has been subjected to rigorous research protocol, it does not seem to be of particular use when compared with newer screening tools. Instead, it seemed to open the door for investigations into ways to assess malingering outside of lengthy clinical inventories and to move later endeavors towards conceptualizing malingering as a particular condition (G. P. Smith, 1997). It was not designed specifically for usage in any single population, but it has been evaluated and has demonstrated promising results as a research instrument with forensic and correctional populations (Beaber et al., 1985; Rogers, Bagby, & Gillis, 1992).

Overall, the test seems to have fallen out of favor as both a research instrument and clinical tool. Understanding the development of this test may help the novice examiner in understanding development of current instruments. While external validity concerns exist, this test has been scrutinized closely for a screening instrument with such a narrow scope, and in this way sets a high standard for future instruments (G. P. Smith, 1997). The remaining instruments are reviewed alphabetically.

Inventory of Problems

Although a self-report instrument, the classification of this instrument as a screening tool is questionable. Consisting of 162 items, the Inventory of Problems (IOP; Viglione & Landis, 1994) is divided into 19 scales, which are further grouped to form 4 categories. Items go beyond the simple true/false dichotomy to include a third response option ("doesn't make sense"). The instrument's purported strength is its versatility, allowing for use across a wide range of clinical settings, although it does not appear to be of more use than other instruments. Further, the instrument takes longer to complete than many other more comprehensive measures (45 to 90 minutes in one estimate). The test is designed to be administered via computer, but the only study was done using a written format. This study did not produce results clearly supporting the use of the instrument, although significant differences were found between honest respondents and simulators on some scales (Viglione & Landis, 1994). At the present time, more research is needed on the instrument and it is not recommended for use in clinical practice.

M-FAST

One of the newer instruments for screening of malingering is the Miller Forensic Assessment of Symptoms Test (M-FAST; Miller, 2001). Described by the author as a structured interview, the test is reminiscent of the SIRS in terms of format, administration, and scoring. Further, it is modeled on the same principles as the SIRS by using validated strategies for detecting malingering (Rogers, 1990, 1997b). The 25-item test is divided into 7 scales, although 3 scales consist of a single item.

The professional manual for the M-FAST notes that the author "recognized the need for a reliable and valid screening instrument to assess malingered mental illness" (Miller, 2001, p. 21). Strengths of the instrument include its quick administration time and standardized administration format. Although psychometrically sound, the author cautions against using the instrument in isolation to draw conclusions, instead suggesting it be followed by additional tests and interviews.

In the tradition of the M Test, the M-FAST has been the subject of a great deal of inquiry including both known-groups and simulation designs. Reliability coefficients (alpha) of M-FAST scales in clinical and nonclinical samples showed a great range of variability (.44 to .82; Miller, 2001). Significant differences were found between honest responders and malingerers in a series of known-groups and simulation designs. Validity studies have compared the instrument to the MMPI-2 and supported its use (Miller, 2001). More recent investigations have moderately correlated the instrument with both the SIRS and MMPI-2 validity indicators in a pretrial jail population (Pietz et al., 2004).

Overall, this is one of the more promising instruments in current circulation. It has good psychometric properties and is quick and easy to use. It has shown utility for both forensic evaluations and standard correctional use.

Malingering Probability Scale (MPS)

The Malingering Probability Scale (MPS; Silverton & Gruber, 1998) contains 139 items designed to assess malingering of depression/anxiety, dissociative disorders, schizophrenia, and posttraumatic stress disorder. Like the IOP, its length calls into question its utility as a screening device, but it certainly does not have the psychometric properties of instruments such as the SIRS. Like the M Test, the MPS includes both actual and pseudo symptoms. This self-report instrument is written at the 3rd-grade level and has demonstrated sensitivity and specificity greater than 85%. It has been standardized with both males and females ranging from 16 to over 90 years of age. Despite important features, including lack of item overlap, rational methods of scale construction, and broad scope (ability to detect feigning of conditions other than psychosis), the instrument seems to have both conceptual and empirical weaknesses, causing one reviewer to give the opinion that it is not presently appropriate for clinical use (Nicholson, 1999).

Malingering Scale (MS)

An intermediate length instrument, the MS purports to detect both mental retardation and "insanity" conditions (Schretlen & Arkowitz, 1990). The 90 items are divided into 4 subtests, of which 2 allow open-ended responding, which may increase administration time. Unlike many other screens, this measure has been subjected to a great deal of research. While studies have been limited by size and confounding variables, the MS has demonstrated the ability to make correct classifications in greater than 90% of cases (Schretlen & Arkowitz, 1990; G. P. Smith, 1997). Additionally, a strength of this instrument is its use of multiple detection strategies (G. P. Smith, 1997).

Structured Inventory of Malingered Symptomatology (SIMS)

A newer screen, the SIMS was designed in the true-false format of many earlier instruments. The 75 items were drawn from existing measures and were written to cover malingering traits discovered in research endeavors (G. P. Smith & Burger, 1997). The test consists of five subscales, which conform mainly to neurological conditions, such as amnesia. Psychosis and general "fake-bad" syndromes are covered as well, making this one of the few instruments to cover both neurocognitive symptoms and psychopathology. This measure has shown promise as a screen for malingering in pretrial forensic evaluations (J. L. Lewis et al., 2002). Although initial investigations displayed efficacy in malingering detection, this test also had some weaknesses (e. g., overlap with true mental illness) that suggest it may not be appropriate for clinical use without further validation (Edens, Otto, & Dwyer, 1999).

Screening SIRS

Although this instrument has not become a tool for clinical use, it deserves mention due to its derivation from the gold-standard malingering instrument, the SIRS. The 40-item test was explored in a correctional setting and evinced sensitivity of 87% and specificity of 73% when compared to the original SIRS (Norris & May, 1998). The Screening SIRS has been the subject of only a single published study, but seems to be an excellent candidate for further investigation as a screening tool.

Tehachapi Malingering Scale (TMS)

The TMS was developed by a correctional psychologist to be used specifically in a jail or prison environment (Haskett, 1995). As such, it is easy to score and can be administered as part of a mental status interview, attending to time constraints present in correctional settings. In fact, this is the most unique quality of the instrument and something that makes it quite promising for use under time-limited conditions. Instead of being administered separate from an interview, the instrument can be scored from ANY standard clinical interview. The questions were gleaned from research and experience and were evaluated and reduced to a 20-item scale. This self-report instrument covers a wide variety of symptoms and focuses on lower threshold behaviors not included by other malingering screens (e.g., sleep problems). Additionally, the format is unique among screens, which rely predominantly on true-false dichotomies. The TMS suffers in its lack of systematic research, but initial studies suggest adequate reliability and validity when compared to the MMPI-2.

In more recent evaluations, a modified version of this instrument (TMS-AC) has demonstrated utility in a correctional setting. McLearen and Zapf (2002) added five items to the protocol to underscore the lower threshold malingering behaviors covered by the instrument, changed the scoring to a 0, 1, or 2 format, and scored the instrument from clinical interviews administered to 136 incoming jail detainees. Results showed significant utility, in that average scoring time after a brief interview was less than 1 minute. Additionally, moderate correlations were found between classifications made through the use of this instrument and later malingering determinations of both officers and mental health staff. Factor analytic procedures conducted with the revised instrument supported the comprehensive definition of malingering involving feigned psychosis, feigned cognitive dysfunction, and feigned minor symptoms or medication-seeking (McLearen, Zapf, & Clements, 2004).

Victoria Symptom Validity Test (VSVT)

This instrument is covered in greater detail in Chapter 5, but deserves mention as a screener for malingering. The test is available only as a computer-administered measure, which is time-efficient, but not cost effective. Developed in the tradition of forced-choice testing, the VSVT contains 48 items designed to confirm or disprove claims of cognitive impairment (Lees-Haley, Dunn, & Betz, 1999). Evaluees are presented with a series of numbers ranging from easy to difficult, and then tested on recognition. Strengths include the fact that even instructions can be given via computer and that incomplete protocols can be scored. Adequate reliability and validity have been shown with the VSVT and normative data exists. Although definitional issues may be problematic (malingering is not defined by *DSM-IV* criteria), this test appears promising as a screen for neuropsychological malingering.

TEST SELECTION

Throughout this chapter, the authors have tried to put special emphasis on the various uses of the malingering-specific instruments. For more information on when to choose a malingering-specific test from other, more comprehensive measures, refer to the conclusion of this volume. However, in this section, we would like to explore some areas to consider once the determination to use a malingering-specific test has been made.

Given the number of strengths of the SIRS, it is hard to imagine a situation when this instrument would not be a good option to enhance knowledge. Along with the excellent psychometric properties and comprehensive nature of the SIRS come lengthy administration time and high cost. Thus, there are situations when the use of the SIRS, particularly as a purely exploratory measure, would be questionable. These situations are discussed in turn.

In jail settings, where budget constraints limit testing of any kind, and time is of the essence, malingering screens can be quite useful. Malingering is extremely common in correctional settings, ranging from 8% to 37% (Haskett, 1995; Hawk & Cornell, 1989; Rogers, 1997a; Wasyliw & Grossman, 1988). In fact, presence of legal incentive or correctional setting are noted in *DSM-IV* as situations where malingering is likely (APA, 1994). Because resources are extremely limited in detention facilities, and due to high rates of mental illness in jails (Teplin, 1990, 1994), identifying malingerers could be of significant advantage to mental health professionals. Thus, the use of screening measures as routine practice in jails is warranted.

Malingering is sometimes an issue in clinical practice. When differential diagnosis is important, for example, when Factitious Disorder is a consideration, personality inventories such as the MMPI-2 may provide the best information. Other times, the clinician may suspect symptom exaggeration or falsification and wish to explore that possibility for use in treatment. Rather than putting the client through the rigor of a lengthy instrument, a screening device could be used quickly, and even in session.

Finally, screening for dissimulation may be helpful in forensic cases, when malingering is being "ruled out." For example, a case that seems to be legitimate mental illness may still benefit from some form of malingering assessment. Additionally, instruments such as the SIRS are costly. When malingering is not suspected or when it is overwhelmingly suspected, screening instruments with sound psychometric properties may suffice in lieu of comprehensive instruments.

In cases where the choice has been made to screen for malingering, there is a wide field from which to make a selection. The instruments presented in this chapter represent the best, most widely studied, and most promising of the malingering screens. Table 1 (pp. 100-101) highlights some of the differences between the various screening instruments.

Table 1: Comparison of Screens on Major Dimensions

	M-Test	IOP	M-FAST	MPS	MS	SIMS	Screening SIRS	TMS-AC	VSVT
Valid for correctional population?	No	No	Yes	No	No	No	Yes	Yes	No
Valid for forensic population?	Yes	No	Yes	No	No	No	No	No	?
Covers psychotic symptoms	Yes	Yes	Yes	Yes	Yes	Yes	Yes	Yes	No
Covers neuropsych symptoms	No	Yes	No	No	Yes	Yes	No	Yes	Yes

Covers physical/anxiety symptoms	No	?	No	Yes	No	No	?	Yes	No
Any reliability studies?	Yes	No	Yes	Yes	Yes	Yes	No	Yes	Yes
Any validity studies?	Yes	No	Yes	Yes	Yes	Yes	Yes	Yes	Yes
Can be given or scored by auxiliary staff?	?	?	No	No	?	No	No	Yes	Yes
Can be done in less than 15 minutes?	Yes	No	Yes	No	No	Yes	?	Yes	Yes

MEASURES OF SOCIALLY DESIRABLE RESPONDING

The Marlowe-Crowne Social Desirability Scale (MCSDS)

In an attempt to improve upon the Edwards Social Desirability Scale (Edwards, 1957) described in Chapter 3, Crowne and Marlowe (1960) developed the Marlowe-Crowne Social Desirability Scale (MCSDS). They wanted to create a scale for measuring socially desirable response bias that was not based on admitting or denying psychopathology, as the Edwards scale was. They came up with 33 items that were seen as neutral with respect to psychopathology. The measure has good internal consistency and test-retest reliability. Andrews and Meyer (2003) cited several studies showing that the internal consistency of the measure ranged from .72 to .96 (i.e., Ballard, 1992; Crowne & Marlowe, 1960; Reynolds, 1982). Test-retest reliability was originally reported at .89 after 1 month (Crowne & Marlowe, 1960).

There is an extremely large body of literature in which the MCSDS is included as a measure in a research project to assess socially desirable responding (Beretvas, J. L. Meyers, & Leite, 2002). Many short forms of the measure have been developed (Ballard, 1992; Reynolds, 1982; Strahan & Gerbasi, 1972). However, while its uses in research are many and varied, its use in clinical practice has been rather limited (Andrews & Meyer, 2003). Meyer and Weaver (2007) suggested using one of the short forms of the measure as a screen for response style in clinical settings and S. R. Smith and Meyer (1987) suggested using it as part of a standard assessment of deception.

There is actually a great deal of controversy regarding the clinical use of the MCSDS to detect response bias. Many studies, such as that by Andrews and Meyer (2003) provide support for the use of the instrument in clinical and forensic settings, and these authors have provided updated forensic norms for the measure. Several studies also suggest that the measure should only be used with caution (Ballard, Crino, & Rubenfeld, 1988) or that it should not be used at all to attempt to control for response bias in other measures (Barger, 2002). Stober (2001) suggested that the MCSDS is out of date and actually developed a new measure (The Social Desirability Scale-17, SDS-17, discussed below) using more current questions.

Basically, as was mentioned previously, the MCSDS has fairly good psychometric properties and has been used extensively to measure socially desirable responding. The measure may well be more out of date than the newer measures discussed in the following paragraph, but its short forms and easy accessibility make it a practical measure to use when socially desirable responding is a concern.

The mean score on the full MCSDS across eight studies with community, student, and adoption applicant samples was 15.16 (Vella-Broderick & V. White, 1997). The mean for the adoption applicants was 21.25 and the mean for the student and community subjects was 15.06. The MCSDS Short Form C consists of 13 items taken from the original 33. In five studies using nonforensic samples the mean score on the Short Form C was 5.37 (Andrews & Meyer, 2003). The forensic sample studied by Andrews and Meyer was divided into different groups, including physical abuse offenders, child neglect offenders, domestic violence offenders, pretrial competency defendants, domestic violence victims, family members in child abuse cases who did not actually perpetrate abuse on a child, disability evaluees, and an "other" group. The mean combined score for these groups on the full MCSDS was 19.42, and the mean score on the Short Form C was 7.61. The highest scoring group was the family members involved in child abuse cases who had not actually abused a child. These individuals were often being evaluated for whether they could have access to or custody of the children involved. The full scale mean for this group was 22.46 and the Short Form C mean was 9.18. These findings provide support for the use of the MCSDS and MCSDS Short Form C in forensic evaluations in which socially desirable responding is suspected or likely.

The Paulhus Deception Scales (PDS)

The Paulhus Deception Scales (PDS; Paulhus, 1998), formerly known as the Balanced Inventory of Desirable Responding (BIDR; Paulhus, 1984) measures the two components of socially desirable responding described by Paulhus, Impression Management (IM), and Self-Deceptive Enhancement (SDE). The PDS can be used in clinical or research settings, to assist with determinations about whether a subject is distorting responses. The measure has been extensively researched and validated (Paulhus, 1998). The scale has demonstrated Cronbach's alpha reliability estimates ranging from .70 to .86 in university students, military personnel, subjects in the community, and a correctional sample (Salekin, 2000). Salekin noted that the scale has fair construct validation, although he noted the absence of divergent validity.

The PDS consists of 40 items, 20 on each of the IM and SDE subscales. The range of scores for each subscale is from 0 to 20. Using a scale of 1 to 5, the respondent is asked to rate the statements on the PDS by the extent to which they apply to him or her. Only the extreme scores, 1 or 5, are scored as 1 point if the answer is given in the coded direction. For example, on the item "I have not always been honest with myself," if the subject circles the number 1, indicating that this statement is "not true," then he or she will receive a score of 1 for this item. However, if the subject circles any other number, 2 through 5, the score on the item will be 0.

The PDS Manual (Paulhus, 1998) suggests the following guideline for interpreting the results of the measure. In terms of T-scores, the Manual states "For both the SDE and IM scales, the administrator should only be concerned with T-scores above 70 or below 30" (p. 10). These scores are described as "very much above average" and "very much below average" (p. 10), respectively. Extremely high scores would suggest self-favorable responding and extremely low scores would suggest negative response bias. Further, the manual suggests that when the PDS is being used as a validity check in part of a battery of tests, raw scores over 12 suggest probable invalidity and scores over 8 suggest possible invalidity in the way of social desirability of fake-good responding. A raw score of less that 1 suggests probable negative response bias, or faking-bad, and a score of less than 2 suggests possible negative response bias.

The pattern of scores on the PDS can also provide some information about the subject. Paulhus (1998) suggests four different patterns of scores. First, if the individual scores low on both IM and SDE, the individual is likely to be responding in an honest fashion, is aware of his or her own problems, and is not likely to be highly influenced by what others think. If the individual scores high on IM and low on SDE, he or she is likely to be well aware of problems and faults, but is attempting to appear in an especially positive light. This may be due to situational demands and could lead to test results reflecting an overly positive self-presentation. If the score on IM is low, but on SDE it is high, the individual is likely to have little insight and presents with "narcissistic tendencies" (p. 10). This type of self-favorable bias results from a personality style, rather than a certain situation. If the scores on IM and SDE are both high, Paulhus calls this the "repressor pattern" (p. 10). This pattern of scoring suggests that the individual is responding in an overly positive way because of both situational demands and a characteristic style of presenting the self in a favorable light.

Paulhus (1984) has demonstrated fairly convincingly the presence of the two factors measured in the PDS. Still, there is much controversy about how many factors actually make up the construct of social desirability. One study found that intentional deception, or IM, was divided into separate factors of positive and negative distortions, suggesting that the Paulhus model is not sufficiently describing the nature of socially desirable responding (Holden et al., 2003). The results of a study by Helmes and Holden (2003) suggested that social desirability could be unidimensional, two dimensional, or even composed of three factors.

Still, the intention of the PDS to measure the two factors of IM and SDE can be seen as a strength of the measure. Some of the other features of the PDS that make it an attractive measure include its quick administration (it only takes 5 to 7 minutes to complete), its 5th-grade reading level, and its use of modern language (Paulhus, 1998), which is a concern with the MCSDS. The PDS can also be administered and/or scored by computer. Salekin (2000) suggested that the test may be a good addition to use in forensic assessments, but indicated that its use in such settings should be undertaken with caution as there is no formal testing of the PDS in forensic samples.

The Social Desirability Scale-17 (SDS-17)

Because of the view of the MCSDS as being outdated, Stober (2001) developed a newer measure of social desirability called the Social Desirability Scale-17 (SDS-17). The scale consists of 17 items scored true or false. It showed convergent validity with other measures of social desirability, correlating between .52 and .85 with these, and it only correlated with the IM items of the PDS. The SDS-17 displayed divergent validity through insignificant correlations with extraversion, psychoticism, neuroticism, and openness to experience. The measure appeared to be sensitive to instructions that would provoke socially desirable responding and it was highly correlated with the MCSDS for subjects age 18 through 80 (Stober, 2001). This measure appears to be promising for the detection of socially desirable responding; however, more information is needed about its use with varying populations at this time.

KEY POINTS

- Malingering-specific tests began to appear in the late 1980s in response to the growth of forensic psychology.
- The SIRS is arguably the most commonly used and psychometrically robust test designed specifically for the assessment of feigned psychopathology.
- In addition to comprehensive interview schedules such as the SIRS, a number of instruments exist to allow examiners and clinicians to screen for malingering.

- The M Test was one of the malingering screens and set the standard for psychometric evaluation of dissimulation tests.
- Several malingering screening tools have been developed, but require further research before being used in clinical settings.
- Currently, the M-FAST is an excellent choice for screening in forensic evaluations, while the TMS-AC appears useful for correctional settings.
- Other screening instruments may be useful to confirm or disconfirm hypotheses or in cases where specific symptoms are of interest, but should not be used alone to draw conclusions about malingering/validity.
- There are several measures available that are specifically designed to detect socially desirable responding. Of these, the PDS seems to be the easiest and most updated for use in clinical populations and it also contains correctional norms. However, the MCSDS is the only one of the three measures described here that has been normed on a forensic population. Both of these measures could be useful for contributing information about response set. The SDS-17 looks promising, but more research is needed on it at this time.

Chapter 5

EXAGGERATION AND FEIGNING OF NEUROCOGNITIVE DYSFUNCTION

Clinical experience and empirical evidence suggest individuals do not exaggerate neurocognitive compromise in a uniform manner, particularly if there is a specific goal in mind. Sweet (1999) noted that "malingering can have variable degrees of intention, selectivity in presentation, variable degrees of exaggeration, and more than one strategy on the part of the malingerer or across malingerers" (p. 277). There very well may be differences in exaggeration styles depending on individuals' IQs, creativity, and certainly access to relevant literature and coaching. Research and clinical experience suggest individuals may exaggerate general intellectual compromise, short-term memory deficits (visual or verbal), long-term memory deficits (e.g., amnesia for a specific period of time), or general somatic issues, such as pain and fatigue (Beetar & Williams, 1995; Goebel, 1983; Iverson, 1995; Tenhula & Sweet, 1996). These domains are in addition to possible exaggeration in more traditional psychiatric realms (depression, anxiety, or psychosis). Lastly, some individuals apparently exaggerate nearly everything in a pan-malingering manner. There is no indication that criminal litigants malinger in a similar fashion as civil litigants (Wynkoop & Denney, 1999). We are able to identify these differences because clinical researchers have developed a number of measures to detect exaggeration corresponding to the above domains. It is difficult to identify base rates of exaggeration for each of these domains because such results are inextricably related to the sensitivity of each detection strategy. It appears that those malingering neurocognitive dysfunction tend to focus on memory-related deficits more often than other cognitive domains, as would be expected given the widely understood truth that head injury most typically causes memory problems (Sweet, 1999). In this chapter, we will review what is known about the prevalence of neurocognitive malingering, a proposed classification system for detecting neurocognitive dysfunction, and review common detection strategies.

<h1 align="center">PREVALENCE OF
NEUROCOGNITIVE MALINGERING</h1>

In order to address prevalence rates for neurocognitive malingering, we must first point out that there is a subtle, yet important difference between malingering and negative response bias (NRB). As we have highlighted throughout this text, individuals have various reasons for dishonest and inaccurate presentations, ranging from poor comprehension to lack of interest to deliberate deception. There are variations in subject response characteristics that fall loosely under the general concept of "poor effort" as it relates to neurocognitive abilities. Unlike other areas of psychological assessment, neuropsychological tests are basically achievement-like tests that require sustained effort from the evaluee. While subjects cannot "fake-good" on neuropsychological tests (apart from "cheating" or having been coached), they can easily suppress their performance by simply not giving their best effort. In more extreme cases, they can give tremendous effort, but in the direction of attempting to appear more impaired than is truly the case. Poor motivation of the subject is the bane of neuropsychological assessment. Without motivation, tests do not reveal the subject's true abilities. Thankfully, there has been a growing awareness of these concerns over the past decade in the field of neuropsychology. With that increased interest, however, came an increase in concepts and terminology that make understanding the issues more complicated. Hom and Denney (2002) made this observation:

> Negative response bias, symptom validity, exaggeration, malingering, and effort testing all relate to the concept of identifying test results that are not a valid reflection of the patient's abilities. Differentiating willful attempts to exaggerate disability for secondary gain (malingering) from willful exaggeration for primary gain (factitious disorder), non-willful exaggeration (conversion or other psychiatric disorder), or simply poor motivation is a complicated process. (p. xii)

Neuropsychological researchers often use the terms NRB and malingering interchangeably. Negative response bias is the broader term. While it reflects systematic bias, it does not reveal the motivation or reason for the bias. Malingering, on the other hand, is a clinical decision which incorporates not only test performance, but also the totality of the clinical situation and ascribes willful intent of the examinee to appear disingenuously more impaired for substantial secondary gain (Slick, Sherman, & Iverson, 1999). One must keep this distinction in mind when reviewing the prevalence of malingering in the literature.

A consideration of base rates is necessary to evaluate the accuracy of malingering determination (Gouvier, Hayes, & Smiroldo, 1998; Rosenfeld, Sands, & Van Gorp, 2000). Neglecting base rate information appears to contribute to the difficulty of malingering detection and misclassification in general (Labarge, McCaffrey, & Brown, 2003; Rosenfeld et al., 2000). Making it more difficult still is the apparent case that malingering base rates vary among settings, with forensic settings having a higher rate of attempted malingering (Mittenberg, Patton, et al., 2002; Rosenfeld et al., 2000). There is no expectation that malingering styles or base rates will remain stable across evaluation settings. Here we review known base rates for the civil forensic arena and later present what little is known about criminal settings.

Negative Response Bias in Civil Forensic Settings

Heaton et al. (1978) cross-validated a previously developed discriminant function on 42 participants who were involved in civil or criminal court actions at the time of testing. Thus, they had a reason to exaggerate pathology during testing. The researchers found that 27 (64.3%) were classified as presumed malingerers. It was not clear if there was a difference between the malingering base rate for criminal and civil cases.

Trueblood and Schmidt (1993) examined 106 neuropsychological evaluations from individuals pursuing litigation using below-chance symptom validity testing (SVT). They were able to identify eight participants who scored below chance on an SVT procedure modeled after the M. Hiscock and C. K. Hiscock (1989) Digit Memory Test. Another eight participants at or above chance on the SVT were identified as presumed malingerers due to highly improbable neuropsychological test results (e.g., zero grip strength, finger oscillation test [FOT] rates of 9 and 13). These findings resulted in an overall base rate of NRB of 15% (16/106).

During a validation study of the Forced-Choice Test of Nonverbal Ability, Frederick and colleagues (1994) used 64 participants who were referred for testing for other than pure clinical reasons, which implied that some motivation to exaggerate their symptoms may have existed. The instrument classified 16 participants as presumed malingerers, resulting in a base rate of 25% (16/64).

Binder and Kelly (1996) used the Portland Digit Recognition Test (PDRT), an adaptation of the Hiscock Digit Memory Test to identify poor effort. The test was given to 103 participants with mild head trauma who had financial incentives to exaggerate. Forty-eight of the 103 participants' performance fell in the below-chance range of responding, resulting in a base rate of 47% (48/103).

Youngjohn, Burrows, and Erdal (1995) examined the neuropsychological performance of 54 individuals presenting with postconcussion syndrome (PCS). When using the PDRT and the Rey Dot Counting Test (see Frederick, 2002) they found 26 of the participants had questionable motivation during testing; this resulted in a base rate of 48% (26/54).

Millis (1992) examined the ability of the Recognition Memory Test (RMT; Warrington, 1984) to detect exaggerated or malingering memory impairment (see Millis, 2002, for a review). The RMT is a forced-choice, two alternative, word and face recognition test. Millis used 10 participants who were mild head injury trauma patients and compared their performance to a group of 20 participants with moderate and severe traumatic brain injuries. He found that 50% (5/10) of the mild head injury participants scored below the worst performance of any moderate to severe head injury participant.

Greiffenstein et al. (1994) compared persistent postconcussive syndrome (PPCS) participants to participants who suffered a traumatic brain injury (TBI). Along with a standard comprehensive neuropsychological test battery, participants were administered validity measures such as the Rey Word Recognition List, Rey's 15-Item Memory Test, a short form of the PDRT, and the Rey Dot Counting Test. The authors also introduced a new measure, which they termed Reliable Digit Span (RDS). Following the standard Wechsler Adult Intelligence Scale administration, the RDS is calculated by summing the longest string of digits repeated without error over two trials on both forward and backward. A score of 7 or less is considered classification for NRB. Using these measures, they classified 43 of the 73 PPCS participants as presenting NRB, resulting in a base rate of 59% (43/73).

Millis, Putman, Adams, and Ricker (1995) examined mild head injury participants who had external incentives to exaggerate symptomatology. In their sample of 92 litigating mild head trauma participants, 23 were found to show NRB based on RMT performances, a base rate of 25%.

J. E. Meyers and Volbrecht (1998) followed up work done by Greiffenstein et al. (1994) involving the validation of RDS. They used 47 mild TBI participants who were also involved in litigation and compared them to a group of 49 nonlitigating referrals for neuropsychological evaluations. Following a comprehensive neuropsychological evaluation each group was compared using the RDS cut off of 7. Only 2 of the 49 (4%) participants in the nonlitigating group were classified as possible malingerers, while 23 of the 47 (49%) in the litigating group were classified as possible malingers by the RDS score.

Grote and colleagues (2000) performed a cross-validation of the Victoria Symptom Validity Test (VSVT; Slick et al., 1997) and identified cut off scores for discriminating compensation-seeking participants with mild traumatic brain injury from noncompensation-seeking participants with intractable seizures. The VSVT classified 22 of the 53 compensation-seeking participants as presenting NRB, a base rate of 42%.

When examining depression and neurocognitive test scores, Rohling et al. (2002) found 299 of their 719 referrals for compensation-related evaluations had to be excluded due to their poor performance on the Computerized Assessment of Response Bias (CARB; Allen et al., 1997) and/or the Word Memory Test (WMT; Green, Allen, & Astner, 1996). These numbers correspond to a NRB base rate of 42%.

Mittenberg, Patton, et al. (2002) surveyed members of the American Board of Clinical Neuropsychology regarding the diplomates' recollections of the incidence of malingering conclusions over the course of the previous year. Mean estimated rates of "probable malingering or symptom exaggeration" were between 28% and 33% for personal injury, disability, and worker's compensation cases. A difficulty with this survey is that it appears to rely on clinicians' recollection of the number of times they identified NRB. This finding is not only weakened by fading memory, but possibly less than thorough efforts of NRB identification in the first place.

Larrabee combined results of 11 of the above malingering studies and found the overall average base rate of NRB among civil forensic cases to be 40% (2003a). Fairman, Denney, and Halfaker (2003) presented a study done using 101 outpatient civil litigants. The researchers compared performances on a variety of NRB indices. They found 39.6% of the sample was classified as NRB using a two or more tests positive rule, which corresponded closely to Larrabee's 40% overall prevalence. A difficulty in this particular study is that many of the presumed NRB subjects were classified by multiple indices within the Booklet Category Test (BCT) alone (a combination of total errors, errors on subtests I and II, Bolter items, easy Items, and subtest VII errors; Sweet & King, 2002). Using these criteria, the BCT was the most sensitive measure. Aside from the methodological difficulties inherent in treating such clearly related indices as separate measures, the correspondence to Larrabee's conclusion was striking. Larrabee's conclusion of 40% appears to be the most robust finding regarding the prevalence for NRB among the civil forensic setting as it combines the actual data from an extremely large set of claimants. Much less literature exists regarding NRB in the criminal forensic setting.

Negative Response Bias in Criminal Forensic Settings

Very little is known about the prevalence of NRB in the criminal forensics arena, and much of the information deals with exaggeration of general psychiatric issues. Rogers (1986) identified rates of 20% for suspected malingering and 4.5% for "definite malingering" among criminal defendants. Cornell and Hawk (1989) considered 8% of their pretrial criminal defendants to be feigning psychosis. J. L. Lewis and his colleagues (2002) identified a base rate of 31.4% for feigned psychiatric presentation among pretrial criminal defendants using the Structured Interview of Reported Symptoms (SIRS; Rogers, Bagby, & Dickens, 1992).

Each of the preceding studies dealt with general psychiatric presentation; even fewer studies exist for exaggerated neurocognitive deficit in the criminal population. The Mittenberg, Patton, et al. (2002) survey included estimates of marked neuropsychological exaggeration for criminal referrals as well, with the mean falling between 19% and 23%. Lastly, Frederick and Denney (1998) estimated a 25% prevalence of below random responding assessed by forced-choice recognition tests for individuals claiming amnesia in a criminal forensic setting.

With the exception of the Frederick and Denney (1998) and Mittenberg, Patton, et al. (2002) estimates, the above criminal related studies focus on general psychiatric presentation only. Ardolf, Denney, and Houston (2004) recently presented the base rate of NRB among 105 pretrial criminal defendants serially referred for neuropsychological assessment and found a significantly higher base rate. The study used a variety of standard neurocognitively related malingering measures. Using a one or more indices positive cut off resulted in a NRB base rate of 91.43%, two or more positive equaled 71.43%, three or more positive equaled 53.33%, four or more equaled 39.05%, and five or more equaled 34.29%. These results suggest that when pretrial criminal defendants present with neurocognitively related diagnostic concerns, the base rate of malingering is much higher than when they just present with psychiatric concerns.

IDENTIFYING DISINGENUOUS
NEUROCOGNITIVE PERFORMANCE

Thus far, we have focused on differentiating forms of invalid performance on neurocognitive measures. We have also explored base rates of cognitive dysfunction-type malingering in various settings. The remainder of this chapter identifies specific tests, indices, and techniques allowing the examiner to evaluate test-taker effort and intent.

Identifying feigned or exaggerated neurocognitive compromise requires more than knowledge of specific malingering tests. Test scores can identify negative response bias and even overall test battery invalidity, but in and of themselves, tests do not identify malingering (Millis, 2004). Like every other area in clinical psychology, the evaluator cannot become test bound. Contextual issues, including behavioral observations, potential motivating factors, clinical test results, and certainly malingering test results all require consideration. In this light various clinical researchers have addressed factors to consider when identifying malingering of neurocognitive deficits.

Greiffenstein et al. (1994) classified probable persistent postconcussive syndrome malingerers in their validation study based on two or more positive hits on these four criteria: (a) two or more impairment ratings of severe on neuropsychological tests in comparison to appropriate age and education standardization groups; (b) an improbable symptom history contradicted by records or surveillance films; (c) total disability in work or in a major social role after 1 year; and (d) claims of remote memory loss.

Nies and Sweet (1994) and Sweet (1999) provided these six clinical strategies to assist in the identification of malingering neurocognitive deficits based on a multidimensional, multimethod approach: (a) use of specific tests of insufficient effort; (b) evaluation of insufficient effort on common measures; (c) examination of nonsensical or unique malingering responses or response patterns on common measures; (d) examination of excessive inconsistency; (e) comparison of test data to real-life behavior; and (f) determination of self-serving versus real-life losses (i.e., evaluating the amount of real world loss the subject has undergone secondary to the "condition" can help determine the difference between malingering and somatoform or genuine neurocognitive deficits).

Pankratz and Binder (1997) presented a threshold model for suspicion of malingered neuropsychological impairment which included positive indication on any of these factors: (a) lying to health care providers;

(b) marked inconsistency between present diagnosis and neuro-psychological findings; (c) marked inconsistency between reported and observed symptoms; (d) resistance, avoidance, or bizarre responses on standard tests; (e) failure on any specific measure of neuropsychological faking; (f) functional findings on orthopedic or neurological exams; and (g) late onset of cognitive complaints following an accident. They suggested a formal decision model was not feasible, but rather, an application of a set of approaches would help in providing a conceptual framework for the clinical formulation.

Larrabee (2000) outlined four questions an evaluator must consider when determining the validity of an examinee's presentation: "1) Are the data consistent within and between neuropsychological domains?; 2) Is the neuropsychological profile consistent with the suspected etiologic condition?; 3) Are the neuropsychological data consistent with the documented severity of the injury?; and 4) Are the neuropsychological data consistent with the client's behavioral presentation?" (p. 308).

Inherent in that clinical formulation is the need to determine "conscious intention" in order to differentiate between malingering, Factitious Disorder, and somatoform/conversion disorders. Faust and Ackley (1998) indicated that various inaccuracies during an evaluation may be viewed as intentional or unintentional. Intentional inaccuracies may include poor effort, false or exaggerated symptoms, false attributions, false baseline of functioning, and denial of positive abilities.

In that light, each index of suspicion has a different level of assuredness, or weight, in support of a conclusion of intention. Denney (1999) proposed five basic clinical strategies, with varying levels of confidence, for determining functional ability in the face of apparent intentional misrepresentation. The most definitive indication of ability is *inconsistency between the subject's demonstrated real-world functional ability and his or her test performance or claims of disability*. As Denney (1997) noted, "real-world functioning always trumps psychological test results." Too many times, neuropsychologists focus solely on the test results, ignoring the fact that the examinee's daily living behavior is incongruous with those test results. Only slightly less definitive is *test performance which demonstrates ability in the face of claimed disability*. Below random performance on forced-choice testing is an example of this occurrence. Below random results on tests based on the binomial theorem actually demonstrate ability because the subject chose the incorrect answer more often than what would have occurred by chance alone (Pankratz, 1979; Pankratz, Fausti, & Peed, 1975). "Positive results on [such tests] is tantamount to having the patient claiming they cannot perform a function in the midst of actually performing that very function" (Denney, 1999, p. 20). Less demonstrable evidence is *the subject's presentation being inconsistent with legitimate neurological illness and more reminiscent of the media's portrayal of such illness.* An example includes a person with mild traumatic brain injury claiming life-long remote memory loss. Malingering strategies based on floor effects (e.g., Rey 15 Item Memory Test) and gross overendorsement and abnormal endorsement (e.g., SIRS, MMPI-2) are examples of such methods. While these procedures can identify poor effort, they do little in the way of demonstrating functional ability. *Inconsistency between tests that measure same or similar functional abilities* is another way of determining invalid results. Lastly, *pattern analysis of test results between nonlitigating head injured groups and simulated malingerers* can identify invalid test results and suggest the person's performance is more similar to that of simulators than to that of genuine injured patients. Each of these methods should be considered, and weighted appropriately, when evaluating the potential presence of malingering.

Slick et al. (1999) pointed out that many methods and measures currently used to determine suppressed neuropsychological performance could be classified into these three categories: "(1) inconsistencies or other signs from the patient's reported symptoms; (2) inconsistencies or other signs from standard neuropsychological test; and (3) measures or indices designed expressly to detect feigning of cognitive deficits" (p. 548). They took this general framework and proposed diagnostic criteria for "malingered neurocognitive dysfunction" (MND).

Malingered Neurocognitive Dysfunction

Slick et al. (1999) proposed a model classification system for identifying malingered neurocognitive dysfunction in research and clinical settings. Prior to this proposed model, we had the general definition of malingering presented in the *DSM-IV* and the above authors' recommendations for conceptualizing inconsistencies suggestive of malingering. Since there is no gold standard for the identification of neurocognitive malingering, the authors recognized the need for a standardized classification system that incorporated various detection strategies outlined in literature into one overall classification scheme. The authors indicate that psychometric limitations in neuropsychological test data and the fact there is no valid and reliable pathognomonic sign for malingering make the task difficult, particularly when one needs to "tease apart legitimate from exaggerated impairment in cases where both may be present" (p. 551). The classification system is starting to be used in malingering research (Bianchini, Greve, & Love, 2003; Langeluddecke & Lucas, 2003; Larrabee, 2003a, 2003b, 2003c, 2003d). While any classification scheme will likely have its weaknesses, the effectiveness of this system is yet to be determined. Slick et al. (1999) define MND in this manner:

> MND is the volitional exaggeration or fabrication of cognitive dysfunction for the purpose of obtaining substantial material gain, or avoiding or escaping formal duty or responsibility. Substantial material gain includes money, goods, or services of nontrivial value (e.g., financial compensation for personal injury). Formal duties are actions that people are legally obligated to perform (e.g., prison, military, or public service, or child support payment or other financial obligations). Formal responsibilities are those that involve accountability or liability in legal proceedings (e.g., competency to stand trial). (p. 552)

The classification scheme includes three levels of diagnostic certainty analogous to identifying other neurological conditions (e.g., Alzheimer's Disease) which include "definite," "probable," and "possible" MND. It also uses a multidimensional approach, which incorporates neuropsychological test results, observations, and tests specifically designed to identify negative response bias (NRB). In this regard, the system identifies NRB as simply one aspect of malingering, thereby revealing the point that simply because a person performs poorly on a test designed to detect poor effort, it does not automatically mean the person is malingering. Consistent with the malingering literature, the conclusion of malingering must take into account the entire clinical situation. See Table 2 (pp. 118-122) for the Slick et al. (1999) diagnostic categories and classification criteria.

Following the development of the Slick MND model, Millis (2004) adapted it to a diagnostic decision tree (see Figure 1, p. 117). In practice, the clinician must first determine whether or not the evaluee has substantial external incentive to feign or exaggerate his or her condition. If he or she does not, then the evaluator must entertain other psychogenic reasons for the poor performance, such as somatoform, factitious, personality, psychiatric, or neurological disorders. The next consideration depends on whether or not there is below random performance on forced-choice testing.

FIGURE 1: Diagnostic Decision Tree for Malingered Neurocognitive Dysfunction*

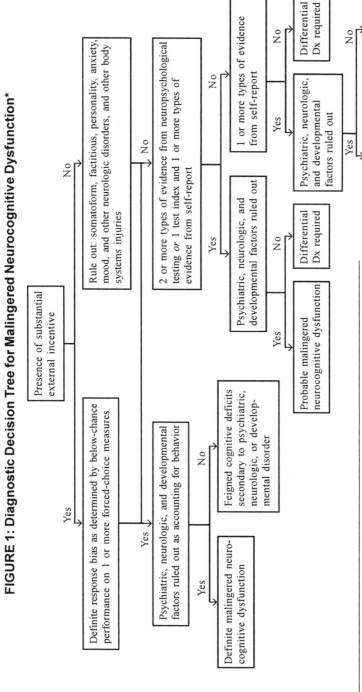

* Reprinted from *Principles and Practice of Behavorial Neurology and Neuropsychology*, M. Rizzo and P. J. Eslinger (Eds.), "Evaluation of Malingered Neurocognitive Disorders" (Figure 53-1, p. 1082), by S. R. Millis, copyright © 2004, with permission from Elsevier.

TABLE 2: Slick et al. (1999) Diagnostic Categories and Classification Criteria*

DIAGNOSTIC CATEGORIES FOR MALINGERING NEUROCOGNITIVE DYSFUNCTION (MND)

Definite MND

This is indicated by the presence of clear and compelling evidence of volitional exaggeration or fabrication of cognitive dysfunction and the absence of plausible alternative explanations. The specific diagnostic criteria necessary for Definite MND are listed below:

1. Presence of a substantial external incentive [Criterion A]
2. Definite negative response bias [Criterion B1]
3. Behaviors meeting necessary criteria from group B are not fully accounted for by Psychiatric, Neurological, or Developmental Factors [Criterion D]

Probable MND

This is indicated by the presence of evidence strongly suggesting volitional exaggeration or fabrication of cognitive dysfunction and the absence of plausible alternative explanations. The specific diagnostic criteria necessary for Probable MND are listed below:

1. Presence of a substantial external incentive [Criterion A]
2. Two or more types of evidence from neuropsychological testing, excluding definite negative response bias [two or more of Criteria B2-B6]

— Or —

One type of evidence from neuropsychological testing, excluding definite negative response bias, and one or more types of evidence from Self-Report [one of Criteria B2-B6 and one or more of Criteria C1-C5]

3. Behaviors meeting necessary criteria from groups B and C are not fully accounted for by Psychiatric, Neurological, or Developmental Factors [Criterion D]

Possible MND

This is indicated by the presence of evidence suggesting volitional exaggeration or fabrication of cognitive dysfunction and the absence of plausible alternative explanations. Alternatively, possible MND is indicated by the presence of criteria necessary for Definite or Probable MND except that other primary etiologies cannot be ruled out. The specific diagnostic criteria for Possible MND are listed below:

1. Presence of a substantial external incentive [Criterion A]
2. Evidence from Self-Report [one or more of Criteria C1-C5]
3. Behaviors meeting necessary criteria from group C are not fully accounted for by Psychiatric, Neurological, or Developmental Factors [Criterion D]

— Or —

Criteria for Definite or Probable MND are met except for Criterion D (i.e., primary psychiatric, neurological, or developmental etiologies cannot be ruled out). In such cases, the alternate etiologies that cannot be ruled out should be specified.

EXPLANATION OF CRITERIA

Criterion A: Presence of substantial external incentive

At least one clearly identifiable and substantial external incentive for exaggeration or fabrication of symptoms is present at the time of examination (e.g., personal injury settlement, disability pension, evasion of criminal prosecution, or release from military service).

Criterion B: Evidence from neuropsychological testing

Evidence of exaggeration or fabrication of cognitive dysfunction on neuropsychological tests, as demonstrated by at least one of the following:

* **Note.** From D. J. Slick, E. M. S. Sherman, and G. L. Iverson (1999). "Diagnostic Criteria for Malingered Neurocognitive Dysfunction: Proposed Standards for Clinical Practice and Research." *The Clinical Neuropsychologist, 13,* 545-561. Copyright © 1999 by Psychology Press Ltd. (http://www.psypress.co.uk/journals.asp). Reprinted with permission.

TABLE 2: Slick et al. (1999) Diagnostic Categories and Classification Criteria (Continued)

Criterion B: Evidence from neuropsychological testing (Continued)

1. *Definite negative response bias.* Below-chance performance (p < .05) on one or more forced-choice measures of cognitive function.

2. *Probable response bias.* Performance on one or more well-validated psychometric tests or indices designed to measure exaggeration or fabrication of cognitive deficits is consistent with feigning.

3. *Discrepancy between test data and known patterns of brain functioning.* A pattern of neuropsychological test performance that is markedly discrepant from currently accepted models of normal and abnormal central nervous system (CNS) function. The discrepancy must be consistent with an attempt to exaggerate or fabricate neuropsychological dysfunction (e.g., a patient performs in the severely impaired range on verbal attention measures but in the average range on memory testing; a patient misses items on recognition testing that were consistently provided on previous free recall trials, or misses many easy items when significantly harder items from the same test are passed).

4. *Discrepancy between test data and observed behavior.* Performance on two or more neuropsychological tests within a domain are discrepant with observed level of cognitive function in a way that suggests exaggeration or fabrication of dysfunction (e.g., a well-educated patient who presents with no significant visual-perceptual deficits or language disturbance in conversational speech performs in the severely impaired range on verbal fluency and confrontation naming tests).

5. *Discrepancy between test data and reliable collateral reports.* Performance on two or more neuropsychological tests within a domain are discrepant with day-to-day level of cognitive function described by at least one reliable collateral informant in a way that suggests exaggeration or fabrication of dysfunction (e.g., a patient handles all family finances but is unable to perform simple math problems in testing).

6. *Discrepancy between test data and documented background history.* Improbably poor performance on two or more standardized tests of cognitive function within a specific domain (e.g., memory) that is inconsistent with documented neurological or psychiatric history (e.g., a patient with no documented loss of consciousness [LOC] or post-traumatic amnesia [PTA], multiple negative neurological investigations, and no other history of CNS trauma or disease consistently obtains verbal memory scores in the severely impaired range after a motor vehicle accident).

Criterion C: Evidence from Self-Report

The following behaviors are indicators of possible malingering of cognitive deficits, but their presence is not sufficient for the diagnosis. However, presence of one or more of these criteria provides additional evidence in support of a diagnosis of malingering. These criteria involve significant inconsistencies or discrepancies in the patient's self-reported symptoms that suggest a deliberate attempt to exaggerate or fabricate cognitive deficits.

1. *Self-reported history is discrepant with documented history.* Reported history is markedly discrepant with documented medical or psychosocial history and suggests attempts to exaggerate injury severity or deny premorbid neuropsychological dysfunction (e.g., exaggerated severity of physical injury or length of LOC/PTA; exaggerated premorbid educational or occupational achievement; denial of previous head injury or previous psychiatric history).

2. *Self-reported symptoms are discrepant with known patterns of brain functioning.* Reported or endorsed symptoms are improbable in number, pattern, or severity; or markedly inconsistent with expectations for the type or severity of documented injury or pathology (e.g., claims of extended retrograde amnesia without loss of memory for the accident, or claims of loss of autobiographical information after mild head trauma without LOC).

3. *Self-reported symptoms are discrepant with behavioral observations.* Reported symptoms are markedly inconsistent with observed behavior (e.g., a patient complains of severe episodic memory deficits yet has little difficulty remembering names, events, or appointments; a patient complains of severe cognitive deficits yet has little difficulty driving independently and arrives on time for an appointment in an unfamiliar area; a patient complains of severely slowed mentation and concentration problems yet easily follows complex conversation).

4. *Self-reported symptoms are discrepant with information obtained from collateral informants.* Reported symptoms, history, or observed behavior is inconsistent with information obtained from other informants judged to be adequately reliable. The discrepancy must be consistent with an attempt to exaggerate injury severity or deny premorbid neuropsychological dysfunction (e.g., a patient reports severe memory impairment and/or behaves as if severely memory-impaired, but his or her spouse reports that the patient has minimal memory dysfunction at home).

TABLE 2: Slick et al. (1999) Diagnostic Categories and Classification Criteria *(Continued)*

Criterion C: Evidence from Self-Report *(Continued)*

5. *Evidence of exaggerated or fabricated psychological dysfunction.* Self-reported symptoms of psychological dysfunction are substantially contradicted by behavioral observation and/or reliable collateral information. Well-validated validity scales or indices on self-report measures of psychological adjustment (e.g., MMPI-2) are strongly suggestive of exaggerated or fabricated distress or dysfunction.

Criterion D: Behaviors meeting necessary criteria from groups B or C are not fully accounted for by Psychiatric, Neurological, or Developmental Factors

Behaviors meeting necessary criteria from groups B and C are the product of an informed, rational, and volitional effort aimed at least in part towards acquiring or achieving external incentives as defined in Criteria A. As such, behaviors meeting criterion from groups B or C cannot be fully accounted for by psychiatric, developmental, or neurological disorders that result in significantly diminished capacity to appreciate laws or mores against malingering, or inability to conform behavior to such standards (e.g., psychological need to "play the sick role," or in response to command hallucinations).

Forced-choice testing, originally called Symptom Validity Testing (SVT), was developed as a means to assess perceptual and short-term memory complaints (Brady & Lind, 1961; Pankratz, 1979, 1983; Pankratz & Binder, 1997; Pankratz et al., 1975). Based on the binomial theorem, the strategy purports that when one of two possibilities of equal probability is selected, results will fall within a predictably random range with approximately normal distribution. Examples include tossing a coin or asking a person with no knowledge questions with only two possible answers of equal probability. Ability affects the results by raising them above random range. Ability is likewise demonstrated when results fall significantly below random as the person must have ability to select the incorrect answer more often than would occur by chance alone. In this way, the procedure does more than simply identify negative response bias; it actually demonstrates functional ability within an established probability range (Pankratz, personal communication cited in Lezak, 1995). The procedure can also work when there are more than two alternatives, but scores need to be more extreme to fall significantly below random when the probability of a correct response is less than .50 (e.g., 25% on a four alternative test such as the Wisconsin Card Sorting Test or Booklet Category Test; Denney & Scully, 1996; Siegel, 1956). Below random responding indicates definite negative response bias. It also demonstrates malingering if the behavior occurred due to substantial secondary gain. In the absence of secondary gain, one must rule out Somatization Disorder and Factitious Disorder.

In the absence of definite MND, Slick et al. (1999) proposed two classifications with less diagnostic certainty, probable and possible MND. Probable MND requires two or more positive findings related to neuropsychological testing or one finding related to testing and one or more findings from self-report. Findings from neuropsychological testing are listed under Criterion B in Table 2. While B-1 refers to below-chance performance on forced-choice tests (FCTs), B-2 describes probable NRB based on tests or indices developed specifically to detect exaggeration and feigning of neuropsychologically related abilities. Larrabee (2003c) and Scott Millis (personal communication, June 1, 2004) interpreted the "two or more positive findings" from Criteria B to also include two or more positive malingering test results from Criterion B-2 rather than two or more "types" of evidence from Criteria B (e.g., B2 + B3 or B3 + B5). Glenn Larrabee (personal communication, May 31, 2004) noted that relying on the criteria other than B1 or B2, as it is strictly written, opens the door to subjective impressions that are difficult to verify. There also appears to be an inconsistency in the classification between the definition of Probable

MND (two or more of Criteria B2-B6) and the explanation of Criteria B: "Evidence of exaggeration or fabrication of cognitive dysfunction on neuropsychological tests, as demonstrated by at least one of the following" (Slick et al., 1999, p. 553). In addition, under Criterion B2, Probable response bias, it is noted, "performance on one or more well-validated psychometric tests or indices designed to measure exaggeration or fabrication of cognitive deficits is consistent with feigning" (emphasis in the original; p. 553). In other words, "one of the following" could indicate "one or more positive well-validated" effort tests such that only one positive effort test would result in Probable MND if there was presence of external incentive and no other logical cause for the finding. It appears Slick et al. (1999) intended to require at least two positive indications, each from different Criteria B evidence, excluding B1 (e.g., B2-B6) to meet this portion of Probable MND.

Probable MND can also be achieved with one or more positive indications from Criteria B (excluding definite response bias, Criterion B1) and one or more types of evidence from Self-Report (Criteria C1-C5). Larrabee (2003c) classified litigants with chronic pain using one or more positive neuropsychological measures of effort and one type of evidence from Self-Report (Criteria C). Specifically, he used scores above cut off scores of the MMPI-2 Lees-Haley Fake-Bad Scale (Lees-Haley et al., 1991) as the indicator of exaggerated self-report, consistent with Criterion C5: *Evidence of exaggerated or fabricated psychological dysfunction.*

Larrabee's (2003c) interpretation of using two or more positive tests of NRB or one positive test of NRB and at least one objective measure of exaggerated self-report (e.g., MMPI-2 FBS) to classify Probable MND appears reasonable. The potential difficulty with this manner of classification is the varying sensitivities for tests of NRB. In this regard, a positive result on one effort test may mean something different than a positive result on another effort test, depending on the sensitivity of the test and strength of its supporting validation literature. Each of the many tests of NRB has a different level of sensitivity and specificity. Further, each test has a different positive and negative predictive accuracy, depending on the expected base rate of NRB, and likely performs differently in various settings (e.g., clinical vs. forensic; civil vs. criminal). Research will need to delineate these differences, and the differences will likely change as people are either coached in how to circumvent malingering detection (Lees-Haley, 1997; Wetter & Corrigan, 1995; Youngjohn, 1995) or obtain information from the Internet prior to the evaluation. We will now turn to a review of a number of these well-validated measures.

FREESTANDING INDICES OF
NEUROCOGNITIVE NRB

Each of the following measures of NRB has different characteristics. Particularly important is the apparent face validity of each. For example, some measures are based on general intellectual ability, while others are based on visual or verbal memory. Although some of these procedures may be termed "floor effect" tests in that they actually measure only a modest level of ability, they, nonetheless, have face validity to the evaluee. In this regard, subjects who wish to exaggerate deficits in certain neurocognitive functions (consistent with their understanding of what true pathology looks like) will likely not exaggerate in every functional domain. This distinction becomes important when psychologists evaluate the meaningfulness of NRB test results.

General Intellectual Ability

The Validity Indicator Profile (VIP; Frederick, 2003) is unique in that it uses performance curve analysis and establishes a four-fold classification system of performance, including compliant, inconsistent, irrelevant, and suppressed. The VIP has nonverbal and verbal components, both of which are based on the combination of two-alternative, forced-choice testing and progressive item difficulty. The nonverbal portion was originally adapted from the Test of Nonverbal Intelligence (Brown, Sherbenou, & Johnsen, 1982) and the verbal portion patterned after the verbal portion of the Shipley Institute of Living Scale (Zachary, 1986). Consequently, it pulls for general intellectual ability. The nonverbal test can be administered separately from the verbal test for those who cannot read. It uses six different classification strategies that were developed with a sample of more than 1,000 clinical and nonclinical subjects. It was cross-validated with an independent sample of 312 individuals in five criterion groups: TBI patients, suspected malingerers, normal subjects, simulators, and random responders. In a recent review, Frederick (2002) reported sensitivity/specificity rates of 73.5/85.7 for the nonverbal subtest and 67.3/83.1 for the verbal subtest during cross-validation. Frederick suggested these rates were underestimates of test performance because of criterion group contamination. The VIP is a major breakthrough in attempting to understand the nature of malingering as more than simply a dichotomous occurrence as it takes into consideration motivation and effort. In addition, there are no other freestanding NRB indices specific to general intellectual function.

Short-Term Memory

The Rey 15-Item Memory Test (Rey, 1958) is the most widely known of Rey's malingering tests. It is a simple memory procedure, which takes little time to complete and has received a great deal of research attention. Frederick (2002) reviewed the procedure and found sensitivity rates to vary from 40% to 89% depending on the cut off, with the specificity generally placing in the mid to upper nineties. There appeared to be a difference in test performance between civil litigants and criminal defendants. K. B. Boone et al. (2002) reviewed the test and found sensitivities to range from 7% to 72 % for volunteer simulators and 5% to 72% for clinical samples of patients in litigation and those suspected of malingering. Boone and her colleagues developed a recognition test to add to the Rey-15 Item Test, which raised the sensitivity by 50% over the rather modest sensitivity of 47% in a known group's design. This change to the procedure adds little additional time to a test that is already quite time efficient. Vallabhajosula and van Gorp (2001) suggested the procedure, as it was originally developed, would not meet *Daubert* court admissibility standards because of low sensitivity, but Frederick (2002) suggested it is a reasonable procedure to use as long as it is not used in isolation. Indeed, Boone and colleagues found that sensitivity increased with the addition of multiple indices. Because of its popularity, its utility has probably become compromised due to an increasingly informed public.

The Portland Digit Recognition Test (PDRT; Binder, 1990; Binder & Willis, 1991) is a forced-choice, two-alternative digit recognition test patterned after the Hiscock Digit Memory Test (M. Hiscock & C. K. Hiscock, 1989) and incorporating three trials of what appear to be increasingly difficult stimuli. The entire test requires about 40 minutes to administer, although an abbreviated form has been developed for individuals who appear to be performing well (Binder, 1993). Binder (2002) recently reviewed the procedure and noted sensitivity rates to vary between 39% to 77% depending on the type of subject, while specificity rates held constant at 100%. The benefit of using such forced-choice, two-alternative tests as the PDRT, is the fact that occasionally subjects will perform below chance and, in effect, demonstrate the very ability they are trying to claim they do not have (Denney, 1999). The Victoria Symptom Validity Test (VSVT; Slick et al., 1997; see Thompson, 2002, for a recent review) and Computerized Assessment of Response Bias (CARB; Allen et al., 1997; see Allen, Iverson, & Green, 2002, for a recent review) are similar strategies, but they use computer administration. The CARB uses antiquated computer software and a confusing and poorly written manual, which can be frustrating to master (Wynkoop & Denney, 2001). The great benefit of the CARB, however, is the fact that it includes norm references which allow the examiner to compare the subject's performance to known neurological, amnestic, and severe brain injury patients. Oftentimes, this comparison by itself provides substantial indication of poor subject effort and presence of clear inconsistency between test results and activities of daily living. In this regard, the CARB appears to be a more effective digit memory test than others currently available.

The Test of Memory Malingering (TOMM; Tombaugh, 1996) is also a two-alternative, forced-choice test of memory, but it uses line drawings rather than digits. In a recent review, Tombaugh (2002) reported 84% and 88% detection rates for simulators with a 100% specificity rate using the recommended cut off. A follow-up study using TBI patients in litigation resulted in a 77% correct classification rate. Specificity dropped to only 90% when including severely impaired neurological patients. Teichner and Wagner (2004) evaluated the performance of the TOMM in elderly patients with cognitive impairment and dementia. Patients with cognitive impairments did not differ significantly from cognitively intact patients (92.7% vs. 100% normal performance, respectively), whereas the false-positive rate for the dementia patients was unacceptably high. There appears to be little effect from depression and anxiety for community-dwelling older adults (Ashendorf, Constantinou, & McCaffrey, 2004). Delain, Stafford, and Ben-Porath (2003) reviewed the performance of the TOMM in a sample of pretrial criminal defendants. In a differential prevalence design, Weinborn et al. (2003) found that criminal defendants referred for pretrial mental health evaluations were more likely to demonstrate below cut off performances on the TOMM than criminal defendants civilly committed and adjudicated not guilty by reason of insanity. While a number of studies demonstrate the utility of the TOMM in the civil forensic arena, these results also suggest it is a valid indicator of poor effort among criminal defendants.

The Word Memory Test (WMT; Green, Allen, & Astner, 1996) is unique in the area of malingering tests as it is a forced-choice, two-alternative procedure that also includes legitimate memory assessment for words and word pairs. It is available as a computer-administered test, which automatically calculates z-score comparisons to a variety of normal and neurologically impaired adults and children. Although the test was initially met with a cool review (Wynkoop & Denney, 2001) due to difficult computer software and lack of peer reviewed, published research, it has now become a widely researched tool with a strong empirical basis (Hartman, 2002; Wynkoop & Denney, 2005). In a recent review, Green,

Lees-Haley, and Allen (2002) note the WMT demonstrates overall sensitivity rates of about 97% and specificity rates of 100% for simulation studies. With the new Windows version, the test is tremendously easy to use and can be performed in six different languages. It appears that, with the current research literature available, the WMT is the most effective freestanding malingering detection strategy available.

EMBEDDED INDICES OF
NEUROCOGNITIVE NRB

Aside from tests and techniques that are designed specifically to assess neurocognitive malingering, there are many NRB indices that are incorporated within widely used psychological and neuropsychological measures. These strategies are beneficial because they take little additional time to administer and the connection is clear between poor performance on the validity scale and poor performance on the genuine test. In addition, these indices can be calculated on testing protocols from evaluations done in the past. The negative aspect is that specificity results will probably not be as strong with these strategies, because they are comprised of tasks designed to be sensitive to genuine brain injury. Vallabhajosula and van Gorp (2001) suggest the best malingering detection strategies will be sensitive to feigning but not genuine impairment. Nevertheless, the trend of designing NRB detection methods within already established neuropsychological measures appears to be a reasonable pursuit. Examples of such malingering detection strategies based on established clinical measures include the Warrington Recognition Memory Test (see Millis, 2002, for a review), atypical pattern analysis on the Wechsler Scales, Wechsler Memory Scale-Revised, and Halstead-Reitan Battery (see Mittenberg, Aquila-Puentes, et al., 2002 for a review of each), Reliable Digit Span (Greiffenstein et al., 1994; Larrabee, 2003a; J. E. Meyers & Volbrecht, 1998), Rarely Missed Index of the Wechsler Memory Scale-III (Killgore & DellaPietra, 2000), California Verbal Learning Test (Millis, Putnam, Adams, & Ricker, 1995; Slick, Iverson, & Green, 2000), Wisconsin Card Sorting Test (see Greve et al., 2002, a review of various methods), Finger Tapping (Heaton et al., 1978; Larrabee, 2003a), Benton Judgment of Line Orientation (J. E. Meyers, Galinsky, & Volbrecht, 1999), Category Test (see Sweet & King, 2002, for review), test-retest changes on the Halstead-Reitan Battery (see Reitan & Wolfson, 2002, for review), and Benton Visual Form Discrimination (Larrabee, 2003a). Readers are referred to each article to learn specifics of computing these indices, as reprinting them here raises test security issues.

Larrabee (2003a) points out that "assessment of effort in medicolegal settings must be multi-variate" (p. 422). J. E. Meyers and Volbrecht (2003) demonstrate that use of multiple embedded NRB indicators within a standard neuropsychology battery can efficaciously identify invalid performance. J. E. Meyers and Volbrecht found 83% sensitivity and 100% specificity in identifying NRB using a two or more positive cut off among a mixed group of clinical cases and analog simulators. There were no false positives using this method. Larrabee (2002) found that using multiple NRB indicators and a two or more positive cut off resulted in an overall sensitivity of 87.8% and specificity of 94.4% for the combined samples of litigating and nonlitigating closed head injury evaluees who were classified based on Slick et al. (1999) criteria. He also demonstrates that use of multiple indicators decreases the chance of false-positive identification errors. The above sensitivity rates rival, and even beat, that of many of the freestanding measures of NRB. Using the above embedded indices facilitates the identification of NRB in this regard with no additional test administration time. Incorporating one or more freestanding indices of NRB would likely increase the sensitivity of this multivariate method without compromising specificity.

IDENTIFICATION OF FEIGNED REMOTE MEMORY IMPAIRMENT

It is not uncommon in the criminal forensic setting for defendants to claim memory impairment for a specific time in the past, usually associated with the commission of a particular crime (Kopelman, 1987). The United States Court of Appeals for the District of Columbia Circuit has dealt with the impact such amnesia has on the trial process (*Wilson v. U.S.*, 1968). In this case, the appeals court affirmed that amnesia does not necessarily eliminate a defendant's ability to remain competent to stand trial, but each case must be evaluated regarding its unique circumstances. Most other jurisdictions have maintained the same position (R. D. Miller, 2003). Research also suggests that a substantial amount of the claimed amnesia in these instances is feigned (Cima, Merckelbach, & Hollnack, 2003; Power, 1977). Identifying feigned remote memory loss, such as for events surrounding a crime, can be difficult, and it has been argued that effective identification of malingered remote memory requires technical skill and understanding of specialized assessment strategies (Cima et al., 2002).

Frederick, Carter, and Powel (1995) applied the two alternative, forced-choice testing method to the assessment of remote memory for an evaluation of a pretrial criminal defendant who claimed amnesia for the alleged offense. They developed two alternative, forced-choice questions based on investigative information and used reasonably plausible alternative answers for the foils. Denney (1996) demonstrated the procedure again with three pretrial criminal defendant case studies. Denney carried the procedure further by administering the three tests from the case studies to naïve undergraduates and demonstrated item probabilities approximated the normal distribution with test means nearly 50% for each. Due to continued concerns that foils developed for such testing do not truly have equal probability to the correct answers, Frederick and Denney (1998) replicated the findings of Denney in demonstrating tests performed in a manner consistent with random probability. In fact, naïve subjects generally performed slightly better than what one would expect from individuals with no knowledge of events in question. This finding suggested the procedure is even more conservative than expected. To address more specifically the concern about unequal item response probabilities, Frederick and Denney (1998) performed a computer simulation for a large number of trials using tests comprised of variable response probabilities. Results revealed that as item response options (correct & foil) deviated from the perfect .50/.50 probability, the likelihood of achieving statistically significant results actually decreases. This finding indicates the test becomes more conservative (in regard to classifying a person as malingering based on below random responding) as test items deviate from perfect equality in probability. Overall, it appeared to be a robust procedure for identifying feigned remote memory loss.

Merckelbach, Hauer, and Rassin (2002) evaluated the procedure in regard to its sensitivity. They pointed out the commonly accepted view that below random performance is actually quite rare even in the feigning population. However, using a sample of undergraduates simulating remote memory loss, the authors demonstrated a 40% rate of below random performance for this very short SVT (15 items). This rate of below random performance regarding remote memory is higher than the 25% estimated by Frederick and Denney (1998). It is possible that malingerers perform at below chance levels with greater frequency when answering questions specific to autobiographical information or information specific to an alleged crime. Additional research is needed to elucidate this possibility.

EXAGGERATED OR FABRICATED PSYCHOLOGICAL DYSFUNCTION BASED ON SELF-REPORT

As noted above, Larrabee (2003d) used the Lees-Haley Fake Bad Scale (FBS) from the MMPI-2 as an objective indicator of exaggerated self-report. The MMPI-2 (Butcher et al., 1989) has long been useful as a measure to identify exaggerated psychological distress (Lees-Haley et al., 2002). The FBS was originally developed to identify exaggeration of emotional distress in personal injury litigants (Lees-Haley et al., 1991), but more recent research indicates it is useful in identifying exaggeration of somatic concerns (Larrabee, 1997, 1998). It is comprised of 43 items focused primarily on somatic concerns. An increasing body of research demonstrates it is more sensitive to exaggerated somatic and neurocognitive symptom complaints than F, Fb, or F(p) (Larrabee, 1998, 2003b, 2003c; Millis, Putnam, & Adams, 1995; Ross et al., 2004; Slick et al., 1996; W. T. Tsushima & V. G. Tsushima, 2001).

A considerable number of simulation and known group studies have addressed the validity of FBS, and it has consistently proven sensitive to the exaggeration of neurocognitive and somatic complaints (see Lees-Haley et al., 2002, for a review of these many studies). Larrabee (1997) concluded that "somatic malingering should be considered whenever elevations on the scales 1 and 3 exceed T80, accompanied by a significant elevation on the FBS" (p. 203). Related to detecting MND, FBS demonstrates superior effect sizes to any other MMPI-2 scale (Larrabee, 2003b). Larrabee's results were consistent with that of Ross and colleagues (2004) with similar cut offs. A greater than 21 raw score yielded a sensitivity of 0.808, specificity of 0.862. Using an estimated base rate (BR) for MND of 40% results in a positive predictive power of 0.669 and negative predictive power of 0.764.

Butcher and colleagues (2003) reviewed FBS performance among various clinical samples based on archival files. In addition, the authors added data from VA patients and personal injury litigants. They concluded that FBS correlated with other clinical scales more than the established validity indicators of the MMPI-2. Further, they concluded that FBS overclassified individuals as malingerers. "The highest malingering classification was for the women in the personal injury sample (37.9%), while the lowest was among male prison inmates (2.3%)" (p. 481). They thought it odd that lower rates of classification occurred for prison males than personal injury females. They concluded the false-positive rate was too high and recommended against use of the FBS in clinical and disability evaluation settings. Greve and Bianchini (2004), Larrabee (2003d), and Lees-Haley and Fox (2004) responded and pointed out the methodological flaws in the study by Butcher et al. (2003). FBS does not correlate with F, Fb, or F(p) scales as much as it does with scales 1, 2, 3, 7, and 8, because these scales are most commonly elevated in personal injury litigants (Berry et al., 1996; K. B. Boone & Lu, 1999; Larrabee, 2003d). Further, Butcher et al. did not control for malingering in their study. It is striking that the FBS positive classification rate of 37.9% so closely approximates Larrabee's (2003a) estimate of 40%. Further, there should be no surprise that incarcerated males complain of somatic related concerns less than female personal injury litigants. It is likely that the predominant majority of those males were sentenced inmates with no significant motivation to exaggerate physical "weakness" or pretrial defendants with motivation to exaggerate psychiatric disturbance. The weight of multiple studies demonstrating the validity of FBS suggests it is an effective tool in the identification of exaggerated somatic and neurocognitive related self-report.

CLOSING CONSIDERATIONS

The identification of malingering during the assessment of neurocognitive abilities requires a multidimensional approach, which incorporates neuropsychological test results, observations, and tests specifically designed to identify NRB. Research by J. E. Meyers and Volbrecht (2003) and Larrabee (2003a) demonstrate the effectiveness of this method. While it is questionable whether or not the method increases sensitivity, it clearly increases specificity. As a result, it decreases the likelihood of obtaining false positives. Applying the Slick and colleagues (1999) classification system in clinical and forensic practice appears reasonable; however, the reliability and validity of this classification method needs further verification. Clinicians need to be aware of the differing sensitivities of various measures of NRB as well as the differing base rates for NRB in various setting (e.g., civil vs. criminal). The difficulty in this particular endeavor is that characteristics of various measures may change depending on the setting. Clearly, additional research is needed not only in the identification of base rates, but test performance as well.

KEY POINTS

- Neurocognitive malingering and Negative Response Bias (NRB) are related terms, with NRB encompassing malingering. Differentiation between these terms is important in discussing base rates of disingenuous neurocognitive performance, which vary considerably depending on definition, method of measurement, and setting.
- A number of authors have proposed general strategies for assessing invalid performance across a neurocognitive battery and interview. The most definitive indication of ability is *inconsistency between the subject's demonstrated real-world functional ability and his or her test performance or claims of disability.*
- Clinicians may use symptom validity testing to assess malingering of neurocognitive deficits. This procedure involves the development of forced choice items, at times specific to the evaluee. Individuals with true deficits will demonstrate random response patterns, while malingerers are likely to obtain scores significantly lower than chance alone would suggest.
- There are several freestanding indices of neurocognitive malingering. The Validity Indicator Profile, a measure of general intellectual ability, is by far the most versatile and empirically sound. Measures of short-term memory malingering including the Rey 15-item test, Portland Digit Recognition Test, Computerized Assessment of Response Bias, Test of Memory Malingering, and Word Memory Test. The current literature base suggests the Word Memory Test is the best choice in this category.
- A number of general and neurocognitive tests included embedded measures of response validity. For example, Reliable Digit Span can be computed from WAIS-III scores, allowing for some estimation of the probability of feigned deficits.
- Despite its function as a personality assessment tool, the MMPI-2 (discussed in detail in Chapter 3) contains scales that are of assistance in assessing NRB.

Chapter 6

HYPNOSIS AND THE POLYGRAPH

HISTORICAL INTRODUCTION TO HYPNOSIS

Hypnosis has been recognized as a phenomenon and as a clinically useful tool since ancient times (C. Bartol & A. Bartol, 2004; Meyer, 1992; H. Spiegel & D. Spiegel, 2004). For example, references to the therapeutic use of "temple sleep," and to being enchanted by the "evil eye," can be traced back to as early as 3000 B.C. Anton Mesmer is credited with introducing the scientific approach to the study of this phenomenon (then termed "mesmerism") in his 1766 medical dissertation at the University of Vienna. James Braid is inaccurately credited with introducing the term "hypnosis" in the early 1840s; the term was clearly applied to the phenomenon as early as 1820 by a Frenchman, Etienne de Cuvillers.

In 1893 Josef Breuer (1842-1925) and Sigmund Freud (1856-1939) published the original chapters of *Studien uber hysterie*, which discussed using hypnosis to encourage spontaneous verbalizations, from the unconscious, that led to catharsis (Forrest, 1999). Freud later seemingly abandoned hypnosis, influencing many mental health practitioners toward the same view in the years hence. However, in 1924 Franz Polgar, a Hungarian born hypnotist-entertainer asserted that he was invited by Freud to Vienna, and while there, "watched" Freud administer hypnosis, later becaming Freud's medical hypnotist, that is, kind of an aide to do the hypnosis work that Freud supposedly did not want to do. Freud was also influential in his strong support of lay hypnotists.

Benjamin Rush, a signer of the Declaration of Independence and the "father of American psychiatry," wrote the first American textbook on psychiatry in 1812, and later developed an interest in hypnosis, which facilitated a degree of acceptance of hypnosis in medical circles in the United States (Forrest, 1999). Interest in hypnosis waned in the United States for many years, except as part of the spiritualistic movement.

Interest by researchers and clinicians began to increase around the turn of the century. In 1923 Clark Hull (1884-1952), the noted behaviorist, asked Milton H. Erickson (1901-1980), still an undergraduate pre-medical student at the University of Wisconsin, to lead a graduate seminar on his informal but interesting research on hypnotism. This event marked the beginning of Erickson's extremely influential career in hypnosis and apparently also helped stimulate Clark Hull's interest in hypnosis (Forrest, 1999).

Much of Erickson's exploratory work with patients took place while he was at the Wayne County General Hospital from 1934 to 1948 in Eloise, Michigan (the post office designation for what was then the hospital grounds, and named after a former superintendent's daughter – the third author [Dr. Meyer] completed the first phase of his internship there). By the 1950s Erickson had attained national renown, being consulted by famous athletes, other media figures, and the military, and in the process achieving what some in the field of hypnosis perceive as a cult status. He was famous for his indirect induction technique, strongly believed that subjects could be made to perform acts that were against their will, and once made a little-known tape in which he caused a young woman to experience severe emotional pain from a memory he inserted by hypnosis (Emery, 1998).

Although in 1930 Hull was forbidden by administrators at Yale to hypnotize students, in 1933 he published *Hypnosis and Suggestibility*. Although the particular behavioral-based theory that Hull promoted ultimately received little acceptance, his international reputation in behavioral research fueled a renewed interest in hypnosis. During the 1940s hypnosis even began to appear in some police journals, and was taught to police as a method to get people to tell the truth by people like the lay hypnotist Harry Arons. He and his followers typically fostered the belief that hypnosis could compel people to act against their will (Forrest, 1999).

Founded by Jerome Schneck, the Society for Clinical and Experimental Hypnosis (SCEH) began publishing the *Journal for Clinical and Experimental Hypnosis* in 1949, with the appellation *International* added 10 years later. In 1955 the British Medical Association designated hypnosis as an accepted treatment modality, and in 1958 the American Medical Association recognized hypnosis as a legitimate treatment technique in medicine and dentistry. In 1961, the American Psychiatric Association endorsed hypnosis as an acceptable treatment modality and the American Psychological Association created an interest-affiliation section in 1969 for psychologists interested in hypnosis.

THE CONTROL OF BEHAVIOR BY HYPNOSIS

Although the media has long been fascinated by the use of hypnosis to force one to tell the truth and on whether one can convincingly fake being hypnotized, these concepts have seldom been directly researched by sound empirical methods. However, underlying these issues is a more basic one, whether by hypnosis one can force someone else to do something against his or her will.

There certainly have been numerous anecdotal reports of people being controlled by hypnosis. The most exhaustive collection of such anecdotal reports was collected by Emery (1998). She detailed a large number of cases wherein people were apparently controlled by hypnotists to the point that they engaged in antisocial, violent, and/or bizarre behaviors. And some noted researchers, such as George Estabrooks (Estabrooks & Lockridge, 1957) reported numerous single-case situations that indicate hypnosis can make individuals perform behaviors they would not do in their normal state of consciousness. Orne (1972) reported a demonstration in which a young woman readily accepted a suggestion to stab people with a pseudodagger and to poison them with what actually was sugar.

There have also been attempts to empirically research this, sometimes by very creative methods. For example, in 1939, Rowland used a box that contained a rattlesnake. It appeared as though one could reach in and grab the snake, but a set of mirrors prevented this from actually happening. People under hypnosis were told they should grab the snake even though it was poisonous. While all 42 nonhypnotized subjects would not try to touch the snake, three out of four hypnotized subjects did so. Young (1952) reports replicating the same experiment and came up with essentially the same results. Young also performed another experiment wherein people were told that someone had done something horrible, and the person was about to enter the room, and that when he or she did, they should throw acid (a harmless concoction designed to look like acid) on that person (a confederate). In virtually all such experiments a small portion of people did the horrible deed. But, as with mock jury research, there is always the valid criticism that those who did these deeds may have known at some level of consciousness that they would not really be asked to do something so horrific. It should be noted, though, that through a bizarre mistake, one of Young's subjects threw actual nitric acid on the confederate, but fortunately, "on account of the promptness of remedial measures, no scars were left on his face" (p. 405). The truth is that we cannot do the research that would definitively answer the question. Even ignoring the criticisms of their experiments, it is unlikely a scientific review board would allow the replication of either Young or Rowland's experiments.

Research by Knight and Meyer (2005) indicates that experts in hypnosis believe that individuals cannot be made to do things against their will while under hypnosis. Questionnaires were mailed to a random sample ($N = 582$) of the 2,700 members of the American Society of Clinical Hypnosis. Responses were received from 251 members for a very respectable return rate of 43%. Only 1% strongly agreed and 15% moderately agreed that a moderately to deeply hypnotized individual can be made to do things against his or her will, while 29% somewhat disagreed and 55% strongly disagreed with this statement. On the other hand, when students in a psychology class were given the same question, 7% strongly agreed and 41% somewhat agreed, while 30% disagreed somewhat and 24% strongly disagreed with the statement. The experts' view that people probably cannot be made to do things truly against their will fits with the majority of scholars who write about this issue (Knight & Meyer, in press).

Control by Hypnosis in the Media and the Courts

In 1894 George du Maurier, an Englishman, authored his last and most famous novel, *Trilby*. Based on his observation of a hypnotic subject, who manifested a complete amnesic dissociation, du Maurier created the classic character of Svengali. Svengali, a middle-aged and unsuccessful musician, gained control over a young female singer, Trilby. Henceforth, she always performed her songs in a hypnotic trance. He controlled her life, including cohabiting with her. Svengali died in the end. However, reflecting a belief of the time that the person controlled cannot survive without the controller, or "Svengali," Trilby died a few hours later. Such was the power of the novel that it generated a popular outcry to ban hypnosis, which only seemed to abate when du Maurier himself died 2 years later (Forrest, 1999).

In 1887, Tardieau reported the case of an 18-year-old female, Marguerite, who became pregnant while receiving daily magnetic treatments, and asserted she could not understand how this could have happened. Tardieau, along with two other expert witnesses, concluded that since such procedures can render one impervious to the pain of "tortures," Marguerite could have been sexually assaulted in a treatment session, and her hypnotist was convicted.

Albert Moll's influential 1892 book, *Der Hypnotisme*, published in 1897 in English (New York: DaCapo), is the classic work of the 19th century on hypnotism. It only mentions one legal case involving hypnosis, in which a physician who allegedly had sex with a hypnotized client was later brought to the attention of the courts when he tried to get her to accept his offer to arrange an abortion. He was acquitted.

A landmark trial known as the Eyrand-Bompard affair stems from the murder on July 26, 1889 of Gouffe, a wealthy Parisian bailiff. The trial attained the status of a landmark case because it elicited conflicting "expert" commentaries from the then predominant theories of the Nancy and Salpetriere schools, and also because it gained notice as it coincided with the First International Congress for Experimental and Clinical Hypnotism in 1889, as well as the World's Fair of 1889 in Paris. Gouffe had been in an affair with Gabrielle Bompard, the mistress of Eyrand, a "businessman." Gabrielle confessed to the murder, but with an indifference that would suggest either an altered state of consciousness or psychopathy. It was known she was being hypnotized by a Dr. Sacreste, a friend of her father's, to cure her of her generally "wild" behavior. However, her lover, Eyrand, a 48-year-old con man, was also hypnotizing her to counteract Dr. Sacreste's efforts, and Eyrand was apparently the victor. All evidence indicates that Eyrand murdered Gouffe. But Gabrielle was at the very least a passive witness, and possibly an active accomplice. Today, we would at least recognize the contributing feature that Gabrielle was apparently repetitively physically beaten by Eyrand.

So the question at hand was whether she acted psychopathically, or as a person hypnotically controlled by Eyrand. The Nancy School argued that as an "automaton," a highly hypnotizable person could enact a behavior suggested by the hypnotist, yet be without either awareness or the associated criminal intent. The Salpetriere School held otherwise, following from their view of hypnosis as having an inherent pathological context. The Salpetriere experts were also not so clear that Gabrielle had been hypnotized, as there was no evidence of "Hysterical crises." Thus, they emphasized her behavioral history. So when both Eyrand and Gabrielle were found guilty, this was seen as an affirmation of the Salpetriere view and a blow to the prestige of the Nancy School. The court did find that Gabrielle acted under mitigating circumstances, sentencing her to jail and forced labor for 20 years. But they sentenced Eyrand to death.

Father Gregory Rasputin, a Siberian monk, gained power and influence in the Russian Romanov monarchy in the period from 1905 to 1918, allegedly by using hypnosis to control bleeding in Alexis, the hemophiliac son of Tsar Nicholas II, and the only available heir to the Russian throne. Revolutionaries used Rasputin's alleged mystical influence as one of the rallying points in the overthrow of the monarchy. Alexander Kerensky commented that "without Rasputin, there is no Lenin."

Pentothal (thiopental) was synthesized in 1935 by Tabern and Volwiler, and Lundy found its application as an intravenous anesthetic. In the following year sodium pentothal was synthesized. Not long after, they were each combined with hypnosis by some practitioners in order to maximize the ability to control behavior.

Ludwig Mayer published *Das Verbrechen in Hypnose* (Berlin: J. F. Lehmanns) in 1937 wherein he discusses 21 previous European court cases that dealt with crimes generated through posthypnotic suggestion. Mayer cited the risks to the public in stating

> a person in somnambulistic hypnosis is not able to take up a critical attitude on his own behalf . . . subordination to the hypnotizer, and dulling of his consciousness takes place, regardless of whether he is the subject of a legitimate experiment or is being hypnotized for other purposes. . . . Just as suggestions can be employed therapeutically . . . they can equally well be used for criminal purposes." (p. 53)

Although never translated into English, it became an extremely influential book throughout Europe.

HYPNOSIS AND THE AMERICAN LEGAL SYSTEM

There are anecdotal reports that the first use of hypnosis to refresh the memory of a witness to a crime occurred in 1845. In 1848 we find the first formal reports of cases in United States courts (in the *American Journal of Insanity*) that focused on hypnosis. In the first case, in a court in Cincinnati, Pascal B. Smith was found insane and incapable of managing his affairs after his wife alleged his involvement in hypnosis had caused him to squander their property.

In the *People v. John Johnson*, tried in 1846, Ann-Augusta Burdock's husband and family physician used hypnosis in an attempt to clarify her testimony about an alleged kidnapping and assault on her by Johnson. The story produced under hypnosis was different from all others, possibly the first case of tainting of an eyewitness by hypnosis, and Johnson was acquitted.

In 1878, the first U.S. case, *People v. Royal*, was heard in which it is argued that sexual abuse occurred under hypnosis (magnetism). The California court, relying on a legal precedent (from *Commonwealth v. Burke*, 1870 - that force is a necessary legal element of rape) concluded that magnetism could not be the legal cause of abuse. Then, in 1894, in *People v. Worthington*, Mrs. Worthington, who had killed her lover, stated that her husband had asked her to do it, and had influenced her under hypnosis to carry it out. One piece of evidence offered for the presence of hypnosis was that "she seemed not at all excited" when apprehended immediately after the shooting. The jury was not impressed, and sentenced her to 25 years imprisonment. Upon appeal, the Supreme Court of California was also not impressed, saying that just because she was told by her husband to kill, and then did it, does not prove she was influenced by hypnosis to do it.

In the case of *State v. Pusch* (1950), following the long tradition first articulated in *People v. Ebanks* (1897), that is, wherein any testimony obtained under hypnosis per se is inadmissable (though this court did not indicate awareness of Ebanks), August Pusch was charged with the murder of his wife, with evidence provided by his mistress as the main witness. It was alleged that August put strychnine into his wife's prescribed Vitamin B capsules. He was administered both a polygraph and a hypnosis session. He reportedly "passed" both, insofar as they supposedly supported his innocence. The hypnosis expert, alleged to be so because he had "a doctorate in psychology from a university," asserted that in hypnosis (a) the subconscious takes over control from consciousness - a legacy from Freud, and (b) the hypnotized person behaves like an "automaton," reminiscent of the concepts of the Nancy school's theory. It was then asserted that these two factors together produced an inability to deceive. However, the North Dakota Supreme Court disallowed the expert testimony, and ignoring Ebanks, asserted that no case was found that dealt with this.

The important case of *Leyra v. Denno* (1954) concerns a confession elicited by hypnosis. Though hypnosis was not formally induced, Justice Hugo Black wrote of "trance-like submission." The decision overturned the defendant's alleged hammer murder of his mother and father. The confession was elicited by a psychiatrist who identified himself to the defendant as his doctor. The psychiatrist told the defendant that he was not morally responsible, massaged his head, commanded him to stare into his eyes, suggested that he did commit the murders, and threatened him with an injection (of at least an implied truth serum) if he did not cooperate.

In *Zani v. State* (1988), there was an eyewitness identification in a murder, elicited via hypnosis by a Texas Ranger who was trained by James Boulch, described as a "teacher of hypnosis at Texas A&M." Like many police officers, his training was via a short course given by Martin Reiser's group, and Boulch was present at the training. Two wrong ideas that were purported were: (a) hypnotically enhanced testimony has consistently proven to be reliable; and (b) the videotape theory of memory is accurate.

This court was impressed by the prior strong precedent set in *State v. Hurd* (1981) wherein hypnotically obtained testimony was deemed admissible as long as specific guidelines were strictly followed, and which stated that as long as such procedures are followed, hypnosis provides a "reasonably reliable means of restoring memory comparable to normal recall in its accuracy."

In *Rock v. Arkansas* (1987), Vickie Rock was charged with shooting her husband. She had partial amnesia for the details of the shooting. She was hypnotized to enhance her memory, and after hypnosis she remembered that the gun had misfired because it was defective. The trial court refused to permit this testimony because it had resulted from hypnosis, and was therefore considered unreliable. The U.S. Supreme Court, in a 5-4 decision, with Rehnquist, White, O'Connor, and Scalia in the minority, held that it is a violation of constitutional rights (based on the 5th, 6th and 14th amendments) to arbitrarily or absolutely preclude the hypnotically refreshed testimony of the defendant in a criminal trial about those memories recalled during hypnosis. The Court asserted that the recognized difficulties with such testimony can be handled through cross-examination or by adopting appropriate rules of evidence. The Court specifically noted that this does not apply to civil trials, and left open the question as to the issue of a nondefendant witness.

In 1993, in *Daubert v. Merrill Dow Pharmaceuticals, Inc.*, regarding the issue of the admission of expert testimony, the Supreme Court provided a clear affirmation of a "helpfulness" standard, rather than the *Frye v. United States* (1923) "scientific acceptance" standard, which had been dominant for 70 years. *Daubert* is a Federal standard, and hence is not compelling on the states, but it has been adopted in many states. It was at first thought that this "helpfulness" standard was likely to allow the admission of highly speculative "syndrome" testimony and other "junk science;" however, most believe that, paradoxically, it has had the opposite effect.

In *Daubert*, the Court provided four factors that it said *could* be used to determine the ultimate criteria of reliability and relevance: (a) is the theory or technique testable, (b) has it been subject to peer review and publication, (c) is there a "known or potential rate of error," and are there "standards controlling the technique's operation," and (d) does the theory or technique enjoy "general acceptance" within a "relevant scientific community" (1509 U.S. at 592-594)? As the Court often does, it waffled by not saying whether one, all, or any of these factors must be applied. Ironically, many courts apply the essentials of all four of these criteria, thus making it more stringent than *Frye*, and less "helpful," which results in disallowing expert witness testimony that would have been admissible under *Frye*. The *Daubert* decision also emphasized the "gatekeeper" role of the trial court judge, in effect giving tremendous latitude to the trial court judge in decisions whether or not to admit expert witness testimony. Unfortunately, many judges do not have the knowledge base to judicially employ this tremendous power.

Then, in 1999, in *Kumho Tire Co. v. Carmichael* an expert witness testified about a tire blowout that caused a minivan to overturn, causing injuries and one death. The expert asserted that his test for tire abuse (which would contradict manufacturer's liability) required two out of four physical symptoms. The Court held that technical as well as scientific-based expertise may be subject to *Daubert* factors. However, the Court also gave indication that expert testimony based strictly on experience (e.g., interview data), may require a lesser standard than scientific or technical-based expertise, but still must be reliable and relevant.

HYPNOSIS AND MALINGERING/DECEPTION

Since malingering typically involves a legal issue, hypnosis and malingering involve the challenge and contention of two disparate areas. Problems stem from (a) the lack of a clear consensus on a definition of hypnosis, (b) the same hypnotic procedure is not used in all research, and (c) the procedures used in research are seldom the same as those used in clinical practice. Some researchers, such as Theodore Barber (Meyer, 1992) even argue that there is no such thing as hypnosis as an altered state of consciousness and, thus, we are only talking about suggestibility. Nevertheless, while there are numerous theories of what hypnosis is, they basically break down into two main conflicting theories of hypnosis as they relate to the concept of deception (Meyer, 1992). The first theory, the "*state*" theory and its variations, is that hypnosis is characterized by a dissociative experience, a special, unique state of being. In this state, the subject's actions are considered to be involuntary. Hypnotic behavior is thought to be characteristically different than behavior performed outside of hypnosis. For example, within this framework, a person does not feel pain as intensely because the part of the person that feels pain is dissociated from awareness at the time of hypnosis (H. Spiegel & D. Spiegel, 2004). This leaves the hypnotic behavior to be experienced as nonvolitional, or out of conscious control. With regards to deception, if one accepts that the client has become truly hypnotized (and behavior is dissociated to some extent), then conscious deception in this model seems difficult to perpetuate. Of course, if the client fakes hypnosis at the outset, such as with Kenneth Bianchi, deception is easier to accept and explain.

The various *"nonstate"* views assert that explaining hypnosis by an altered state of consciousness is unnecessary and not parsimonious. Instead, behavior that occurs during hypnosis is explained as a purposeful, goal-directed action that can be understood in terms of how the "hypnotized" individual interprets the situation. These theorists are careful not to interpret the differences found between hypnotized and simulating subjects as evidence of a special state. Instead they say that the task demands of simulating instructions are so distinctive that they can account for any group differences. Faking hypnosis would be consistent with a nonstate view of hypnosis.

Historically, there has been no clear consensus as to whether malingered hypnosis can be detected, although it does appear that the majority of experts over the years believe that hypnosis could be malingered. As early as 1888, Binet (also famous for his work on intelligence testing) and Fere argued that hypnosis in forensic settings could always be faked. More recently, the Connecticut Supreme Court (*State v. July*, 1991) held that a trial court, even absent expert testimony, has the discretion to determine whether not a witness in a criminal trial has actually been hypnotized. The court emphasized that even experts cannot consistently distinguish between malingered and actual hypnosis since no reliable criteria exist for such an assessment. However, as will be seen in the foregoing discussion, certainly progress has been made.

Also, the recent research by Knight and Meyer (2005) noted earlier in this chapter indicates that experts believe that individuals can fake hypnosis and can lie while under hypnosis. Of the 231 questionnaires returned by the hypnosis experts (43% return rate), 32% of the American Society of Clinical Hypnosis (ASCH) members strongly agreed and 47% somewhat agreed with the statement "It is possible to successfully fake a hypnotic state even with an experienced hypnotist," while 15% somewhat disagreed and 6% strongly disagreed. Somewhat comparably, in the student sample 25% strongly agreed and 56% somewhat agreed, while 15% somewhat disagreed and 3% strongly disagreed with the statement.

In their expert sample, 48% strongly agreed and 36% moderately agreed with the statement "It is possible for a subject to lie while at least moderately to deeply hypnotized," while 11% somewhat disagreed and 5% strongly disagreed with the statement. The student sample differed to a degree as 15% strongly agreed and 60% somewhat agreed with the statement, while 28% somewhat disagreed and 8% strongly disagreed.

Anecdotal Signs of Deception/Simulation

Over the years there have been anecdotal reports of methods for assessing simulation in hypnosis. One of the best summaries is provided by H. Hall and Pritchard (1996), although they reasonably do not provide much empirical data to support their suggestions. Some methods are noted later in this chapter as empirical data has emerged for them. In addition, they indicate that simulators (a) will show variation in susceptibility scores over time, (b) are less likely to show distress in prolonged physical challenges, such as arm levitation, (c) track moving objects with head fixed rather than tracking by moving the head, and (d) show increased physiological arousal (e.g., pulse and respiration rate) over the hypnosis period.

Models for Assessing Deception/Simulation

The first empirically acceptable and still the most common strategy is the "real-simulating" model devised by Martin Orne (1971), wherein a control group of subjects who were not hypnotized were asked to fake hypnosis, but were not given instructions how to do so, yet were treated in the identical manner as hypnotized individuals. Subjects were divided into two groups, based on high or low scores on various measures of hypnotizability, allowing the assumption that the simulators (the low hypnotizables) do not hypnotize easily and would not enter hypnosis while in the experiment.

The main criticism of the real-simulating model is that it does not use high hypnotizables in the simulator group, and by doing so, draws subjects from essentially different populations. However, Orne (1971) argues that high hypnotizables would have a hard time simulating as they have problems determining whether they were following directions for faking or entering hypnotized state. Therefore, if no differences are found between the real and simulating groups, it could be because both had in fact entered hypnosis.

The majority of research conducted using Orne's real-simulating model utilizes a single experimental session with multiple subjects in a group format for the purpose of attempting to detect group differences, and this has produced mixed results. In a single session one group of high hypnotizables is hypnotized, while a second group of people screened to be resistant to hypnosis is asked to simulate being hypnotized. However, Blum and Graef (1971) used this design over six training sessions rather than one, and it was over time that the experimenter was able to detect the simulators from the "reals." Although there has been no substantial replication of Blum and Graef's design, it does suggest that this approach might help detect malingered hypnosis.

The Surreptitious Observer Design

Kirsch et al. (1989) note that Orne later expressed surprise upon realizing that when he took the role of the blind experimenter, he was shocked to discover that even with his extensive clinical experience, he could not always distinguish between the two groups. Therefore, Kirsch et al. (1989) used the "surreptitious observer" design wherein subjects are first divided into reals and simulators. Then the groups are combined and a hypnotist blind to the design hypnotizes the group as a whole. Subjects are told they will experience a tape-recorded hypnotic induction two times, the first with the experimenter present and the second time alone. However, both hypnosis sessions are secretly videotaped in order to compare the subjects' responses between the two conditions. Generally, simulating subjects are significantly less responsive to hypnotic suggestions when alone. This is especially true when simulating subjects do not figure out the actual experimental design, as revealed during debriefing. Yet, most of the high hypnotizables continue to respond when alone, indicating they are not simply responding to demand characteristics. Further research (Spanos et al., 1993) suggests this design could be helpful in detecting clients who are faking hypnosis.

Exaggerated Responses

It appears that the most consistent and reliable finding across various designs is that exaggerated responses to suggestion indicate deception. Simulators consistently "overact" in response to some suggestions. However, one potential problem is that very high hypnotizables (i.e., "high virtuosos") tend to enter into a very deep trance and thus may display behaviors which may be characterized by what appears to be exaggerated responding.

Hypnotic Analgesia

The tolerance of painful stimuli has been researched as a marker that subjects are truly hypnotized. It was once believed that this tolerance would be able to distinguish reals from simulators. However, early research proved this "traditional" view is not true, at least for nonsevere pain stimuli. Watching a hypnotized individual go through a Caesarean section or extensive dental surgery without anesthesia leads the present authors to believe that virtually no one could do this with simple repeated suggestions to do so, and then later report any absence of pain. However, there seems no way to empirically validate this since no scientific review board is going to approve the experiment that would definitively answer this.

Self-Report Measures

To date, only one self-report measure has shown any significant success in discriminating truly hypnotized subjects from simulators, the Hypnotic Simulation Index (HSI; Martin & Lynn, 1996). Martin and Lynn (1996) created a 31-item self-report scale of subjective experience based on the premise that "simulators would over-endorse, exaggerate, overplay questions but that real participants would fail to endorse subjective experiences that are not directly suggested to them" (p. 341). They found that the HSI correctly classified 94% of their participants into the two groups. Basically, simulators passed more suggestions than did hypnotizables on the index measure of hypnotizability, likely because they overplayed the role of hypnotized persons. Further research is needed to clarify if the HSI is distinguishing between simulators and "hypnotic virtuosos" who are extremely hypnotizable, since both would demonstrate extreme responses and score high on the scale.

Physiological and Nonverbal
Behavioral Cues of Deception

Although there have been many efforts, no one has found a physiological sign that defines a hypnotic trance, especially what one would define as "light" or "moderate" trance, at least in part because induction and deepening methods can vary markedly in their physiological emphasis (H. Spiegel & D. Spiegel, 2004). Computerized interpretation of brain wave patterns, MRIs, and the like offer some promise of defining "deep" hypnosis, but this research is in its early stages (Knight & Meyer, in press). It is also logical to use physiological measures to define if one is faking hypnosis (e.g., using a polygraph). The polygraph is discussed in an upcoming section of this chapter. Kinnument, Zamansky, and Block (1994) used electrodermal skin response (SCR), similar to the galvanic skin response (GSR) that is part of a standard polygraph. They asked highly hypnotized subjects to lie while under hypnosis and then also to lie while in a waking condition. SCR measurements were recorded for both conditions. They found that, based on SCR data, it was possible for the hypnotized subjects to consciously lie while under hypnosis.

Some researchers have attempted to rely on the various nonverbal behavioral cues of deception, sometimes referred to as "body language." However, to date no consistently effective cues that are discernible to the naked eye have received consistent support, at least to the point that would allow admissibility in most courts. For example, Kennedy and Coe (1994) found no significant differences between truly hypnotized individuals and simulators on measures of asymmetry of the mouth, frequency of eye blinks, eyebrow raising/lowering, arm or leg symmetry, hand relaxation, sideways lean, or incidents of smiling or eye contact. Other research is consistent with this (Knight & Meyer, in press).

On the other hand, the research of Paul Ekman (2003) on subtle facial cues "micro expressions, very fast facial movements lasting less than one-fifth of a second" (p. 15) offers much promise here, as they appear to not be under conscious control, and especially as these cues are apparently similar across all ethnic groups. The computer analysis of videotaped interviews of these micro-expressions, still in the development phase, offer substantial promise for assessing deception not only for assessing hypnosis but for numerous other applications. Paul Ekman's extensive research on facial and other behavioral cues to deception in nonhypnotized individuals is reviewed at length in Chapter 1.

Specific Hypnotic Procedure Cues

The classic case of Kenneth Bianchi (*Bianchi v. Blodgett*, 1979) initiated an inquiry into methods specific to hypnosis that might be used to assess malingered hypnosis. This derived in part from the notoriety of the "Hillside Strangler" case, but largely because the experts in this case included two of the most prominent hypnosis experts in the world, John Watkins and Martin Orne, as well as several others with significant reputations, such as Ralph Allison and Donald Lunde (Watkins, 1984). It also helped that Bianchi was apparently higher than average intellectually and had some sophistication about psychological techniques.

The essential issue arose when Dr. Watkins apparently discovered a second personality in Bianchi while Bianchi was under hypnosis, and this second personality admitted to the murders. Other experts agreed, but the prosecution believed Bianchi was malingering and brought in Dr. Orne to assess this. He used several of the techniques discussed below and eventually concluded Bianchi was malingering. The jury apparently believed Orne, as Bianchi was convicted. Some excellent counterarguments to the general consensus that Bianchi was faking are presented in an elegant paper by Watkins (1984).

Orne's first technique was to offer an offhand remark while Bianchi was within earshot that it was extremely rare for a Multiple Personality Disorder (MPD) to only have two personalities. During a hypnosis session the following day, Bianchi produced a third personality. Orne also used the Double Hallucination Test, the Single Hallucination Test, and suggested anesthesia with Bianchi.

Double Hallucination Test (DHT)

In the DHT the hypnotized person is asked to hallucinate someone sitting in a chair facing him or her, and deeply hypnotized subjects report they do. Then they are asked to turn around and respond to the actual person who is sitting behind them, which they easily do, as under deep hypnosis, "trance logic" allows the acceptance of this seeming impossibility. A malingerer, however, will often note the incongruity of this situation, although Bianchi did not do so.

Single Hallucination Test (SHT)

In the SHT the hypnotist asks the subject to hallucinate someone sitting in a chair in front of him or her. Deeply hypnotized subjects can be made to mix "percept and hallucination," that is, they will agree they can see the outline of the chair through the person. Bianchi failed to see this, even when prompted. Also, consistent with the characteristic of exaggerated responding, Bianchi did several things that are uncharacteristic for a truly hypnotized person interacting with a hallucination. He extended his hand and shook hands with the hallucinated person, he asked the hypnotist to engage in conversation with the hallucination, and appeared to try hard to convince the hypnotist of the existence of the hallucination.

Suggested Anesthesia

A classic form of suggested anesthesia is the circle-touch test. A circle is drawn on the back of the hypnotized person's hand, and total local anesthesia within the circle is suggested. The subject is told to close his or her eyes and instructed as follows, "The area inside the circle on the back of your hand is completely numb. . . . When you are touched in an area you can feel, respond with a 'Yes' and when you are touched in an area you cannot feel, respond with a 'No.' " Bianchi, like the majority of simulators, realizes these instructions are paradoxical and rationalizes that if his hand is numb he will not feel anything and consequently would not know when to say "No," and he does not do so. However, again using "trance logic," truly hypnotized subjects accept the logical aberration and respond "No."

Source Amnesia

In Source Amnesia the hypnotized subject is asked a series of easy questions, which are easily answered, and then a question that the person will not be able to answer. The hypnotist then provides the correct answer, and then before hypnosis is terminated, the subject is told he or she will forget all that occurred during hypnosis. Then, all of the questions are again asked. Hypnotized subjects can provide all the correct answers, but are unable to provide the source of the answer to the difficult question. Simulators typically will not provide the answer to the difficult question. Source Amnesia and the following technique were not used with Bianchi.

Age-Regression Inconsistencies

Again following from the concept of "trance logic," truly hypnotized age-regressed individuals will act as children, while at the same time writing words that only an adult would be able to understand or spell. Also, about 50% of hypnotized age-regressed individuals (and also about 50% of nonhypnotized very high hypnotizables) report alternately feeling like a child and like an adult while in hypnosis, whereas simulators virtually never report such an experience.

Recommendations for Detecting Malingered Hypnosis

1. Assess level of hypnotizability using a test specifically designed to assess hypnotizability, such as a respected performance-based scale (e.g., one of the Stanford scales, and/or a questionnaire scale such as the Tellegan Absorption Scale).
2. Use oral inquiry, written inquiry, and any collateral information to assess the individual's expectancies and information about hypnosis. Collateral information may also help to assess motivation for hypnosis and general characterological patterns.
3. Use psychological tests that assess any general proclivity to malinger. See Chapters 2 and 3 for a discussion of these. Consider physiological tests such as the polygraph or newer brain wave measures.

4. Use multiple hypnotic sessions in order to obtain a longitudinal sampling and look for inconsistencies in the individual's behavior.
5. Utilize the surreptitious observer design when feasible. Allow the person to believe he or she is alone while still hypnotized and secretly observe his or her behavior.
6. Administer the Hypnotic Simulation Index while keeping aware of its limitations and any new relevant research about it.
7. Be watchful for evidence of exaggerated responses.
8. Use specific tests for malingering, such as the double hallucination test, single hallucination test, circle-touch test, source amnesia, and any other evidence of trance logic. Here it is especially important to be sensitive to individual differences and to the individual's sophistication about hypnosis.
9. Keep up with the research on malingering deception in hypnosis, and in general.

THE POLYGRAPH AND LIE DETECTION

When people think of the assessment of deception, not unreasonably one of the first things that comes to mind is the use of the polygraph, since it has a kind of "magic bullet" connotation to it. Indeed, an interesting question is how would courts, legislatures, and private citizens react if an apparatus was developed that assessed deception at a validity rate of 95% or better? Would we put all witnesses through the process? Would we even need certain trials? (And would the legal system tolerate such efficiency?)

> The polygraph literature variously attributes the origins of the modern polygraph machine to Benussi in 1914 or to Larson, who constructed the prototype of the multi-channeled polygraph in 1921. . . . But in many ways we can trace the idea of using psychophysiological recordings–in particular, systolic blood pressure–to measure deception in laboratory and legal settings to William Moulton Marston, largely while he was a graduate student at Harvard University from 1915 to 1921. (Precursors for recording from other channels to detect deception go back even earlier). (National Research Council, 2003, p. 291)

However, his possible testimony in court based on this data was rejected in the famous case of *Frye v. United States* (1923) because of a lack of its "scientific acceptance." Marston eventually left this field but went on to fame when, along with his wife, he developed the cartoon character "Wonder Woman" – recall that one of her powers was her "Lasso of Truth" – if you were caught in her lasso, you were compelled to tell the truth.

In approximately 1947 John Reid introduced the "control question" technique, wherein questions like "Did you ever steal something of value in your life?" are used. Allegedly, this established a physiological baseline for comparison to innocuous questions and directly relevant questions like, "Did you steal the $500 from the petty cash drawer?" Reid also drew up a list of behavioral indicators of lying, so if one was administered a polygraph by someone trained in his school, it is likely the decision was not based purely on the physiological results. Leonard Keeler brought fame to the polygraph by developing an operational mobile unit, and he started the first polygraph school.

A central problem in the use of the polygraph has been the split between polygraphers (those licensed by the state to give such an exam) and those researchers in various fields like physiology and psychology who more skeptically look at the value of the "evidence" generally accepted by polygraphers. The National Research Council (2003) has published what is no doubt the most definitive review of polygraph research, using three separate panels ("Scientific Evidence," "Behavioral, Cognitive, and Sensory Sciences," and "National Statistics") composed of the most respected experts in the field. Their 2003 report notes that "a polygraph examiner subculture exists, complete with its own institutions (e.g., professional societies), norms, values, etc." (p. 19), and "Another aspect of the polygraph mystique that creates difficulties for scientific analysis is the strong, apparently unshakeable, beliefs of many practitioners in its efficacy on the basis of its experience" (p. 20), and

> The American Polygraph association, the largest polygraph association consisting of examiners in the private, law enforcement, and government fields, claims that the polygraph has a high degree of accuracy in detecting truthfulness or deception, with research studies published since 1980 reporting average accuracy rates ranging from 80 to 98 percent. (p. xiii)

Clearly, the polygraphers have been far more politically effective and active, to the point where some state laws even mandate the modalities (e.g., blood pressure, respiration) that must be used to administer a polygraph. For comparison, consider what it would be like for laws licensing medicine to dictate the procedure that must be used for certain operations. Also, polygraphers typically have focused, but very limited training, again, often mandated by state law, thus disallowing the administration of a polygraph by individuals who have far more sophistication in the relevant physiological and psychological data. Parallel to this, polygraphers have consistently ignored data from sciences like physiology and psychology that would suggest that newer modalities (e.g., measures of brain waves) and techniques (e.g., the sophisticated Guilty Knowledge Technique developed by David Lykken) should be integrated into the day-to-day practice of polygraphy. As a result, "research on the polygraph has not progressed over time in the manner of a typical scientific field. It has not accumulated knowledge or strengthened its scientific underpinnings in any significant manner" (National Research Council, 2003, p. 213).

From the beginning, there has been marked skepticism about the effectiveness of the polygraph in detecting deception, including from John Larson himself. There are two things that most experts agree on (C. Bartol & A. Bartol, 2004; Moore, Braga, & Petrie, 2002; National Research Council, 2003; Office of Technology Assessment, United States Congress, 1983). First, the polygraph is effective in eliciting confessions, particularly to the degree the client believes in the infallibility of the machine, and to the degree the polygrapher (on occasion stretching the truth) indicates that the machine suggests deception, for example, when after a certain response the polygrapher frowns and says "We seem to have a problem here." Second, jurors are likely to be overly impressed with the results of the polygraph; that is, the prejudicial value of such testimony is likely to outweigh its probative value. As a result, it has typically not been admissible in court, and to do so usually requires prior stipulation by both sides that the results will be admissible. Not surprisingly, one side immediately becomes suspicious about the potential outcome if the other side suggests allowing it.

This, and questions about validity, led to the 1988 Employee Polygraph Protection Act that essentially ended all preemployment polygraph screening by private employers. Ironically, it allows the continued use of the polygraph for applicants for sensitive government positions, such as in the FBI and CIA, and arguably they employ the best-trained polygraphers. Yet, Aldrich Ames, a member of the CIA, was eventually detected as a spy by other means, but had passed four polygraphs. The National Research Council (2003) concluded that the polygraph was ineffective in catching spies, was often inaccurate in general, and should only be used as an investigative tool, rather than a method that produced conclusive evidence for the legal arena or other important decisions.

This appears to answer the central question – does the physiological data provided by the standard polygraph detect malingering? Yet, virtually all practicing polygraphers and several respected scientific experts, such as Charles Honts and David Raskin (2004), have argued that it does in all or at least the overwhelming majority of cases. However, as noted, most true experts view the standard polygraph as unacceptably inaccurate for lie detection (C. Bartol & A. Bartol, 2004; National Research Council, 2003), although it is a good measure of physiological arousal. For example, those individuals who are physiologically overactive and/or are prone to anxiety reactions may appear guilty, even though they are innocent. Secondly, those individuals who tend to be very underreactive physiologically, or who do not process emotional content in a normal fashion (such as a psychopath), may appear innocent even if they are guilty.

Also, the National Research Council (2003) notes

> that individual differences in the mode of autonomic activation to acute psychological stressors have been identified, with some individuals showing primarily sympathetic increases, others primarily vagal withdrawal, and others showing reciprocal sympathetic activation . . . findings call into question assumptions about cardiovascular signals of arousal that are consistent across individuals (p. 287) . . . even when measuring skin conductance, however, stimuli that elicit the responses are so numerous as to make it difficult to isolate its specific psychological antecedent (p. 288). . . . Respiration is easily brought under voluntary control. (p. 289)

The other problem is defining an acceptable level of detection. Although some practicing polygraphers have argued that the polygraph is close to infallible, and many might assume it is at least close to 90% accurate, few, if any, respected scientists who have worked with the polygraph accept that figure, and are more likely to assert it is in the 60% to 85% range when administered in the field, as opposed to research (Meyer & Weaver, 2007).

The National Research Council (2003) examined 52 sets of subjects from 50 studies, for a total of 3,099 individual examinations. Although there was wide variance, it concludes that the "central box" [average] accuracy estimate was .81 to .91. However, the council emphasizes that many of these studies, especially those with very high estimates, were poorly designed, and that the prior noted accuracy range is "an overestimate of likely accuracy in field applications even when highly trained examiners and reasonably well standardized testing procedures are used" (p. 149).

But, for the sake of argument, assume it is 90% accurate, that 1,000 suspects have been rounded up, that 50 are guilty, and that all 50 deny guilt. If the polygraph works at a 90% rate, of the 50 who are guilty, 45 will be detected, and 5 will go undetected. Of the 950 who are innocent, 855 are accurately detected. However, 95 will be misidentified as guilty. Most would argue that this is unacceptable, especially if we agree with the political premise that it is more important that we do not identify someone as guilty when they are not, than it is to let a guilty person go free. Curiously, the obvious standard to which we should compare this is the effectiveness in detecting guilt or innocence in our present set of legal procedures (i.e., trials, plea bargains, etc.). The rather bizarre problem, and one that is conveniently overlooked by almost everyone in the legal system, is that we don't have any data on how effective it is.

There are a variety of psychological, pharmacological, and physiological methods that are available that may mute or disrupt the client's responses to the point that an inaccurate or at least noninterpretable result may occur. As early as 1983, the U.S. Congress' Office of Technology Assessment panel of experts concluded that certain techniques might "beat" the polygraph. The National Research Council (2003) report asserts

> basic science and polygraph research give reason for concern that polygraph test accuracy may be degraded by countermeasures. (p. 5) . . . basic psychophysiology gives reason for concern that effective countermeasures to the polygraph may be possible. All of the physiological indicators measured by the polygraph can be altered by conscious efforts through cognitive or physical means, and all the physiological responses believed to be associated with deception can also have other causes. As a consequence, it is possible that examinees could take conscious actions that create false polygraph readings (p. 101). . . . It is entirely plausible, from a scientific viewpoint, to develop a range of countermeasures that might effectively mimic specific physiological response patterns that are usually the focus of a polygraph test. (p. 141)

Charles Clifton (2002) has devoted an entire book to methods of beating the polygraph. Anyone who has thoroughly read that book ought to be able to easily produce a protocol that is "noninterpretable," and very likely pass as innocent when he or she is, in fact, guilty. One of the best ways to "pass," whether one is guilty or not, is to take the polygraph a number of times. People are more likely to fail the first time they take a polygraph, because they do not know what to expect, which leads to some anxiety. It is not unheard of for people who are accused in the media to go to several polygraphers in succession until they finally "pass" and then report that last one through the media, knowing that it will not be used in court and knowing the prior "failures" or noninterpretable results will remain confidential.

As already noted, the legal system has long been skeptical of the polygraph, and for two very good reasons: First, the problem of accuracy noted previously and second, the reasonable fear that jurors in particular are likely to give it undue credence; that is, the prejudicial value outweighs the probative value. The Supreme Court has seldom fully deliberated a case that focused on the polygraph. One of the most recent in which it did was in *U.S. v. Scheffer* (1998). Airman Edward Scheffer was convicted by a general court-martial of several charges, but one was of particular significance. He was working with the Air Force's Office of Special Investigations to investigate drug allegations, so it was routine to ask him to also take a drug test. He asked for a 1-day delay, saying that he urinated only once a day and had done so already. He was given a delay, but a few days later was asked to take a polygraph test, and was asked: (a) Did you ever use illegal drugs while in the Air Force? (b) Have you ever lied in any information given to the OSI? (c) Have you ever told anyone but your parents that you worked for OSI? He answered "No" to all of these questions, and the examiner concluded there was no deception. However, the subsequently available results of the drug test indicated he had used methamphetamine. The trial judge would not allow the introduction of the polygraph evidence, Scheffer was convicted of this charge at his court-martial, and the USAF Court of Criminal Appeals affirmed. However, the higher USAF Court of Appeals set the conviction aside, and it was sent to the Supreme Court where it was heard, resulting in an 8 to 1 decision, with Justice Thomas writing the decision and Justice Stevens dissenting. The Court set aside both appeal court decisions and said there was no constitutional right to present the lie-detection evidence; that is, the right to present evidence has reasonable restrictions.

One of the few modern cases with some recognized positive precedent value for the introduction of polygraph evidence into the courtroom is *U.S. v. Galbreth* (1995). In a tax fraud case psychologist David Raskin convinced a federal trial judge that the "Directed Lie Control Question Technique" met the admissibility requirements set forth in the Daubert decision (discussed earlier in this chapter) and thus Raskin was allowed to testify that the polygraph data indicated that the defendant was not being deceptive when he asserted that he was unaware that certain items should have been reported as taxable income. In his testimony Raskin asserted that the technique he used was accepted in the scientific community as 80% effective. Many believe the testimony was allowed in large part because of Raskin's impeccable credentials as both a psychologist and a polygrapher.

The "lie detection examination" using a polygraph does have vast potential. But, this will only come to fruition if there is more emphasis placed on developing new measures and implementing a combination of the best of those that are not so amenable to conscious, unconscious, or situational manipulations, for example, measures of brain stem responses to questions, measures of retinal changes, and thermography (the measure of radiant energy emitted from an examinee's face), and so forth. The difficulty is that polygraphers presently have a strong political lobby, which would be opposed to most changes, and there is no significant political opposition that could neutralize their efforts. Education of the public as well as those in the legislative and legal arenas offers the best chance for change in this area.

KEY POINTS

- Though there is significant controversy about whether behavior can be controlled by hypnosis, and, thus, whether an individual can be forced to tell the truth when hypnotized, the general consensus among experts on hypnosis is that behavior cannot be controlled by hypnosis.
- The Supreme Court has ruled it unconstitutional to arbitrarily and absolutely disallow memories reported during hypnosis in a criminal trial. However, expert witness testimony on such issue must meet the relevant standard in the jurisdiction, be it *Daubert*, *Frye*, the Federal Rules of Evidence, or some other standard.
- Experts on hypnosis generally believe that individuals can fake being hypnotized and also can lie while under hypnosis. The famous case of Kenneth Bianchi is a classic example of this.
- There are many techniques for detecting malingered hypnosis, including the surreptitious observer design, examining exaggerated responses, assessing hypnotic analgesia, using self-report measures of hypnotizability, noting physiological

and nonverbal cues to deception (much like that discussed in Chapter 1), various specific hypnotic procedure cues, and age-regression inconsistencies.

- There is a great deal of controversy about the effectiveness of the polygraph for detecting deception.
- There are two things most experts agree on, that the polygraph can be useful at eliciting confessions from individuals who think it is infallible, and that jurors tend to be excessively impressed with the results of a polygraph examination, perhaps leading to prejudicial impact of the measure if used in court.
- Similar to many of the cues discussed in Chapter 1, the polygraph is a good measure of physiological arousal, but cannot necessarily tell us when an individual is lying, versus when that individual is simply nervous about the interview or aroused for some other reason.

Section III

SPECIAL
POPULATIONS

Chapter 7

THE DETECTION OF MALINGERING AND DISSIMULATION IN CHILDREN AND ADOLESCENTS

THE RELEVANCE OF MALINGERING AND DISSIMULATION IN CHILD AND ADOLESCENT POPULATIONS

Clinicians who specialize in treating children and adolescents are required to use their expertise to formulate opinions about the well-being of the children, the children's families, and the communities. Is the teenager a threat to the community or amenable to psychotherapy on an outpatient basis? Should the child remain in special education or be mainstreamed into a regular classroom? Should the child's father have visitation rights? Is the adolescent best served by inpatient or outpatient services? These decisions are based, largely, on children's self-reports. Thus, given the far-reaching consequences of such decisions, it becomes imperative that the evaluator be able to rely on the veracity of a child's self-report; any form of dissimulation (e.g., malingering, denial, defensiveness, overreporting) can undermine the therapeutic and/or psychoevaluative process.

Although both child and adult specialists face the challenge of detecting dissimulation in clinical practice, research on dissimulation has focused almost exclusively on adult populations. To our knowledge, no empirically based classification model of malingering exists for children and adolescents. Furthermore, there is no systematic assessment protocol with which to approach the question of dissimulation in children and adolescents. Thus, the primary purpose of this chapter is to provide a context in which the clinician may approach a suspected case of dissimulation. More specifically, this chapter will (a) consider the impetus behind the growing interest in the assessment of malingering in children and adolescents, (b) consider the current research on the use of interviewing techniques and psychological tests in the detection of child and adolescent dissimulation, (c) consider the clinically relevant factors that critically impact a child's ability to dissimulate, and (d) provide clinicians with a basic assessment strategy with which to approach suspected cases of malingering.

The Increasing Need for Assessment of Deception in Children and Adolescents

During the past several decades, clinicians have expressed a growing interest in the assessment and detection of dissimulation in child and adolescent populations. McCann (1998b) theorized that this increased interest is reflective of three, late 20th century trends: (a) an increased emphasis on the promotion of child welfare, (b) the increasing number of juveniles involved in the justice system, and (c) the expanding role of managed care in the provision of mental health services.

Increased Emphasis on the Promotion of Child Welfare

The late 20th century witnessed a proliferation of laws and social programs designed to protect the rights of children. As a result of this proliferation, societal vigilance for child abuse increased; since the 1970s, there has been a steady increase in the number of sexual abuse allegations (Quinn, 1991). Consequently, clinicians have been called upon more frequently to evaluate legal questions related to the veracity of children's claims of child abuse.

Increased Numbers of Juveniles Involved in the Criminal Justice System

Although arrest rates for juvenile offenders have declined in recent years, the latter half of the 20th century witnessed an alarming increase in the arrest rates of juveniles for violent crimes (Federal Bureau of Investigation, 1993). As a result, evaluators are more frequently asked to testify about appropriate placements for adolescents; evaluators may be asked to distinguish those offenders who may benefit from psychological services and rehabilitative treatments from those offenders who may not be responsive to such interventions.

The Expanding Role of Managed Care

Changes in the health care system have forced clinicians to justify their treatments to insurance providers. Thus, the truthfulness of a client's claim may be called into question because clinicians must justify that resources are being allocated to those clients who genuinely need care.

BUILDING AN ASSESSMENT STRATEGY FOR THE DETECTION OF MALINGERING AND DISSIMULATION IN CHILDREN AND ADOLESCENTS

Despite the need for research-based assessment strategies and diagnostic techniques for dissimulation in child and adolescent populations, current classification models of malingering are based on research with adult populations. Although these models may provide a basic framework for evaluating suspected dissimulation in children and adolescents, we caution against their strict application to these youthful populations. Notably, these models do not take into account developmental and contextual factors specific to childhood and adolescence that can play critical roles in the interpretation of response style.

As there is no empirically supported assessment protocol for the assessment of malingering and dissimulation in children and adolescents, how should an evaluator approach the question of dissimulation in these populations? Although the dearth of research in this area prevents the establishment of a clinical decision model at this time, information about clinically relevant factors that influence children's response styles gives the evaluator a context within which to approach the question of dissimulation. In the following pages, data relevant to the detection of malingering in child and adolescent populations are summarized into six guiding principles. Under each principle, we have provided a brief response to commonly asked questions pertaining to that principle. These principles should not be thought of as inclusion or exclusion criteria for the classification of malingering or for any specific dissimulatory response style; rather, the clinician may think of these principles as a context within which to approach suspected dissimulation.

Guiding Principles for the Assessment of Malingering in Children and Adolescents
Principle 1: Understand the Professional and Ethical Issues
Arguably, a thorough understanding of the professional and ethical issues that are specific to the referral question forms the foundation of any comprehensive assessment. In any evaluation, it is important that the clinician's assessment strategy, conclusions, and recommendations are

concordant with theoretical and scientific principles. Before pursuing a dissimulation assessment, we advise the clinician to consult the *Ethical Principles of Psychologists and Code of Conduct* (American Psychological Association, 2002). Forensic psychologists will need to consult the *Specialty Guidelines for Forensic Psychologists* (Committee on Ethical Guidelines for Forensic Psychologists, 1991).

Given the lack of research in this area, many clinicians have asked whether it is ethical to classify children and adolescents as malingerers. The diagnostic classification of malingering in both clinical and forensic settings may have far-reaching consequences; a child who is genuinely suffering may not receive the care needed; an adolescent who is, in fact, being abused by a parent may be labeled as "unreliable;" or a teenager who is experiencing bona fide cognitive deficits as the result of a head injury may be incorrectly classified as "feigning."

Even if the adolescent is feigning symptoms, McCann (1998b) argued it is not always true that malingerers are "liars that should be cast away in favor of those who are more worthy of treatment and other valuable resources" (p. 123). He further argued that symptom exaggeration, bizarre symptom reporting, and symptom overreporting may be indicative of an underlying, genuine psychopathology. Thus, from an ethical perspective, when dissimulation is suspected, it is incumbent on the evaluator to distinguish between malingering and overreporting as a product of psychopathology. McCann (1998b) maintained that the following factors are indicators that the overreporting is suggestive of underlying psychopathology:

> (a) a clinical as opposed to forensic setting, (b) identifiable environmental stressors that would create distress in most adolescents (e.g., physical abuse), (c) clinical presentation that is consistent with severe psychopathology, (d) intellectual deficits, (e) prior psychiatric history, and (f) secondary gain that has psychological significance (e.g., attention from an ex-boyfriend or ex-girlfriend, removal from an abusive household) opposed to material significance (e.g., release from custody, time off from school). (pp. 167-168)

Despite these cautions, McCann (1998b) maintained that malingering evaluations need not be avoided; rather, clinicians should undertake them "using adequate information, good clinical judgment, and diligent adherence to professional ethics" (p. 130).

In general, as mentioned in the "Introduction," we concur with Rogers (1997a) that evaluators tend to rely on clinical indicators of "speculative" and "tentative" certainty to form the basis of their determination of malingering (p. 15). Diagnostic classification of child and adolescent malingering is unethical if it is based primarily on clinical judgment, and/ or on clinical decision models that have been substantiated on research with adults, and/or on performance on one psychological test (Rogers, 1997a).

Principle 2: Consider the Setting in Which the Evaluation Takes Place

The strategy with which the clinician approaches the question of possible dissimulation in children and adolescents should be determined largely by the context of the evaluation. Professionals evaluating the veracity of a child's self-report in forensic contexts must be prepared to support their conclusions with scientific evidence. Such contexts include custody proceedings, competency evaluations, disposition hearings, and investigations of abuse allegations.

In clinical settings there may be less emphasis on the systematic assessment of malingering (McCann, 1998b). Still, dissimulation may threaten successful treatment because it undermines accurate diagnosis and identification of the symptoms that should be targeted during treatment. Clinicians who suspect dissimulation in a therapeutic context will need to consider the child's possible motivations to deceive and how such deception confounds underlying psychopathology. Additionally, the clinician will need to determine whether or not the deception presents an obstacle to the child's success in therapy.

Principle 3: Consider the Developmental Phase of the Child

First, one should consider whether or not the child is developmentally capable of malingering. The ability to deceive requires mastery of certain developmental skills. Specifically, to deceive, a child must (a) understand the concept of a false belief, (b) recognize that false statements can mislead others, and (c) be able to successfully convince others of the "veracity" of the false statement (Oldershaw & Bagby, 1997, p. 155).

Although it was originally assumed that very young children were incapable of deception, research has suggested that children as young as 3 are able to deceive adults without detection (M. Lewis, 1993). Nonetheless, children's deceptive capabilities improve during the first 6 years of life; deceptive strategies of very young children are generally limited to misleading confirmations or denials of information, while older children and adolescents are capable of more sophisticated deceptive strategies (M. Lewis, 1993; Oldershaw & Bagby, 1997).

Next, the evaluator will need to consider the child's general intellectual functioning when addressing the possibility of malingering or dissimulation. Children and adolescents may lack the vocabulary to describe complex emotions, such as guilt, frustration, or anxiety. Thus, the clinician may mistakenly interpret the child's inability to express himself or herself as denial or defensiveness. Additionally, clinicians should be vigilant of the reading level required for certain assessments. Bizarre and/ or inconsistent responding may be indicative of the child's inability to understand the content of the questions (McCann, 1998b). In cases in which dissimulation or malingering is suspected, the evaluator is advised to administer measures of both general intelligence and academic achievement to obtain a sense of the child's verbal abilities and reading competency.

It must be determined whether or not very young children have the *neurological* capacity to remember events over time. Forensic psychologists can provide information about children's memory capacities to help courts decide whether or not events occurred (e.g., when a child makes an abuse claim). The following summarizes B. K. Clark's (2002) review of the literature concerning the accuracy of children's memory and its relevance to the child's self-report:

- In general, the development of a child's memory is variable (Fivush & Shukat, 1995). The accuracy of children's memories may be contingent on individual differences and basic cognitive capacities. Therefore, there appears to be no strictly defined age at which a clinician may consider a child's memory of an explicit event accurate or inaccurate. Given this variability, individual assessment of a child's memory is recommended.
- Most professionals agree that very young children (i.e., under the age of 2), do not have the neurological capacity to form explicit memories of particular events in their lives. In general, clinicians should be skeptical of older children, adolescents, and adults claiming to remember events occurring before the age of 3.
- As children get older, their abilities to encode, remember, and report events improve.
- Similar to adults, older children tend to accurately remember the general meaning of an event, rather than the details. Their memories of past events are based on information from scripts (i.e., a long-term memory representation of a complex event that

guides interpretation and comprehension of daily experiences), as well as information from the actual event.
- Younger children tend to forget more quickly than do older children (Bruck & Ceci, 2002).

In summary, when a clinician is asked to assist the court in determining the accuracy of a child's memory of an event, we advise the clinician to be knowledgeable about the literature on memory development and to assess the child's individual memory abilities.

Finally, consider whether or not any generalities can be made about the impact of developmental phase on response style. Exaggeration, self-delusion, denial, oppositionality, and symptom-minimization may prevent the evaluator from accurately assessing clinical and forensic issues. Although there is a dearth of research on response styles and test-taking attitudes in child and adolescent populations, some generalities can be made about the impact of developmental phase on response style. The following summarizes these generalities:

- Some research suggests that preschool-aged children are prone to exaggeration, tending to perceive themselves as more competent than they actually are. Thus, the clinician should be cautioned against interpreting exaggerations as deliberate distortions on the part of the youth (Oldershaw & Bagby, 1997).
- Importantly, characteristics associated with adolescence may impact youths' response styles. Social and family issues, as well as the psychological and physical changes experienced during this developmental phase, may confound the adolescent's perception of his or her psychopathology. Additionally, adolescents may be mistrustful of adults, particularly adult authority figures, such as a forensic evaluator; they may fear that adults will not understand their problems and, consequently, may respond defensively. Additionally, adolescents may fear social rejection if they appear mentally ill and, therefore, may attempt to minimize their symptoms. A youth may be angry that she has been compelled to attend therapy or an evaluation. Thus, rather than being indicative of malingering or deception, irrelevant or inconsistent responding may reflect an adolescent's oppositionality or an attempt to assert control over a situation in which he or she does not wish to participate.

Principle 4: Consider the Child's Motivation to Dissimulate

Arguably, a key task for an evaluator in a malingering evaluation is to correctly identify the youth's motivation to dissimulate: Is an adolescent denying symptoms because of fears of being ridiculed by parents or a peer group? Is a child overreporting as a cry for help? Is there an attempt to avoid punishment or to protect a parent? Has the young individual been coached by a parent to report false symptoms? Assessing the child's motivation to dissimulate has direct implications for diagnostic considerations and treatment choices.

The accurate identification of the child's motivation to dissimulate poses a challenge to the evaluator, as the child himself may not be fully aware of the reasons for feigning. Furthermore, the child may not be conscious of the fact that his or her self-report represents an exaggeration or minimization of symptoms.

The child's motivation to deceive may reflect his or her developmental stage. Young children may be motivated to deny problems by the fear of upsetting their parents or losing their approval. Adolescents may be particularly concerned about maintaining a favorable impression with peers, thus, denying psychological symptoms, such as depression, thought disturbances, or anxiety.

As with adults, the youth's motivation to deceive may be strongly contingent on the context of treatment and/or evaluation. In custody, divorce, and child welfare proceedings, the evaluator may ask the child to provide negative information about a parent. In such a situation, the child may be motivated to withhold information to protect a parent; similarly the youth may provide false information to incriminate a parent in order to please or protect the other parent (Oldershaw & Bagby, 1997). Youth receiving evaluations in juvenile justice settings may be motivated to feign psychiatric symptoms in order to obtain a therapeutic, rather than punitive, disposition. Many youth perceive therapeutic placements as far less restrictive. Conversely, other youth may deny psychological disturbance with hopes that the judges will allow them to return home.

The child's perceptions of the assessment and of the evaluator contribute to the child's motivation to deceive. Oldershaw and Bagby (1997) argued that an appraisal of the child's perceptions of the assessment "enables clinicians to better grasp potential motives to deceive or malinger" (p. 158). For instance, if a gifted child believes that "superior performance" on an intelligence test will lead to further isolation from peers at school, this may create motivation to underperform on the test. Thus, Oldershaw and Bagby contended that probing the child's perception of the assessment could allow the evaluator to rectify misperceptions, thereby increasing the likelihood of honest responding. Similarly, such a probe could allow the assessor to identify possible motivations to deceive.

Additionally, Oldershaw and Bagby (1997) noted that "children typically assume a subordinate role relative to adults and, therefore, are more easily influenced by them than other adults" (p. 158). Additionally, some children may feel compelled to express whatever they believe adults will respond to positively, "regardless of its truthfulness" (p. 158). Oldershaw and Bagby cited a Fuchs and Thelen study that suggested that if children believe their parents will respond negatively to their expressions of negative emotions, the children will be less likely to express negative emotions during an assessment. Thus, to avoid negative evaluations, children may use cues from the evaluator to determine how the evaluator would like them to respond during the assessment.

Principle 5: Consider the Role Parents May Play in Influencing Their Child's Self-Report

Parents may consciously or unconsciously influence their child's self-report. Some research suggests that specific parent characteristics and parenting styles may influence children's responses. Specifically, children with depressed parents may underreport their own psychopathology (Cole, Barrett, & Zahn-Waxler, as cited in Oldershaw & Bagby, 1997). Additionally, children tend to be more defensive during evaluations when they are raised by religious families or have mothers who work outside the home (Francis, Lankshear, & Pearson, as cited in Oldershaw & Bagby, 1997).

Symptom coaching refers to the deliberate attempt by a parent or caregiver to influence a child's self-report by coaching the child to present as physically or sexually abused, learning disabled, or mentally ill. Stutts, Hickey, and Kasdan (2003) documented a case of a 13-year-old who malingered a disability as a result of the parent instructing the child to do so for the purpose of obtaining financial gain. Although most clinicians recognize the existence of this phenomenon, to our knowledge there are no empirically supported indicators of symptom coaching. McFarlane advised clinicians to consider the possibility of symptom coaching when the child (a) describes incidents that are lacking in detail, (b) uses adult language, (c) is repetitive, and (d) when the child's description of the event lacks authenticity (as cited in Quinn, 1991).

Quinn (1991) also suggested that (a) a history of false allegations by the custodial parent against the noncustodial parent, (b) "chronic visitation restrictions," (c) "a late arising sexual abuse complaint," (d) evidence of brainwashing, and (e) "the absence of substantiating factors," are consistent with false allegations (p. 149).

Principle 6: Consider the Research That Suggests Children Are Not "Mini-Adults"

It was once assumed that children and adolescents manifested the same symptom presentation as adults. As a result, children were often administered assessment tools that had been normed on adults. In general, research suggests that children and adolescents may endorse a greater number of pathological symptoms (Archer, 1992). Thus, assessments that have been developed for and normed on adults tend to overpathologize adolescents (Conkey, 1999).

Furthermore, considerable research has suggested that the symptom presentation and age of onset of major psychiatric illnesses are different in children and adolescents than they are in adults. For instance, as described in the *DSM-IV-TR* (American Psychiatric Association, 2000), depression in children may manifest as irritability, and children's symptoms of social phobia and specific phobia may be expressed through crying, tantruming, or freezing. A clinician should be familiar with the manifestations of Axis I disorders in children to avoid mistakenly believing the child is dissimulating.

The clinician also should have a general knowledge of the typical age of onset of the Axis I disorders and the prevalence of these disorders in child and adolescent populations. For instance, the age of onset for Schizophrenia is typically between the late teens and mid 30s. Although cases of Schizophrenia have been documented in children as young as 5, onset of the disorder prior to adolescence is rare (American Psychiatric Association, 2000).

ASSESSMENT STRATEGIES FOR THE DETECTION OF MALINGERING AND DISSIMULATION IN CHILDREN AND ADOLESCENTS

Evaluators conducting malingering evaluations in forensic contexts will need to provide psychometric data for their conclusions. Although no standardized assessment protocol for the evaluation of malingering by children and adolescents exists, we have compiled the relevant data on empirically supported techniques for the detection of dissimulation in youth. This section considers (a) the use of structured and unstructured interviews in these evaluations, (b) the use of psychological testing in the assessment of dissimulation, and (c) general guidelines for the assessment of dissimulation in these populations.

Unstructured Interviewing Techniques

The clinical interview is a key component of assessment and evaluation. The interview allows the evaluator to gather relevant information from the client's perspective, while also affording an opportunity for direct observation of the client's communication behaviors and response style.

Basic Interviewing Techniques

To our knowledge, no research substantiates the use of unstructured interviewing techniques in the detection of malingering. Thus, the evaluator should not rely on the unstructured interview to make conclusions about the accuracy of the child's self-report. However, unstructured interviewing can afford the clinician an invaluable opportunity to assess the child's general response style, expressed self-perception of the presenting problem, and values regarding honesty (McCann, 1998b). Thus, information garnered from the unstructured interview can provide the clinician with critical information that may be used to generate hypotheses about the accuracy of a self-report.

We have compiled the following list of interviewing techniques that can assist the clinician with dissimulation assessments:

- *Use open-ended questions.* Open-ended questions increase the likelihood that responses will be spontaneous and decrease the likelihood that responses will be "contaminated" by suggestibility or the adolescent's attempt to please the examiner (McCann, 1998b, p. 74). Bruck and Ceci (2002) reported that the verbal and nonverbal dimensions of the interview may influence the accuracy of the child's self-report. Verbal dimensions include the way in which a question is asked (e.g., asking the child, "Mr. Smith touched you inappropriately, didn't he?" vs. asking the child, "What happened when Mr. Smith picked you up at school?"), and the number of times a question is repeated (e.g., repeatedly asking the child, "Have you been having nightmares about this event?" despite the child's persistent denial of experiencing nightmares). Nonverbal dimensions include the use of anatomical dolls, line drawings, and props to elicit responses. The investigators point to evidence that suggests young children interviewed with these tools tend to make more errors of commission than do children who are interviewed without these media (Bruck et al., Gordon et al., Salmon et al., Steward & Steward, as cited in Bruck & Ceci, 2002).

- *Consider interview questions carefully.* Although open-ended questions increase the likelihood of an accurate response, young children tend to provide more information when prompted with pointed questions. B. K. Clark (2002) noted the dilemma here: "Does one take the risk of getting an inaccurate report that may be harmful to a person being accused, or does one risk missing important information about actual abuse, placing the child at further risk?" (p. 134). To address this dilemma, B. K. Clark advised that the clinician begin the interview with open-ended questions and use information the child provides to form prompts for specific questions. She further advised, "any reports or testimony about information received following leading questions should be accompanied by statements making clear that this information may be less accurate than information obtained under free recall conditions" (p. 134).
- *Focus the questions on the child's behaviors, rather than the child's emotions.* As previously discussed, children may lack the vocabulary to discuss the complicated emotions that are often associated with mental illness. Asking children to describe their behaviors, as opposed to their emotions, may yield a more comprehensive picture of the presenting problem (Oldershaw & Bagby, 1997).
- *Be wary of possible symptom coaching.* Although there are no empirically supported indicators of symptom coaching, a child's report that is lacking in detail, repetitive, and expressed using sophisticated vocabulary should send a signal to evaluators that further investigation into the veracity of the child's report will be necessary (Quinn, 1991). McCann (1998b) also warned that endorsement of a symptom only in the presence of a parent might serve as a sign that the child is being coerced.
- *Explore the adolescent's perception of the evaluation.* The youth's perception of the evaluation's purpose (e.g., believing that the results of a cognitive evaluation will be used to determine whether the child can remain at his or her current school) may affect the youth's response style. Therefore, it is important that the evaluator assess the child's perception of the evaluation and dispel unnecessary anxiety that could confound honest responding (McCann, 1998b).
- *Explore the adolescent's values and social group norms.* This exploration may reveal to the evaluator the youth's values regarding honesty, and the likelihood of the individual being

influenced by others (McCann, 1998b). In two experiments in which children were asked by their parents to lie about something the parent did, the children were more likely to tell the truth if they were asked questions about telling the truth and telling a lie, and then asked to promise to tell the truth (Talwar et al., 2004).

- *Look for consistency in the presentation of the client's presenting problem.* Do the child's symptoms manifest only in certain situations? In cases in which dissimulation is suspected, the evaluator should always conduct collateral interviews with the youths' family members, peers, and teachers. Information provided by those close to a youth could confirm or disconfirm self-reported information. In forensic contexts, the manifestation of symptoms only in the presence of the evaluator, judge, or detention staff may be regarded with suspicion and warrant further evaluation.

- *Obtain a comprehensive psychosocial history* (McCann, 1998b). A comprehensive psychosocial history offers a context for the presenting problem by providing the evaluator with an understanding of the client's baseline level of functioning. Within this context, the evaluator may ask the following questions: Given the child's baseline level of functioning, is the presenting problem believable? Are there periods in the child's history when similar problems/symptoms were experienced? If so, in what ways is the current problem similar to or different from the previous episodes? Does the child's presentation of the problem make sense given the current stressors the child is experiencing? Furthermore, a psychosocial history allows the evaluator to explore the child's prior exposure to psychopathology. For instance, has the juvenile offender been in a detention facility in which a suicidal youth got preferential treatment?

Structured Interviews

The Structured Interview of Reported Symptoms (SIRS; Rogers, 1992) is a 172-item structured interview designed to assess feigning and related response styles. The SIRS is discussed at length in Chapter 4. Although it was normed entirely on adults, some research has suggested that the SIRS may effectively detect malingering in adolescents. Rogers, Hinds, and Sewell (1996) investigated the use of the SIRS to detect feigning among a sample of adolescent offenders ages 14 to 17. Participants were dually diagnosed with a substance use disorder and at least one other diagnosis.

Participants were administered the Minnesota Mutiphasic Personality Inventory for Adolescents (MMPI-A), the SIRS, and the Structured Inventory of Malingered Symptomatology (SIMS). The MMPI-A is described in greater detail below. The SIMS is an adult measure described in Chapter 4. Participants in the honest condition were asked to be honest and forthright in their responses. Participants in the feigning condition were asked to feign either schizophrenia, major depressive disorder, or generalized anxiety disorder.

Investigators found that the SIRS effectively detected feigning in adolescents. Using the adult cut off score criteria, that is, one scale in the "Definite Range" or two or more scores in the "Probable Range," produced optimal negative and positive predictive powers, suggesting that cut off scores listed in the SIRS manual may be appropriate for use with adolescents. Thus, although more research is needed, preliminary data support the use of the SIRS with adolescent populations.

THE USE OF PSYCHOLOGICAL TESTING IN THE DETECTION OF MALINGERING IN CHILDREN AND ADOLESCENTS

Psychometric data provides information about the reliability, validity, and norms of assessment tools; thus, the psychometric properties of an assessment tool provide a basis for evaluators to draw conclusions about an individual through his or her performance on the assessment instrument. Given the necessary heavy reliance on psychometric data in forensic contexts, there is insufficient research examining the psychometric properties of malingering and dissimulation assessment instruments with child and adolescent populations. Furthermore, of the tests for which there is some empirical basis for use in the assessment of malingering and other dissimulatory response styles, none of these instruments meet all of Heilbrun's (1992) guidelines for selecting test instruments in forensic settings (i.e., the test has been peer-reviewed, produced a reliability of .8 or greater, demonstrated relevance to the legal issue, has standardized administration procedures, has been normed on the population being evaluated, and includes validity indicators).

Nonetheless, in this section we discuss the use of psychological tests in the assessment of dissimulation. We consider research instruments for which any psychometric data has been collected with children or adolescents and/or which contain at least one scale designed to detect malingering or dissimulation in these youthful populations. Specifically, we have included information about the use of the Minnesota Multiphasic Personality Inventory for Adolescents (MMPI-A; Butcher et al.,1992), the Millon Adolescent Clinical Inventory (MACI; Millon,1993), and the Personality Inventory for Children (PIC; Wirt et al., 1984) in the detection of malingering.

Despite the lack of empirical evidence for the MACI modifier indices, we have made the decision to include this instrument because it was normed on juvenile justice populations and because it includes scales that assess self-report biases. It should be noted, however, that the MACI has not been the focus of extensive research, nor are we aware of any research supporting its use in the detection of malingering. Similarly, although the use of the PIC to detect dissimulation has not been substantiated by research, we have included it here because the normative sample included young children (the PIC is normed on parents with children ages 3 to 16).

After reviewing the personality assessments, we summarize research regarding the ability of neuropsychological tests to detect dissimulation.

Minnesota Multiphasic Personality Inventory for Adolescents (MMPI-A; Butcher et al., 1992)

The MMPI-A is a 478-item personality inventory designed for teenagers 14 to 18 years old. The MMPI-A profile provides an empirically supported, descriptive summary of adolescent psychopathology (Archer, 1992).

MMPI-A Scales Relevant to the Assessment of Malingering

The MMPI-A contains 10 clinical scales and 7 validity scales. The validity scales are designed to measure "inconsistent responding, over- and under-reporting of pathology, and various other response sets" (McCann, 1998b, p. 90). These scales include: Cannot Say (?), the Lie (L), Infrequency (F), Infrequency Front (F1), Infrequency Back (F2), Defensiveness (K), Variable Response Inconsistency (VRIN), and True Response Inconsistency (TRIN) scales.

Research Supporting the Use of the MMPI-A in the Assessment of Malingering

The assessment of response style has direct relevance to the assessment of malingering; the adolescent's approach to test taking, level of defensiveness, and tendency to over-/underreport symptoms have a significant impact on the interpretability of the test. Thus, there is "substantial interest" among clinicians in the use of the MMPI-A in the assessment of malingering (McCann, 1998b, p. 90). Two studies provide support for the use of the validity scales on the MMPI-A in the assessment of malingering.

Stein, Graham, and Williams (1995) examined the extent to which the validity scales on the MMPI-A could identify adolescents who had been instructed to respond to the test to give the impression that they had "very serious emotional problems" (p. 420); more specifically, the investigators examined whether the validity scales could differentiate between adolescents who were instructed to "fake bad" and clinical and nonclinical adolescents who received standard instructions. In general, results indicated that the F, F-K, F1, and F2 scales could successfully differentiate between fake-bad profiles and profiles obtained under standard instructions from both clinical and nonclinical student populations.

Stein and colleagues (1995) found that a raw F score of 23 seemed to optimize the ability to distinguish fake-bad profiles from both nonclinical and clinical participants taking the test honestly. A score of 23 correctly classified approximately 97.5% of girls and 100% of boys in the clinical sample, and 80% of girls and 72.4% of boys in the simulation sample. The researchers concluded that these percentages "illustrate the F scale's utility in detecting faked profiles" (p. 425).

Rogers, Hinds and Sewell (1996) examined the utility of the MMPI-A in detecting the feigning of schizophrenia, major depression, and generalized anxiety disorder in a clinical population of adolescents. Results underscored the problem of high rates of false-positives (i.e., miscategorizing an adolescent as a malingerer). Specifically, results highlighted the fact that the MMPI-A's true positives (accurately classifying someone who is malingering as a malingerer) only slightly exceeded its false-positives (inaccurately classifying someone who is not malingering as a malingerer). Although commonly used validity scales (F, F1, and F2) were ineffective at distinguishing honest responders from simulators, the results indicated that the F-K scale was useful in differentiating malingerers from bona fide patients. Specifically, using a score greater than 20 on the F-K scale optimized predictive power (i.e., this score yielded a positive predictive power of .83 and a negative predictive power of .91). The authors concluded that, "the application of F-K > 20 as a screen for feigning appeared promising" (p. 255).

Conclusions Regarding the Use of the MMPI-A in the Assessment of Malingering

Clearly, there is not enough research to establish trustworthy cut off scores for the detection of malingering on the MMPI-A. However, the preliminary data does appear to support the use of the MMPI-A as one source of data in the assessment of malingering. The MMPI-A can be used to produce corroborative data when one has other evidence of deception. It can also be used as an initial screening tool for adolescent malingering or dissimulation. However, Rogers, Hinds and Sewell (1996) recommend that psychologists "explicitly caution referral sources that even extreme scores on the MMPI-A validity indicators may denote confusion, severe psychopathology, and/or illiteracy" (p. 255).

The Millon Adolescent Clinical Inventory (MACI; Millon, 1993)

The MACI is a 160-item personality inventory developed specifically for the assessment of clinical symptoms and personality characteristics of adolescents, ages 13 to 19, in inpatient, outpatient, correctional, and residential treatment settings. The MACI is comprised of 31 scales that are grouped into five sections: Personality Patterns, Expressed Concerns, Clinical Syndromes, Modifying Indices, and Validity. The Personality Patterns and Clinical Syndromes Scales are designed to parallel *DSM-IV* criteria for Axis II and I disorders, respectively. The Expressed Concerns Scales identify common concerns and attitudes of emotionally troubled youth (Tringone, 2002).

MACI Scales Relevant to the Assessment of Malingering

Four scales on the MACI, The Modifier Indices, are relevant in the assessment of deception. These are Reliability, Disclosure, Desirability, and Debasement. These scales "assess self-report style and test-taking attitudes" (Tringone, 2002, p.126).

Research Supporting the Use of the MACI to Assess Malingering

In general, as very little research supports the use of the MACI Modifier Indices in the assessment of malingering, we recommend that evaluators use the Modifier Indices only to generate hypotheses about the adolescent's response style and test-taking attitudes, not to provide any confirmatory data.

Specifically, McCann (1998b) suggested the following interpretation strategies:

- Use the Reliability Scale as a screen for possible malingering. Endorsement of the items on this scale may reflect random responding, reading comprehension problems, or confusion. However, endorsement of these items may also reflect attempts

to appear mentally ill, prompting the clinician to administer a
full malingering evaluation.

- A raw score of 589 or greater on the Disclosure Scale may indicate
  overreporting of pathology. Although an elevated score on the
  Disclosure Scale may be interpreted by the evaluator as a "cry
  for help," it may also be suggestive of malingering.
- A raw score of 201 or less on the Disclosure Scale may indicate
  underreporting, denial, or an unwillingness to appear forthright.
- Extremely elevated scores of 90 or above on the Desirability Scale
  may indicate the extreme minimization or denial of emotional
  concerns. Elevated scores may suggest unrealistic self-appraisal
  or the adolescent's need to appear socially desirable. Thus, this
  scale may be used to generate hypotheses regarding the
  adolescent's test-taking attitudes.
- Extremely elevated scores of 90 or above on the Debasement
  Scale may indicate "over-reporting of symptoms, malingering,
  exaggeration, or a similar response set" (p. 104).

Conclusions Regarding the Use of the MACI in the Assessment of Malingering

As no empirical research supports the use of the indices in the
assessment of malingering, McCann (1998b) cautioned against using these
indices as conclusive tests of malingering. Rather, we recommend that
information from these indices be used only to generate hypotheses about
response styles. Caution should be employed not to overrely on this
speculative data, and evaluators should be forthright in reports about the
limitations of this data, should it serve as a basis for any conclusions
about malingering or deception.

The Personality Inventory for Children (PIC; Wirt et al., 1984)

The Personality Inventory for Children is a 600-item, True-False
inventory. Questions on the PIC are answered by the child's parent or
caregiver.

PIC Scales Relevant to the Assessment of Dissimulation

The PIC includes 3 primary scales to assess response style: the Lie
(L) scale, the Frequency (F) scale, and the Defensiveness (DEF) scale.
Two experimental scales, the K scale and the Social Desirability (SD)
scale, also assess informant response style.

The Frequency (F) Scale is specifically designed to assess malingering.
It is comprised of 42 items that both the clinical and normative samples
rarely endorsed.

Research Supporting the Use of the PIC in the Assessment of Malingering or Dissimulatory Response Styles

In general, the scales used to assess informant response style on the PIC are not well researched (Oldershaw & Bagby, 1997). McVaugh and Grow found that when a cut off score of 59 was used for the L scale, 82% of honest parents and 86% of parents instructed to be defensive were correctly identified (as cited in Oldershaw & Bagby, 1997). In this same study, a cut off score greater than or equal to 110 correctly identified 93% of malingerers and 100% of honest responders (as cited in Oldershaw & Bagby, 1997).

USE OF NEUROPSYCHOLOGICAL TESTING IN THE ASSESSMENT OF MALINGERING AND DISSIMULATION

While the research supporting the use of personality measures in the detection of dissimulation in child and adolescent populations is, at best, minimal, even fewer studies have examined the use of neuropsychological tests in the detection of feigned cognitive deficits in these youthful populations. Notably, although Rogers, Harrell, and Liff (1993) determined six indicators of possible malingering on neuropsychological tests in adult populations (floor effect, performance curve, magnitude of error, symptom validity testing, atypical presentation, and psychological sequelae), these strategies have not been evaluated with child and adolescent populations (McCann, 1998b).

Two studies (Faust, Hart, & Guilmette, 1988; Faust, Hart, Guilmette, & Arkes, 1988) investigated whether neuropsychologists would be able to detect malingering from the test protocols of children and adolescents who had been instructed to feign cognitive deficits. Results from these studies suggested that neuropsychologists were unable to detect feigning from protocols alone. Although these studies have been criticized for their methodological limitations (e.g., neuropsychologists were not given collateral reports or medical records, information that is critical to the detection of malingering), these studies may suggest that neuropsychological assessments have "not escaped the limitations inherent in attempting to uncover feigned psychological deficits" (McCann, 1998b, p. 115).

Given the paucity of research on the use of neuropsychological tests in the assessment of malingering with children and adolescents, we include here only information about the one instrument for which we found research supporting its use with youth, Raven's Standard Progressive Matrices.

Raven's Standard Progressive Matrices (SPM)

Raven's Standard Progressive Matrices (SPM; J. C. Raven, Court, & J. Raven, 1999) is a measure of one's ability to reason by analogy, independent of language and formal education, which was developed for use with individuals age 6 to adult. The SPM consists of 60 items arranged in 5 sets of 12 (e.g., A, B, C, D, E) with each item missing a piece. Each set involves a different theme to solve the missing piece, and sets are arranged in order of increasing difficulty. The raw score is converted to a percentile rank, which is based on age-based norms, including those for children and adolescents. Studies of internal consistency, using either the split-half method corrected for length or the Kuder-Richardson (KR20) coefficient of reliability estimates, resulted in values ranging from .60 to .98, with a median of .90. Furthermore, the median test-retest correlation value was approximately .82.

Research Supporting the Use of the Raven's SPM in the Assessment of Malingering or Dissimulatory Response Styles

To date, one study examined the use of the SPM to detect malingering in 44 children and adolescents ages 7 to 17 (McKinzey, Prieler, & J. Raven, 2003). When asked to perform as badly on the test as possible without getting caught for faking, all but two of the children and adolescents were able to follow instructions and produce malingered results. Cut off scores validated for adults yielded inaccurate results, producing a false-positive rate of 7% and a false-negative rate of 64%. However, a rule was employed that if a child or adolescent missed at least one very easy item (items A3, A4, or B1), then it was concluded that the youth was malingering; this rule yielded a hit rate of 95%, with equal false-positive and false-negative rates of 5%. Therefore, this research suggests the SPM may be a useful tool for detecting malingering in children and adolescents. However, given the limited research on this tool and the small sample size in the one empirical study evaluating its use, evaluators should use caution in generating conclusions based on results of the Raven's SPM.

CONCLUSIONS AND SUMMARY

The detection of dissimulation is a challenge that faces evaluators in forensic and clinical settings. Despite the increased need for empirically supported strategies for detecting dissimulation in these populations, the majority of research continues to focus on adult populations.

Although it is tempting to apply adult research to children and adolescents, we argue against strict application of current models to this youthful population. Notably, current models do not take into account clinically relevant factors that may impact the response styles of children and adolescents. The clinically relevant factors we identified were (a) the setting of the evaluation, (b) the developmental phase of the child, (c) the intellectual functioning of the child, (d) the memory abilities of the child, (e) parental influence, and (f) the unique manifestations of Axis I disorders in childhood. Given the magnitude of influence that these factors may have on a child's self-report, we argued that a dissimulation evaluation of youth must include basic knowledge of these factors, wherever relevant.

Evidence for the use of clinical interviewing and psychological testing in the detection of dissimulation was also provided. It was noted that there is insufficient research on these techniques; thus, no model assessment protocol for the detection of dissimulation in children and adolescents can or should be established at this time.

Nonetheless, using the extant research on deception detection strategies, we provided a basic framework for evaluators to approach the question of dissimulation in youthful populations.

KEY POINTS

Given our analysis of both the relevant factors that may influence a child's self-report and the status of psychological tests and tools to detect dissimulation in these populations, can any generalities concerning the assessment of dissimulation in children and adolescents be drawn?

Although research in this area does not support a model assessment protocol at this time, the data do suggest some basic guidelines with which an evaluator may approach suspected dissimulation in children and adolescents. For practical purposes, we have summarized the data presented in the chapter into a basic framework.

An Assessment Framework for the Detection of Malingering in Children and Adolescents

When dissimulation is suspected:

- Consider the ethical issues associated with classifying malingering in children and adolescents. Consult the *Ethical Principles of Psychologists and Code of Conduct* (American

Psychological Association, 2002), and the *Specialty Guidelines for Forensic Psychologists* (Committee on Ethical Guidelines for Forensic Psychologists, 1991).
• Consider the context in which the evaluation is taking place. Be familiar with the general guidelines for conducting assessment in specialized contexts (e.g., clinical, forensic, neuropsychological).
• Consider the possible motivations for deception.

   ▪ Consider the ways in which the context of the evaluation may influence the child's motivation to dissimulate.
   ▪ Assess current stressors in the child's life and consider how these stressors may influence response style.

• Consider the general intellectual functioning, basic reading ability, and memory capacity of the child. Administer an intelligence test, achievement test, and memory assessment.
• Consider how the child's perceptions of the assessment's purpose may impact the child's response style. Assess the child's perceptions of the assessment.
• Look for consistency in the presentation of the presenting problem.

   ▪ Clarify the nature of the presenting problem using open-ended questions.
   ▪ Supplement open-ended questions with pointed questions, using information provided by the child during the initial interview.
   ▪ Obtain a comprehensive psychosocial history.
   ▪ Conduct collateral interviews with parents, teachers, and those close to the child to examine reliability of information provided by the child.
   ▪ Interview the parent(s) and child separately and jointly.

• Use psychological testing to generate hypotheses.

   ▪ Use tests that have been normed on children and/or adolescents.
   ▪ Do not use adult cut off scores unless these scores are empirically supported for use with child and adolescent populations.

Chapter 8

THE ASSESSMENT OF PSYCHOPATHY AND ITS RELATIONSHIP TO DECEPTION DETECTION

When conducting an assessment in which malingering or other deception is suspected, an important variable to consider may be the level of psychopathic traits present in the individual being assessed. Although the presence of psychopathy does not automatically suggest that an individual is malingering or being otherwise deceptive, psychopathic traits have been found to be highly correlated with being willing and able to engage in deception, especially in males (Edens, Buffington, & Tomicic, 2000). In fact, lying and deception are key characteristics of psychopaths (Hare, 1991, 2003) and tend to be expressed in two main ways in these individuals. One way the psychopath lies seems to be quite compulsive and unrelated to any external gain. In this way, the psychopath lies for the sake of lying. This type of deception is described as Pathological Lying and is the focus of an item by the same name on the Psychopathy Checklist-Revised (PCL-R; Hare, 1991). The other type of deception that psychopaths often engage in is more instrumental, or related to achieving some external gain. This type of deception is more closely related to malingering. This instrumental deceit is described in the PCL-R item "Conning/Manipulative" (Hare, 1991).

Although deceitful behavior is a hallmark of psychopathy, it is unclear what the relationship is between this construct and malingering. In part, this lack of clarity is due to some confusion in the literature between Antisocial Personality Disorder (APD; APA, 1994), psychopathy, sociopathy, and criminal behavior in general. Much of the research that has been done to attempt to clarify the issue has used questionable samples of "psychopathic" individuals, defined by unclear means. We will return to this issue later. First, the construct of psychopathy and various methods for assessing it will be discussed in detail. Then, the implications of psychopathy on deception and the detection of deception will be explored. Finally, some practical suggestions will be provided for deciding how and when to assess for psychopathy as part of an effort to determine the presence of deceptive responding, as well as determining what to do with this information when it is obtained.

DEFINING PSYCHOPATHY

The construct of psychopathy was well defined by Cleckley (1976) in *The Mask of Sanity*, and its empirical measurement was later refined by Hare and his colleagues with the development of the Psychopathy Checklists (PCL, PCL-R; Hare, 1991). Any continued debate and confusion surrounding the concept stems primarily from the inconsistent ways in which the term is used (Gacono et al., 2000). An example lies in the way that it is used interchangeably with the *Diagnostic and Statistical Manual of Mental Disorders, 4th Edition (DSM-IV*; APA, 1994) diagnostic category Antisocial Personality Disorder (APD) by some researchers and clinicians. The two constructs are certainly related, but they are not synonymous.

Hare (1991) described psychopathy as being composed of three main categories of symptoms: interpersonal, affective, and behavioral, while the *DSM-IV* criteria for APD revolve primarily around the presence of antisocial behaviors (APA, 1994). Essentially, the interpersonal and affective characteristics, which are key in distinguishing psychopathy from other criminal behavior, are left out of the APD definition. Subsequently, the relationship between these two constructs is asymmetrical. Most criminal psychopaths will meet the criteria for APD, but many individuals with APD are not psychopaths. Approximately 50% to 75% of those in forensic populations could be diagnosed as having APD, so this diagnosis does not provide much useful information in these populations because it is so common (Gacono & Meloy, 1994). Only 15% to 25% of the forensic populace are psychopaths, a much more useful distinction (Hare, 1996). The focus of this chapter will be on deception in psychopaths as this construct has been carefully defined in the literature, not on APD or general criminal behavior.

ASSESSING PSYCHOPATHY

The PCL-R

The Hare Psychopathy Checklist-Revised (PCL-R; 1991, 2003) is the most comprehensive instrument for assessing the level of psychopathy. The measure consists of a comprehensive file review, followed by a semi-structured interview. The information obtained is used to score the subject on 20 items making up the measure. Scored on a scale of zero to two, the number reflects to what extent each item applies to an individual. If there is uncertainty or insufficient information to score the item, a score of omit is given and the total score is prorated to account for this (Hare, 1991). No more than five items can be omitted. This 20-item PCL-R (Hare, 1991, 2003) consists of the following items:

- glibness/superficial charm
- grandiose sense of self worth
- need for stimulation/proneness to boredom
- pathological lying
- conning/manipulative
- lack of remorse or guilt
- shallow affect
- callous/lack of empathy
- parasitic lifestyle
- poor behavior controls
- promiscuous sexual behavior
- early behavior problems
- lack of realistic, long-term goals
- impulsivity
- irresponsibility
- failure to accept responsibility for own actions
- many short-term marital relationships
- juvenile delinquency
- revocation of conditional release
- criminal versatility

The PCL-R measures a unitary clinical construct as shown in part by mean inter-item correlations above .2 (see Harpur, Hakstian, & Hare, 1988). Alpha coefficients of internal consistency range from .85 to .87 (Hare, 1991); however, these measures have consistently produced a two-factor structure (Hare et al., 1990; Harpur et al., 1988). Factor 1 represents the interpersonal and affective components that appear to be the core of psychopathy, while Factor 2 describes an unstable and antisocial lifestyle component. The relationship between the factors has been shown through a correlation of approximately .5 (Hare, 1998a).

More recent research has found that there may actually be three factors composing the PCL-R. Factor 1, which represents the interpersonal components of psychopathy; Factor 2, measuring the affective component; and Factor 3, comprised of the behavioral variables associated with psychopathy (Cooke & Michie, 2001; Hart, 2000). The initial two-factor structure was based on exploratory factor analyses, while the three-factor structure arose from confirmatory factor analysis, and appears to fit even better than the old structure.

Though Cooke and Michie (2001) suggested three factors as the best fit, when Multi-Health Systems revised the manual for the PCL-R, they incorporated an expansion of the original two-factor model to a four-factor model. This includes subdivisions of the original model based on Hare's recent research (Hare, 2003; Hare & Neumann, 2005). Also, Hare (2003) notes "though they may represent a different level of discourse, traits are not completely independent of the behaviors used to define them" (p. 82). In a related fashion, the manual also incorporates a new five-level scoring system: Level 5, PCL-R, 33-40 (Very High); 4, 25-32 (High); 3, 17-24 (Moderate); 2, 9-16 (Low); 1, 0-8 (Very Low) (Hare, 2003). It is not an unreasonable breakdown, although these authors find it hard to label a person with a PCL-R score of 15 to 16 as Low.

J. R. Hall, Benning, and Patrick (2004) provided evidence of the convergent and discriminant validity of the three factors, further supporting this model. Interrater reliabilities of the PCL and PCL-R vary from .88 to .92, and test-retest reliabilities fall in the range from .85 to .90 (Cacciola, Rutherford, & Alterman, 1990; M. L. Schroeder, K. G. Schroeder, & Hare, 1983). The PCL-R is currently the gold standard in the assessment of psychopathy.

The validity of the PCL-R has been demonstrated consistently throughout the research literature. Its predictive validity is particularly well established. The PCL-R has been shown to be predictive of recidivism, which is generally defined as charges or conviction for a new offense after release, or violation of terms of release (Hemphill, Hare, & Wong, 1998). This predictive power has also been shown for sexual recidivism among released sex offenders. For this reason the PCL-R is often used in actuarial risk assessments of sex offenders prior to their release from prison. PCL-R scores have also been found to be higher in perpetrators of violent crimes of a predatory nature.

Use of the PCL-R With Other Adult Populations

The majority of the research using the PCL-R has been done with male offender samples; however, some research has been done with females. Strachan, Williamson, and Hare (1990; as cited in Salekin, Rogers, & Sewell, 1997) found that incarcerated adult females had scores on the PCL-R that were similar to men's scores, but suggested that two of the test items were not as applicable to women: juvenile delinquency and revocation of conditional release. Salekin and colleagues (1997) administered the PCL-R to 103 female inmates and found that 15% scored above 29, the cut off for psychopathy that they used. They factor analyzed the scores of the women and determined that the factor structure was slightly different for females. They suggested that the characteristics which best described Factor 1, for females as opposed to males, were "lack of empathy or guilt, interpersonal deception, proneness to boredom, and sensation seeking" (p. 583). These characteristics for Factor 2 were "early behavioral problems, promiscuity, and adult antisocial behavior" (p. 583). The construct of psychopathy and the PCL-R are valid for use in female offender samples (Salekin et al., 1997), but more research needs to be done to determine more specifically what limitations, if any, of the PCL-R need to be considered when it is used to identify psychopathy in women.

Kosson, Smith, and Newman (1990) were interested in investigating the applicability of the construct of psychopathy to adult, male Black offenders. Completed PCL protocols for 232 White male and 124 Black male inmates found 23.7% of Whites and 36.3% of Blacks scored 31.5 or greater and were considered to be psychopathic. Additionally, 54.7% of Whites and 54.8% of Blacks were in the middle group with scores between 20 and 31.5. Scores of 20 or less were obtained for 21.6% and 8.9% of Whites and Blacks respectively (Kosson et al., 1990). Black inmates in this study received significantly higher ratings. Two items, glibness or superficial charm and poor behavior controls, had item-to-total correlations of .18 for the Black offenders, which does not reach the minimum of .20. The coefficient of congruence between White and Black Factor 1 scores was .67. This did not meet the researcher's strictest criterion of .82. However the correlation between the Factor 2 scores was .93. The construct validity of psychopathy does not appear to be affected by race, ethnicity, or culture in highly significant ways (Kosson et al., 1990; Wong, 1984). Research using item response theory has shown that the PCL-R generalizes well across settings, ethnicity, and culture (Cooke & Michie, 1997). Rogers (1995) suggests that PCL-R scores may be used for description of Blacks but not for prediction.

Clinical Applications of the PCL-R

The recommended strategy for scoring the PCL-R is to develop a prototype for each item based on Hare's criteria and then determine to what extent the subject being rated matches it (Hare, 1991). It is important to recognize the difference between basing a prototype on the criteria given by Hare and basing it on preconceived ideas about the items on the scale (Hare, 1998a). The latter is inappropriate. If the rater is unsure about whether to score some items 0 or 1, or 1 or 2, Hare (1991) has suggested that half of the items be given the higher score and half the lower. More recently, Hare and Forth (1998) have recommended using what has been termed the "slider method" when scoring uncertainties arise. With this method, if the rater is unsure which score to give, he or she can note this hesitancy by placing an arrow, or "slider," next to the score given. For example, if the rater thinks that a subject probably rates higher than a score of 1 on an item, but is not quite sure that a score of 2 is warranted, he or she can note this by giving either a score of 1 with a slider up to 2, like 1 >, or a score of 2 with a slider down to 1, like < 2, whichever seems most appropriate. When it is time to actually add all of the ratings to arrive at a subject's total score, this method does not actually affect the scores given, but it can be helpful in revealing if the rater has any biases, or tendencies to score high or low.

When administering the PCL-R, the file review should be completed before proceeding to the interview (Gacono, 2000). Hare (1991) has provided the Interview and Information Schedule to aid in the PCL-R interview. This schedule is divided into 10 sections: school adjustment, work history, career goals, finances, health, family life, sex/relationships, drug use, childhood/adolescent antisocial behavior, and adult antisocial behavior. The questions in this schedule do not correspond directly to specific items on the PCL-R; so the interview must be completed, then the rater must go back and score it (Gacono, 2000). The PCL-R Clinical Interview Schedules (CISs; Gacono & Hare, 2000) are less time consuming. The questions are linked to specific items or clusters of items and are scored as the interview progresses. The rater should first obtain a life history of the individual being assessed. Then items 20, 19, 18, 12, 17, 11, 3/14/ 15, 6/7/8/16, 10, 4/5, 9, 13, and 1/2 should be assessed in that order (Gacono, 2000; Gacono & Hutton, 1994). This order of the items progresses from more structured to less structured items, and the information gleaned from questions about earlier items can help with the scoring of later items. The less threatening, behavior-related items are assessed first, which helps the rater to establish rapport with the subject early in the interview (Gacono & Hutton, 1994).

When the PCL-R score is obtained, it can be used for a variety of purposes, either by itself or as part of a risk assessment. These scores can "influence decisions about sentencing, treatment and management, and eligibility for parole . . . [and be used] in civil commitment and dangerous offender proceedings" (Hare, 1998a, p. 106). Gacono (1998) suggests that PCL-R scores can be used for treatment planning, by looking at the overall score and the scores on each item. He states,

> For example, in a low scorer (PCL-R < 20), 0 points on Items 1 (*glibness/superficial charm*) and 2 (*grandiose sense of self worth*) coupled with a score of 2 on Items 3 (*proneness to boredom*), 14 (*impulsivity*), and 15 (*irresponsibility*) rules out a narcissistic or psychopathic disorder, suggests borderline features, and indicates the clinical need for structure and interventions designed to increase impulse control and problem-solving skills. One or 2 points on Item 10 (*poor behavior controls*) signal the need for anger management training. (Gacono, 1998, p. 52)

Insight-oriented therapies have not been shown to be effective with psychopaths, and possibly can even increase their level of dangerousness in some cases. Wong and Hare (2000) propose a model of treatment, which would employ cognitive-behavioral techniques to teach psychopaths that they are responsible for their own behavior and that there are ways of utilizing their strengths in less antisocial ways. To date, this approach to treating psychopaths has not yet been attempted on a large scale.

The PCL-R has also been found to be useful in predicting outcomes of methadone maintenance programs. Alterman et al. (1998) administered the PCL-R to 139 male outpatients with opiate dependence at a Veteran's Administration methadone clinic. They found that the PCL-R identified 61% of participants who completed treatment and 66% of those who failed to complete treatment. This level of prediction was higher than other measures of antisociality used by Alterman and colleagues. The PCL-R looks promising as a tool for predicting which patients are likely to be successful in methadone maintenance programs.

There is considerable debate regarding the appropriate cut off score to use for a diagnosis of psychopathy. The recommended cut off which has been used in most research on psychopathy is 30 (Hare, 1991). With White male inmates this cut off has a sensitivity of .72 and a specificity of .93 (Hare, 1985). However, the mean standard error of measurement (SEM) is 3.14 (Hare, 1991), and it has been suggested that, for clinical purposes, a cut off of 33 be used for a psychopathy diagnosis (Meloy & Gacono, 1992;

Rogers, 1995). However, this would remove a number of people, who clinician-theorists would clearly see as fitting the construct of psychopathy, especially where the Factor 1 score is relatively high. Gacono and Hutton (1994) provide suggested ranges for reporting PCL-R scores, which are not empirically derived but may be useful. These ranges are as follows: > 33 Severe, 30-32 Low Severe, 27-29 High Moderate, 23-26 Moderate, 20-22 Low Moderate, < 19 Low (Gacono & Hutton, 1994). Rogers (1995) cautions against the use of these ranges, stating "such a classification, at the present time, is an overrefinement of PCL-R interpretation" (p. 241).

Other Measures Related to the PCL-R

Following the success of the PCL-R in assessing psychopathy, several other measures have been derived from the scale with modifications to allow them to be suitable for various other settings or populations. In the following sections these modified psychopathy checklists will be examined, beginning with the Psychopathy Checklist: Screening Version (PCL:SV). An even shorter and easier to administer version of the PCL-R is just emerging in the literature. This Self Report Psychopathy Scale-II will be presented as well as some other self-report measures of psychopathy and the problems associated with using these measures.

The focus will then shift to the assessment of psychopathy in younger populations. The PCL-R adaptation used with adolescents, the Psychopathy Checklist: Youth Version (PCL:YV) will be presented as well as some controversial issues surrounding the assessment of psychopathy with this population.

The PCL:SV

The PCL-R takes several hours to complete, which may not be feasible in some situations. A shorter version of the PCL-R, the Psychopathy Checklist: Screening Version (PCL:SV; Hart, Cox, & Hare, 1995; Hart, Hare, & Forth, 1994) was developed to alleviate this time problem. The PCL:SV has 12 items from the full PCL-R and the same factor structure as the PCL-R, with each factor being measured by 6 items (Hare, 1996). The items from PCL-R Factor 1 are: *superficial, grandiose, manipulative, lacks remorse, lacks empathy,* and *doesn't accept responsibility.* From Factor 2 the items are: *impulsive, poor behavior controls, lacks goals, irresponsible, adolescent antisocial behavior,* and *adult antisocial behavior* (Hart et al., 1995). The newer 3 factor structure of the PCL-R has also been found with the PCL:SV (Hart, 2000). The same scoring format as that used for the PCL-R is used for the PCL:SV, so the total score can range from 1 to 24. Up to two items, one from each of the six items per factor, may be omitted if necessary (Hart et al., 1995). The descriptions of two of the PCL-R items, adolescent and adult antisocial behavior, were changed so that behaviors could be included even if they did not result in an official encounter with law enforcement officials. This made the items more appropriate for use with noncriminals (Hart et al., 1995). The PCL:SV has been found to be predictive of risk for recidivism in mentally ill offenders, particularly Factor 2 of the scale (Gray et al., 2004).

The PCL:SV can be used alone for research with noncriminals or in civil litigation, or to screen for psychopathy in forensic populations (Hare, 1996). For research purposes, the PCL:SV can be completed without the use of criminal file information. The scale can also be used in other nonforensic settings such as "civil psychiatric evaluations . . . and personnel selection (e.g., screening of law enforcement, correctional, or military recruits)" (Hart et al., 1995, p. 2). However, when used in these applied settings, although criminal file information will most likely not be available, some type of collateral information should be used, such as interviews with family, friends, or former employers. These sources can be used, along with prison or hospital records, when using the PCL:SV to screen for psychopathy in forensic settings.

The PCL:SV takes approximately 1 to 1½ hours to complete compared with 2½ to 3 three hours for the PCL-R. Thus, the PCL:SV was thought to be able to save valuable time and money when used to screen inmates or forensic psychiatric patients for psychopathy. Concurrence between the PCL-R and the PCL:SV is fairly high, but the latter scale overestimates psychopathy more frequently. The PCL:SV, however, almost never classifies an individual as a nonpsychopath who is actually a psychopath. So false-negative errors with this instrument are practically nonexistent, and only those with high PCL:SV scores need be reevaluated with the PCL-R to weed out the false positives (Hart et al., 1995). In practice, individuals with scores of 12 or less on the PCL:SV can safely be considered nonpsychopathic. A score of 13 to 17 indicates possible psychopathy and the need for further evaluation. Individuals who score 18 or higher are very likely psychopathic and should certainly be evaluated further by the PCL-R (Hart et al., 1995). A cut off score of 18 on the PCL:SV is considered equivalent to the cut off of 30 on the PCL-R (Hare, 1998b).

Gacono (2000) suggests several instances in which a PCL-R evaluation may be warranted. These include instances in which an individual has an extensive criminal history, an APD diagnosis or a history of violence, or is suspected of malingering, or is being considered for parole or placement in a less secure facility. Boyd (2003) also suggested that individuals should be screened for psychopathy before entering certain treatment programs, such as correctional sex offender treatment programs, because of the difficulty in treating these individuals and their ability to feign progress in treatment. These cases could easily cover a large number of individuals, and it would be very costly to administer the PCL-R to all of them. Using the PCL:SV first, and then the PCL-R only for the high scorers, can significantly reduce the time and money spent on this process in instances when many individuals need to be screened for psychopathy. However, because the PCL:SV is also relatively time consuming to administer, and its results should only be used for screening purposes, in cases where only a few psychopathy evaluations are needed, or if there is a high probability that an individual has a high level of psychopathy, it is more economical to just go ahead and administer the full PCL-R instead of spending the time to do both measures.

Self-Report Measures of Psychopathy

Self-report measures of psychopathy can be useful in research with noncriminal samples. However, these scales should not be used to make diagnoses of psychopathy, because their use has several problems, one of which is the lack of control these instruments have over respondent deceitfulness, an important feature of psychopathy (Hart & Hare, 1997). Furthermore, the focus of the majority of these scales, such as the Minnesota Multiphasic Personality Inventory, 2nd Edition (MMPI-2) Psychopathic Deviate (*Pd*) scale (Butcher et al., 1989) and the California Psychological Inventory (CPI) Socialization (So) scale (Gough, 1957), is primarily on the antisocial behaviors associated with PCL-R Factor 2 rather than the personality traits, which are paramount in the assessment of psychopathy (Hart & Hare, 1997; Lilienfeld & Andrews, 1996). Two exceptions to this are Hare's Self-Report Psychopathy Scale-II (SRP-II; Hemphill & Hare, 2004) and the Psychopathic Personality Inventory (PPI; Lilienfeld & Andrews, 1996). These two measures will be examined further here.

The SRP-II

The SRP-II consists of 59 items and is theoretically based on the PCL-R (Hemphill & Hare, 2004). Each item is rated on a 7-point scale with a score of 1 indicating strong disagreement with the item and a score of 7 showing strong agreement. The SRP-II includes items focused on both Factor 1 and Factor 2 traits of psychopathy. In an early study using the SRP-II with 100 criminal offenders, it was correlated .54 with PCL-R total scores (Forth et al., 1996). This measure is not widely available for use at this time.

The PPI

The Psychopathic Personality Inventory (PPI; Lilienfeld & Andrews, 1996), although not specifically derived from the PCL-R as were the PCL:SV and SPR-II, deserves mention here. This scale is a self-report measure that focuses on psychopathic personality traits rather than antisocial behaviors. It consists of the following eight factor derived subscales: Machiavellian egocentricity, social potency, cold-heartedness, carefree nonplanfulness, fearlessness, blame externalization, impulsive nonconformity, and stress immunity. Each of these factors is measured by between 11 and 30 statements, which are rated from one to four on a Likert-type scale indicating how true or false each item is for the individual. The measure also includes two validity scales, the Deviant Responding (DR) scale, which is intended to assess for malingering, random responding, or subjects who have trouble understanding the items or directions. A Variable Response Inconsistency (VRIN) scale was also included and compares answers on correlated item pairs to detect careless responding (Lilienfeld & Andrews, 1996). In early studies using this measure, Cronbach's alpha of internal consistency ranged from .90 to .93 for PPI total scores, and from .70 to .90 for the eight PPI subscales. Test-retest reliability for the total score was .95, and ranged from .82 to .94 for the subscales. Several correlations were reported to establish convergent and discriminant validity for the PPI. For example, the measure correlated .91 with the Self-Report Psychopathy Scale-Revised (Hare, 1985).

The PCL:YV

Although the majority of research on psychopathy has been done with adult samples, the disorder usually emerges early in life, and studying its manifestations in adolescence is important to the understanding of the development of the disorder. Early work in attempting to study psychopathy in adolescents used an 18-item modified version of the PCL-R (Forth & Burke, 1998). This version was made more appropriate to the study of adolescents with the deletion of two items: Item 9 (parasitic lifestyle), and Item 17 (many short-term marital relationships). These items were removed because the nature of adolescence requires some level of parasitic behavior, and many marital relationships are highly unlikely to have occurred for an individual in this stage of life (Brandt et al., 1997). The scoring for Item 18 (juvenile delinquency) was revised, because all adolescent offenders meet the criteria for this item. The scoring was changed to 2 points for violent crimes, and 1 point for nonviolent crimes (Forth, Hart, & Hare, 1990). The scoring of Item 20 (criminal versatility) was also changed because adolescents have a relatively short amount of time to accumulate a criminal history. The scoring for this item was changed to 2 points for four or more kinds of offenses, 1 point for three kinds, and 0 points for one or two kinds (Brandt et al., 1997). A cut off of 27 points was used on this scale to determine psychopathy (Brandt et al., 1997).

In 1994, Forth, Kosson, and Hare made further revisions to this version to create the Psychopathy Checklist: Youth Version (PCL:YV). The descriptions of the items were changed to allow for the limited experiences of adolescents, and the scoring of the items was changed so that their focus was placed more on family, peers, and school. Scoring was kept the same as on the earlier adolescent version for Items 18 and 20 (juvenile delinquency and criminal versatility, see above). Many short-term relationships (Item 17) was replaced but focused on sexual rather then marital relationships. A score of 0 was given for long-term relationships (4 months or longer) that were stable, 1 for problems with stability in sexual relationships, and 2 for severely unstable long-term relationships or three or more short sexual relationships. Parasitic lifestyle (Item 9) was also replaced but focused on parasitic behaviors toward peers, parents, and romantic partners. Scoring criteria was also modified for several other items. Cut off scores for psychopathy have not yet been established, but 30 has been used in research, because this allows for comparison with the adult PCL-R (Forth & Burke, 1998).

A relationship similar to that found between APD and PCL-R scores in adults has been found between Conduct Disorder (CD; APA, 1994) and PCL:YV scores. Forth (1995; as cited in Forth & Burke, 1998) ran a study in which all of the subjects who were found to be psychopathic, using a score of 30 on the PCL:YV as the cut off, met the criteria for CD, but only 30% of the adolescents with CD were psychopathic. This study also provided preliminary evidence that the factor structure of the PCL:YV is very similar to the two-factor structure of the PCL-R. This information may be important in determining that the construct of psychopathy, as it is manifested in adolescence, corresponds closely with its presentation in adults. Alpha coefficient of internal consistency for the PCL:YV ranged from .75 to .88, inter-item correlations ranged from .13 to .29, and interrater reliabilities ranged from .91 to .98. This suggests that the scale is reliable among raters, has adequate internal consistency, and is fairly homogenous (Forth & Burke, 1998).

Some of the traits, which characterize psychopathy in adults, such as impulsivity, sensation seeking, and irresponsibility, may be a natural part of adolescence (Forth & Burke, 1998). It might be expected that noncriminal male adolescents would generally score more highly on these traits than adults. Forth (1995; as cited in Forth & Burke, 1998) and Toupin et al. (1996) assessed psychopathy in community samples of adolescents using the PCL:YV. In these studies, the items with the highest mean scores were Item 3 (need for stimulation), Item 10 (poor behavior controls), Item 12 (early behavior problems), and Item 14 (impulsivity). These findings provide information, which might be useful in developing norms for adolescent samples.

Moffit (1993) distinguished between two antisocial behavior patterns in adolescence. Relatively few adolescents will continue their highly antisocial behavior into adulthood. Moffit labeled those who do the "life-course-persistent" group. Theoretically, the psychopathic young offender fits into this group. The nonpsychopathic adolescent offender is more likely to be involved in criminal activities only in adolescence, and possibly because of environmental influences such as peer pressure. Moffit called this the "adolescence-limited" group. The PCL:YV looks promising as a tool to distinguish between these groups, therefore making it possible to provide interventions that are more appropriate to their different needs.

Assessment of Psychopathy in Practice

The Hare PCL-R is the most reliable and valid instrument available for the assessment of psychopathy in adult male forensic populations. PCL-R scores are strong predictors of recidivism, particularly violent and sexual recidivism (Hemphill et al., 1998; Quinsey, Rice, & Harris, 1995). Scores on the PCL-R are also consistently correlated with violence and criminal behavior (Hemphill et al., 1998). Because the limitations of the PCL-R have not been clarified for its use with female or minority offenders, a good rule of thumb is to use the PCL-R scores for description of women and minority inmates, but not prediction, as Rogers (1995) has suggested when using the PCL-R with African Americans.

Important modifications have been made to the PCL-R so that an estimate of psychopathy level can be obtained more quickly and in nonoffender populations with the PCL:SV and the SRP-II. The SRP-II is still only available for use in research, but hopefully, it will soon be possible to affordably assess psychopathy in community populations. With the PCL:YV, the early assessment of psychopathy will perhaps aid in the prevention of some of the devastation caused by psychopaths.

Although psychopathy assessments need to be completed carefully and responsibly because of the potential for serious implications for the individual being assessed, these assessments are valuable in risk assessment and should not be feared to the extent that they are not used. In prisons and forensic psychiatric hospitals, early identification of psychopathic inmates and patients can increase protective measures for staff and other inmates (Gacono, 2000). This identification can aid in the development of treatment plans specifically designed for monitoring and keeping antisocial behaviors under control. Using the PCL-R can identify high-risk inmates and possibly prevent inappropriate and premature release into the community, thereby preventing further crimes from being committed. This is an essential tool to be incorporated into risk assessments prior to release (Gacono, 2000).

PSYCHOPATHY AND DECEPTION

Using the scales described previously will not necessarily provide an assessment of deception. As was described, two of the characteristics of psychopathy are pathological lying, and conning and manipulative behavior. So, as part of an assessment of psychopathy, these general tendencies are assessed. Knowing these traits are present can provide some useful information about an individual's tendency toward and skill in utilizing these particular types of deception. However, knowing this will not necessarily allow easy assessment of truth or deception at any given time. Just because a psychopath's lips are moving does not necessarily mean he or she is lying.

It is often assumed that psychopaths are good liars. The fact that psychopathic individuals are callous and manipulative leads to the belief that individuals with a high level of psychopathic traits not only tend to lie more often, but are better at it. We will examine the research as it applies to the question of whether psychopaths are better at deceiving others, and in particular, if they are more skilled at malingering.

Characteristics of Psychopaths That Might Make Them Good at Deception

It was previously stated that psychopathic individuals tend to have a greater tendency to be deceptive, and research has supported this assumption (Seto et al., 1997). They are more likely to lie for the sake of lying, or to be pathological liars. They are also more likely to use deception for a specific purpose, to manipulate and con others for some sort of gain. Psychopaths also tend to be charming, to have little experience of guilt or remorse, and to display shallow emotions.

In Chapter 1 there was much discussion about how emotions can reveal deception. Ekman (1992) has suggested that some people are better at deceiving others because they are able to conceal their emotions well. He stated that psychopaths are one group of people who can hide emotions and feel confident about their ability to deceive. Therefore, they are more able to lie convincingly. Psychopaths do not typically have to worry about their guilty feelings being betrayed by their expressions, because they usually lack these feelings altogether.

Research has shown that psychopaths are deficient in their responding to emotional stimuli (Verona et al., 2004). Individuals with higher levels of psychopathy do not show differences in their autonomic responses or facial expressions when imagining emotional versus nonemotional stimuli (Patrick, Cuthbert, & Lang, 1994). In terms of voice inflection, psychopaths have been shown to speak more quietly than nonpsychopaths and also to show no difference in voice pitch when speaking emotional versus neutral words (Louth et al., 1998). Remember from Chapter 1 that higher voice pitch is often associated, and indicative of, deception. Therefore, it would seem that psychopaths' lack of emotional expression would make it easier for them to deceive, since they would not have the problem of emotional leakage. However, much of the research discussed below suggests this is not the case.

Psychopaths' Ability to Deceive Effectively

There are many different ways in which individuals can attempt to deceive. Much of the research on psychopaths' ability to successfully deceive has focused on their ability to malinger severe mental illness. Additional research has examined their ability to engage in positive impression management and to lie in general. We will first examine the research on the ability of psychopaths to effectively malinger mental illness, and then look at each other type of deception in turn.

Psychopaths and Malingering

Research on the question of whether psychopaths can effectively malinger major mental illness has been conflicting. As early as 1942, Good reported that individuals in the military who feigned symptomatology to be relieved from duty were psychopathic and without remorse. As was noted previously, part of the confusion on this topic has stemmed from the inclusion of psychopaths, sociopaths (questionably defined), individuals with APD, and criminal defendants or incarcerated individuals in general in summaries of the research in this area. For example, in his chapter on the subject, C. R. Clark (1997) cited Rogers and McKee's (1995) study as evidence that few sociopaths malinger, because although most of the subjects (criminal defendants being evaluated for insanity) had elevated scores on the MMPI-2 Psychopathic Deviate Scale, few of them were found to be malingering. C. R. Clark also cited Rogers, Gillis, Dickens, and Bagby (1989) and Rogers, Gillis, and Bagby (1990) who found that inmates do not tend to malinger on the SIRS (see Chapter 4) when given standard instructions. This was suggested as indirect evidence that sociopaths do not malinger any more frequently than other individuals. C. R. Clark reasoned, "Although these studies do not address the prevalence of malingering among sociopaths as such, the correctional status of an individual (i.e. indirect evidence of sociopathy) does not lead to any greater likelihood of malingering" (p. 73). Though C. R. Clark's definition of a sociopath is unclear, we would assert that there are crucial distinctions between the general prison inmate and the psychopathic individual, and therefore, the research cited here cannot be used to draw any conclusions about the tendency of psychopaths to malinger.

We would hypothesize that psychopathic individuals are very unlikely to malinger mental illness unless there is a significant external gain for doing so. This is because psychopaths tend to be grandiose and would not be likely to want to present themselves as having anything "wrong" with them, including a mental illness. However, if the incentive is great enough, such as avoiding prison by being found not guilty by reason of insanity, one would expect the psychopathic individual to be more willing to feign illness. One study, which used the PPI to assess psychopathy, found a significant relationship between a psychopathy score and attitudes about malingering (Edens et al., 2000). These findings suggested that the more psychopathic an individual was according to the PPI score, the more likely that individual was to report being willing to engage in deception in various forensic or correctional situations. C. R. Clark (1997) cited Hinojosa's 1993 study using the MMPI-2 validity indices with a group of individuals instructed to simulate illness, mentally ill patients, criminal defendants with sociopathy diagnoses (though the criteria for these diagnoses were not clear), and individuals acquitted on an insanity plea. The study found that the sociopathic group minimized psychopathology rather than malingering. With the idea that psychopaths would only malinger in the presence of a significant prize, it is not surprising that the sociopathic group denied pathology when lacking sufficient incentive to fake it.

In terms of research evaluating the effectiveness of psychopaths' attempts to malinger, again there is some conflicting evidence. Psychopathy (assessed with the PPI) was not found to lead to greater ability to malinger on the SIMS, the SIRS, or the PAI in a study done by Poythress, Edens, and Watkins (2001). This study used prison inmates as subjects and found low, nonsignificant correlations between psychopathy and malingering, suggesting that such a relationship does not exist.

Meloy and Gacono (1995) reported that when psychopaths malinger, they often perform below the levels at which true patients perform on neuropsychological tests, and behave in ways that do not fit with the symptoms they endorse on psychological tests. Psychopathic individuals were found to be no better at malingering than nonpsychopathic individuals, but there was some support found for the hypotheses that psychopaths would be better at malingering and would report more symptoms in the condition in which subjects were instructed to respond honestly (Kropp, 1994; as cited in C. R. Clark, 1997).

Some other research seems to possibly support the idea that psychopathic individuals may be better malingerers. In a sample of 18 individuals acquitted on an insanity defense and hospitalized, but then found to be malingering as they had no current Axis I diagnosis, were not on any psychotropic medications, and had a history of admitted exaggeration of symptoms or malingering, the mean PCL-R score was found to be 34.9, well above the traditional cut off score of 30 for psychopathy (Gacono et al., 1995). One hundred percent of the individuals in the malingering group met criteria for APD. A later study also reported that the group of hospitalized insanity acquittees who had malingered mental illness were more likely to be psychopathic (Gacono et al., 1997). This provides indirect support for the idea that psychopathic individuals are skilled at malingering mental illness, since being found not guilty by reason of insanity is certainly evidence of successful malingering. Of course, we recognize that showing that successful malingerers have high levels of psychopathic traits after the fact does not necessarily allow the conclusion that psychopaths are better at malingering than nonpsychopaths.

Psychopathy and Deception in General
In terms of psychopaths' general ability to deceive, the research is again conflicting. Individuals who obtain high scores on the PPI are able to significantly decrease their scores, and therefore appear less psychopathic, when instructed to "fake good" (Edens, Buffington, Tomicic, & Riley, 2001). However, higher scores on the PCL-R have been shown to be associated with lower perceived truthfulness based on observer ratings of individuals trying to convince interviewers about their participation in socially desirable and undesirable situations (Cogburn, 1993). Even when they were being truthful, those with higher psychopathy scores were seen as untruthful.

The research cited earlier regarding psychopaths' lack of emotional response might suggest that psychopaths would be more likely than nonpsychopaths to be able to pass a polygraph test. Research has actually found that this is not the case. In a study by Patrick and Iacono (1989), psychopathy was measured in prison inmates using the original Psychopathy Checklist (PCL; Hare, 1980). Those who scored in the highest one-third of the sample, with a mean PCL score of 35.95, were found to be no better at passing a polygraph examination using the control question technique (see Chapter 6) than those scoring in the lowest one-third of the sample, who had a mean PCL score of 19.36.

We would hypothesize that perhaps psychopathic individuals high in more Factor 1 traits would be more likely to be better liars than individuals higher in Factor 2 traits. Research has shown that sex offenders higher in psychopathic traits are more likely to be able to fake positive treatment gains than those with lower levels of psychopathic traits (Boyd, 2003; Seto & Barbaree, 1999). Further, when Factor 1 and Factor 2 scores were tested separately, the effect of the difference for higher Factor 1 scores was greater than the difference for Factor 2 scores, suggesting that individuals with more Factor 1 traits were better liars than individuals with more Factor 2 traits.

SUMMARY

Psychopathy is a construct that can be reliably assessed using the PCL-R. Key characteristics of the construct include pathological lying and conning or manipulative behavior. Psychopaths show shallow affect and little, if any, guilt or remorse for their actions. All of these characteristics combined suggest that psychopathic individuals would be more likely to engage in deception and would be more skilled at doing so. Research about this is conflicting. Psychopaths do seem more likely to attempt to deceive, but they are not necessarily better at it. Particularly in the case of malingering, psychopaths are not necessarily any more likely than nonpsychopaths to be able to convincingly feign mental illness.

It is also important to point out that, though we mentioned that the combination of characteristics listed previously would lead to the assumption that psychopaths would be skillful liars, not all psychopathic individuals will possess all or even any of those listed characteristics. It does appear that a high level of Factor 1 traits of psychopathy may lead to a greater ability to successfully deceive. A psychopathic individual with primarily Factor 2 traits might be highly impulsive and tend to speak with many contradictions or leaks of information that would lead to poor ability to deceive. Additionally, the characteristic of pathological lying does not necessarily indicate that an individual is a good liar. In fact, the pathological liar often lies so much and about such easily checked facts that he or she is easily found out. Unfortunately, even after being caught, the pathological liar will usually just tell another lie to try to cover up the other.

When deciding whether or not to assess for psychopathy in an attempt to detect deception, it is important to consider the conditions under which an evaluation is being done. In a forensic evaluation, there is a high level of motivation to deceive, and, therefore, an assessment of malingering and deception should always be included. This will not necessarily start with the PCL-R, since this measure is very time consuming to complete. However, if the more direct measures of deception described in earlier chapters are not providing a clear picture of whether an individual is being deceptive or not, assessing psychopathy level might provide useful information.

Psychopaths probably have a greater ability to "fake good," so assessments in which this type of response set is prevalent might indicate an evaluation of psychopathy. For example, if it is suspected that an individual is engaging in positive impression management in a custody evaluation or an employment screening, but the results of indices measuring such response sets are not necessarily clear, assessing psychopathy may allow for a clearer picture of this. Of course, assessing psychopathy in such populations is often extremely difficult to do with much confidence, because the records necessary for scoring the PCL-R are typically not available.

Assessing psychopathy as a standard part of a measure of motivation and truthfulness might be indicated for referral to correctional treatment programs. As was noted earlier, psychopaths have been found to be able to get into sex offender treatment programs, successfully fake their way through the programs, showing what was perceived as treatment gains by treatment providers, and then complete the programs, displaying higher levels of recidivism, particularly violent recidivism, than nonpsychopaths (Seto & Barbaree, 1999). Therefore, if a correctional treatment program provides significant incentives for participation (i.e., eligibility for parole, early release from confinement, etc.), assessing level of psychopathy might be warranted in order to assist with determining truthfulness about motivation for treatment. While it might not be possible to exclude individuals from treatment based on PCL-R score, it would at least allow treatment providers to more accurately assess treatment gains and be alert for faking if the level of psychopathy is known up front.

KEY POINTS

- Psychopathy level is best measured using the PCL-R.
- Psychopaths may be more likely to attempt to engage in deception, though they may not be more skilled at this deception.
- Research shows that psychopaths are not likely to be any better at malingering mental illness than nonpsychopaths.
- There is some support for the idea that psychopaths can be better at deception than nonpsychopaths, particularly if the psychopathic individual has more Factor 1 traits as opposed to Factor 2 traits of the construct.
- Because psychopaths are not necessarily better at malingering than nonpsychopaths, assessing psychopathy is very time consuming, and determining that one is psychopathic does not necessarily mean he or she is malingering; completing an assessment of psychopathy as part of a forensic assessment of malingering would likely only be warranted to add to other assessment information more specifically aimed at detecting malingering.
- Assessing psychopathy in an evaluation in which "faking-good" is suspected might be more useful.
- An area where knowledge of psychopathy score might be especially useful is in screening prospective participants for a correctional treatment program, since psychopathic individuals have been found to be able to fake improvement in sex offender treatment. This is particularly true if the program provides strong incentives for participation.
- Assessing psychopathy may augment an evaluation of deception. However, it is critical to remember that a high level of psychopathy does not automatically mean that an individual is being deceptive. It does mean that it might be necessary to further explore the possibility of deception if one has not already done so.

Conclusions

PUTTING IT ALL TOGETHER

This book has explored many different types of deception and ways of assessing them. We discussed causes of negative response bias, including malingering and Factitious Disorder, random and careless responding, and two types of socially desirable responding, positive impression management and self-deceptive enhancement. We will now turn to a more deliberate presentation of when and how to conduct an assessment of deception and what to do with the results of such an assessment.

Understanding these issues means that one must first take a look at the context of the assessment. Different situations and settings will include different implications for assessing deception. We will examine various settings and types of assessment and the special considerations within each. Then we will discuss the importance of utilizing multiple data sources in an assessment of deception. We will further discuss the issue of test selection, and then provide examples of three different types of assessment and how deception plays a role in each.

SETTINGS AND TYPES OF ASSESSMENT

Perhaps the most obvious type of assessment in which deception should always be considered is the forensic assessment. There are various settings in which forensic assessments can be done. For example, a pretrial evaluation may be conducted in a jail, forensic hospital, or federal prison. In such an evaluation, typically one would be looking for malingering, or a deliberate attempt to feign some illness or disability so as to appear not competent to stand trial or not responsible for one's criminal actions. Of course, there are also cases in which the defendant is truly ill and is attempting to hide this or present in an overly positive manner. More often, socially desirable responding is likely to take place in parole or risk assessment evaluations where the goal is to appear as well-adjusted as possible so as to be seen as a good candidate for release from custody.

Other types of forensic evaluations that typically do not occur in a correctional setting include child custody evaluations, or any of the various types of assessments described by Andrews and Meyer (2003), which are presented in Chapter 4. In these evaluations, as reported by Andrews and Meyer, the tendency is for socially desirable responding to occur and negative response bias would be rare. An example of a similar type of case is presented below. Also forensic in nature but occurring outside of a correctional or criminal setting is the disability evaluation. In this type of evaluation the subject is evaluated for his or her ability to return to work or need to remain on long-term disability payments. An example of this sort is presented later in this chapter. Also, a subject may sue for damages due to some alleged negligence by another party. Often the degree of suffering or psychological damages needs to be determined and can be assessed in a similar way.

There are other types of evaluations in which deception may be present that are not forensic in nature. One example of such a setting would be employment evaluations. In such evaluations, individuals may be likely to present themselves in a socially desirable manner. However, it is important to remember that, just because an individual is responding in a socially desirable fashion, this does not necessarily mean that the person would not be a good candidate for the job. Remember, some level of socially desirable responding is normal in such settings. Simply reporting the results of the assessment, including deception if it is present, and allowing the employer to make decisions based on the information is more appropriate.

In general treatment settings, it is possible that a client may present with some sort of response bias. This could be social desirability of negative response bias. An individual responding in an overly pathological manner may be presenting with a Factitious Disorder, or may be seeking medications or admission to a special treatment program. Motivation is key in determining whether an individual is malingering, displaying a Factitious Disorder, or simply making a cry for help. An example of a correctional treatment setting in which malingering is suspected is presented below.

MULTIPLE DATA SOURCES

In this volume, we have presented a variety of methods for uncovering deception in behavior and psychological presentation. At times when we have discussed a single test or observation practice, we have alluded to the importance of using multiple methods of assessment. The reasoning for this is simple: No single method is 100% accurate. Furthermore, the conclusions drawn from an assessment can be used in the formulation of life-altering consequences. It is easy to see the potential ramifications of incorrectly identifying deception in employment settings, pretrial contexts, and custody or personal injury disputes. While some testing is done in private practice therapy settings simply to clarify diagnostic issues, even that form of investigation can have lasting effects. Clinicians must be careful of labeling an individual as mentally ill, knowing the stigma attached to such a label. The same is true of categorizing a client as malingering. Inept practice in assessment certainly violates ethical standards. Thus, we proffer the belief that deception rarely occurs in a vacuum. By this, we mean that an evaluee who feigns illness or misrepresents himself or herself on one measure is likely to do so at more than one time, on more than one measure, and even in more than one setting.

In exploring motivation and examining the possibility of deception in psychological evaluations, we propose the use of the Multiple Data Sources Model (McLearen, Pietz, & Denney, 2004; Mrad, 1996). Through the use of this model, the assessment process can be seen as an attempt to determine where the evidence converges, while explaining any divergent information.

Applications of this model tend to be forensic in nature, but the idea behind the model is simple: Assessment should involve review of as much data as is feasible given time, budget, and other constraints. Applications of the model can be complex, and the reader is referred to original sources for more information (McLearen et al., 2004; Mrad, 1996). In this tome, we use a loose interpretation of the model because it can be broadly applied across settings and referral questions. We recognize that dependent on setting, referral question, and other aforementioned concerns, various components of the model will be of greater or lesser importance.

Basically, the Multiple Data Sources Model suggests that information be collected based on two dimensions: time and source. With regard to the time variable, this means a thorough assessment should involve a review of both past and present functioning. Additionally, likely future functioning should be noted. For example, consider a vocational rehabilitation evaluation following an automobile accident. Information regarding premorbid functioning of the injured party allows for a determination of the effects of the accident and provides a context for discussion of current functioning. The combination of information collected at those two times can then be used to suggest the examinee's potential future functioning, and ultimately, the feasibility or necessity of rehabilitation. Information should come together to form a cohesive picture of this person based on the time events. The presence of deception would interrupt the transition from one time to the next.

The Multiple Data Sources Model indicates that information should not be gleaned from only a single moment in time. Additionally, the model suggests that, when feasible, data should not come only from a single source. Three potential sources of information exist: self-report, clinician observation, and third party data. Typically, when we think of assessment, we think of self-report information. Test performance falls within this category, and self-report data usually comprises the bulk of an evaluation. When deception is a possibility, and in any thorough examination, other sources of information should be reviewed. These other sources can be in the form of records (e.g., criminal, school, medical) or as interviews of parties known to the evaluee (e.g., relatives, friends, employers). Again, deception shows up in the model as something that interrupts consistency.

At this point, we should note that the model is not a model for detecting deception. Instead, it provides a framework for conducting evaluations in which the consideration of response bias, malingering, impression management, or other disingenuous performance may occur. It allows the examiner a way to tell the story of the evaluee, and highlights areas that should be consistent or inconsistent, which then isolate potential dissimulation.

Application of the Multiple Data Sources Model provides a conceptual structure to the evaluation process, and can be of assistance in report writing. For example, it makes sense for a report to flow from past to future. Information in each category can be further divided by source, which may add clarity when the time comes for clinical formulation.

Additionally, the Multiple Data Sources Model allows the clinician some assistance in self-monitoring. In an effort to ensure quality control, the evaluator needs only to look and see whether the various dimensions have been adequately covered, and if not, to provide the rationale in the final report or documentation. At times, past records may be unavailable or, as many practitioners have found, previous providers may be loathe to release them. Accurate conclusions can be drawn without such information, but the reason for its absence from the clinical formulation process should be noted.

TEST SELECTION ISSUES

In terms of test selection, there are several different issues to consider. Many types of assessments will benefit from the initial use of a general measure of personality functioning, such as the MMPI-2. This measure is relatively inexpensive, and though it takes some time to administer, it can provide valuable information about response set as well as actual areas of clinical concern if the respondent does not appear to be responding with bias. If the individual does appear to be responding with some sort of bias, then additional measures can be selected based on the type of bias suggested by the MMPI-2. For example, if the MMPI-2 suggests negative response bias of a psychiatric nature (i.e., elevations on F, Fb, and F[p]), a more sensitive measure of malingering may be warranted, such as the SIRS, or one of the screening measures discussed in Chapter 4. If FBS is significantly elevated on the MMPI-2, neuropsychological measures of negative response bias, such as those discussed in Chapter 5, will, perhaps, be warranted. If social desirability is suggested, based on elevations on L, K, SD, Sd, S, Mp, and/or Tt, additional measures, such as the PDS or the MCSDS may be indicated. In addition to providing direction for additional measures to use, the MMPI-2 may provide information to use in a clinical interview about the possible response set of the individual. Depending on the setting, the clinician may want to conduct a clinical interview prior to administering any testing, so that the interviewer will not be biased. This might be the case, especially in treatment settings.

Another way to approach test selection is to look at the type of evaluation and the setting in which it is occurring. Many different types of evaluations and settings in which they occur were presented previously. In each of the different types of assessment, there will be differing issues of importance. For example, in disability evaluation involving a head injury, it may not be necessary to first use a general measure to guide the direction of the rest of the assessment. It is likely that a full neuropsychological battery would be indicated to assess for genuine deficits, with some measures of negative response bias added to determine if the subject is exaggerating or feigning symptoms or disability. Likewise, in a child custody or employment evaluation, while the MMPI-2 or similar general measure may be indicated, it may be prudent to go ahead and also administer other measures of social desirability, given the high incidence of such responding in these types of evaluations.

Another issue to consider in test selection is resource allocation. Depending on the resources available in the setting in which the evaluation is taking place, certain considerations of time and financial limitations may need to be considered. Some tests like the MMPI-2, the SIRS, and the PCL-R take quite a bit of time to administer. Spending the time to administer such tests is worthwhile if the test in question clearly seems to be the most appropriate one to use. However, if there are other shorter measures that can provide a screening to determine if these longer measures are necessary, it might be smart to do so. Similarly, some measures are very expensive, such as the SIRS. It may be prudent to use a screening measure of malingering, such as one of those discussed in Chapter 4, prior to using the expensive SIRS in order to save unnecessary money being spent on such an expensive measure if it is not indicated.

CASE EXAMPLES*

We now turn our attention to three case examples designed to cover practice in a variety of settings and specialty areas. Each example contains differing amounts of information, consistent with assessment in the real world. Despite the major differences in setting, available information, and referral question, it should be clear that the fictional examiners are adhering to the Multiple Data Sources Model framework by exploring various sources of information and looking at chronological information.

Example One – Neuropsychological Evaluation of Disability

Mr. Singer was a 52-year-old, left-handed, Caucasian man referred for Independent Neuropsychological Evaluation by his disability carrier. He underwent liver transplantation 6 years previously. Since that time he has complained about memory, concentration, and word-finding difficulties.

Mr. Singer underwent clinical interview and was administered the tests listed in the table on page 209. A corroborative interview was done with his wife of 30 years. Medical records reviewed included all records related to his liver transplant preparation, surgery, and follow-up; notes from psychiatric outpatient visits; neurological examination, including MRI of the brain; and neuropsychological report (done 2 years previously).

Medical Data

Medical information suggested that prior to the development of liver disease, Mr. Singer had no history of neurological or psychiatric concerns. He had no history of substance abuse. He initially presented in 1998 with

---

* The clients described in these case examples are fictional. They are composites of a wide range of cases and bear no relationship to actual clients, living or deceased.

TABLE 3: Neuropsychological Test Results for Example 1

Rey-15 Item Test
Recall: 15
Recognition: 15
Passed

K-BIT
IQ: 118
Vocabulary: 117
Matrices: 115

CARB
Block 1: 86.5%
Block 2: 81.1%
Block 3: 70.3%
Failed

WMT
IR: 80%
DR: 77.5%
CNS1: 77.5%
MC: 55%
PA: 65%
FR: 27.5%
LDFR: 35%
Failed

Trail Making Test
Part A: 24"; T54
Part B: 74"; T45

Booklet Category Test
38 errors; T43

Thurstone Word Fluency
57 words; T49

Finger Tapping
Dom: 54.5; T54
Ndom: 39.7; T38

Grip Strength
Dom: 42kg; T40
Ndom: 42.5; T44

Grooved Pegboard
Dom: 69"; T49
Ndom: 90"; T39L

WMS-III
Auditory Immediate:	105
Visual Immediate:	88
Immediate Memory:	96
Auditory Delayed:	102
Visual Delayed:	91
Auditory Recog. Del.:	85
General Memory:	92
Working Memory:	108

MMPI-2	Raw	T		
L:	4	52	Hs:	86
F:	14	79	D:	91
FB:	4	59	Hy:	101
K:	13	45	Pd:	72
VRIN:	10	69	Mf:	68
FBS:	24		Pa:	57
			Pt:	61
			Sc:	84

Rey Complex Figure
Copy: >16th percentile
Immediate Recall: T49

chronic ulcerative colitis and sclerosing cholangitis, and he was developing cirrhosis. He developed pancreatitis and was in and out of the hospital several times with septicemia. He eventually went through liver transplantation, but the transplant failed within the first 72 hours. He then received a second transplant. His course was further complicated by inferior vena cava thrombosis and wound infections. He was rehospitalized 6 months after the transplant due to elevated liver function test results. He underwent bile duct reconstruction shortly thereafter. He developed autoimmune cholangitis, and his immunosuppressive medication was changed. Follow-up clinic and transplant coordinator notations revealed that his condition progressed satisfactorily and without significant difficulty thereafter.

Records, dated 2 years later, indicated he complained of side effects after changing his immunosuppressive regimen. He complained of exhaustion, low energy, decreased stamina, fluid retention, headaches, and memory problems. Follow-up notes and laboratory results revealed stable and normalizing findings. His ammonia was normal and stable.

Neurological examination found no conclusive evidence to support his contention that he suffered "irreversible brain damage as a result of the transplant complications." MRI of the brain was normal. The neurologist concluded it may have been possible he sustained irreversible and disabling brain injury; however, it is not possible to draw the conclusion from currently available information. He was then evaluated by a neuropsychologist. Results revealed a WAIS-III FSIQ in the superior range at 121, WMS-III Working Memory Index in the high average range at 118, Immediate Memory Index in the low average range at 89, and delayed memory performance in the borderline range with a General Memory Index of 79. His poor memory scores were considered due to depression and anxiety.

Mr. Singer continued under psychiatric care and received various antidepressant medications. He was considered to have significant depression and occasional anxiety.

Historical Data

Mr. Singer graduated nearly top in his high school class. He then achieved a Bachelors of Science degree with a double major in mathematics and economics. He later obtained an MBA from a prestigious business school. He developed a specialty for himself as a trade analyst and hedge funds manager. He enjoyed the quick pace and challenge of this work and provided services to a variety of banking institutions. He is currently on long-term disability.

Daily Activities

Mr. Singer said his typical day varies a great deal because of his wife's schedule. Typically he gets up at 6:00 a.m. and fixes breakfast for his wife. He spends considerable time going through their tax and insurance paperwork. He takes care of all the bills, and he handles most all of their investments. He receives myriad medical insurance copays and bills, which he deals with 3 days per week. He also checks his stock portfolio. He does not perform day-trading, but he uses his background in trading to maximize their investments by trading shares online.

He is preparing his own taxes and has been working on it for a month now and said he is still finding things he forgot. He said prior to transplantation completing the taxes took only 1 week to finish.

On nice days, he plays golf. He drives to the course and completes 18 holes. He said he is trying to get back to walking 18 holes for health reasons, but currently walks nine and rides nine.

He said he does most of the grocery shopping and 90% of the cooking. He said he is not supposed to clean the house or do gardening due to a weakened immune system. However, he does clean now and then.

Mental Status and Behavioral Observations

Mr. Singer arrived on time after traveling from a nearby city with the assistance of a hired driver. The examinee was dressed in a nice, but casual, manner. His hygiene was very good. His posture and fluidity of gait were normal. His speech was normal in rate, form, and content. His affect was euthymic and mood congruent throughout the majority of the examination. He demonstrated good eye contact.

He demonstrated a behavioral episode during the latter portion of the CARB, where he stated he did not wish to continue the test and was shaking both upper extremities in a large, and mirrored, tremor. With encouragement, he completed the test. He later stated he had never experienced an episode like that before. He attributed it to the stress and difficulty of the task.

During the seventh subtest of the Booklet Category Test, Mr. Singer demonstrated nearly word-for-word recollection of the subtest instructions when he pointed out the presence of an odd and not previously seen item. During the WMS-III Logical Memory Recognition subtest, he refused to answer a question even after multiple requests, saying, "I don't know that information, so I don't have enough information to answer that question."

He was oriented to his name, age, birth date, current and past president, year, month, day, location, and time. He had no difficulty counting from 1 to 20, reciting the alphabet, reciting the days of the week forward and backward, and reciting the months of the year forward and backward. He accurately counted by serial sixes when pairing the results with the days of the week. His speed during each of these tasks was excellent enough to gain bonus points.

Validity Issues

Mr. Singer was administered more than one test sensitive to poor effort. He made a perfect performance during the recall and recognition portions of the Rey 15 Item Memory Test, which is a rather transparent malingering measure. In contrast, his performance during the CARB, a more sophisticated measure, suggested significant negative response bias. He scored below the criterion-related cut offs for detection of improper effort on all three trials. In addition, his performance worsened with each trial. This worsening pattern of performance is not seen with people who are appropriately applying themselves. His overall performance on this measure was over seven standard deviations below the average of severely brain injured patients. Such a score is statistically impossible for an individual giving their best appropriate effort – especially an individual who was not obviously, and grossly, impaired in their activities of daily living.

Mr. Singer performed in a similarly unrealistic manner during the Word Memory Test. This test is comprised of scales that are sensitive to improper effort, but are not sensitive to all but the most severe brain dysfunction. In addition, it contains legitimate memory scales that allow identification of genuine and disingenuous memory patterns. The pattern of his performance is consistent with the pattern obtained by individuals attempting to simulate cognitive deficits. His performance fell multiple standard deviations below the average performance of severely brain-injured individuals on the easiest of scales, while his performance was within the low normal range on the most difficult aspect of this test. This overall pattern of performance is not consistent with genuine memory disorder.

The claimant's performance during these tests of effort allowed little doubt that the validity of the remaining neuropsychological test results was questionable. Even though he may have performed reasonably well on many other tests in this battery, his performance was likely not reflective of his true abilities given the apparent inconsistencies. Last, on the MMPI-2 he produced a Lees-Haley Fake Bad Scale score of 24 which suggested overreporting somatic concerns, even for an individual who is living with a transplanted liver.

Clinical Formulation

Performance during validity testing reveal his clinical results are not valid, due to improper effort. His behavior during testing suggested he may have been attempting to appear disingenuously impaired. Given the context, there is significant secondary gain in continuing to live in a "medical retirement" status.

Results of this testing are not consistent with legitimate brain injury. He performed implausibly poor during simple memory tests, while performing in the average and low average ranges in difficult memory tests. The course of Mr. Singer's "deficits" also do not appear consistent with legitimate brain injury when comparing this performance obtained here with that obtained during the previous neuropsychological evaluation.

By all accounts, his liver function has been stable. Barring elevations in ammonia level, liver disease patients have predominantly normal cognition. There is only a small amount of research on the presence of neurocognitive compromise after liver transplantation. The results of this research suggest no neurocognitive compromise in this population of individuals.

Regarding depression, he did not appear significantly impaired by depression. He elevated scales sensitive to depression on the MMPI-2 to a significant level, but the problem is he overendorsed items of severe pathology to such a degree the results were meaningless. His wife noted his personality has changed in that he has lost his sense of humor and is pessimistic. Irritability and pessimism may be due to depression, but it does not appear to meet the diagnostic criteria for major depression. He displayed no lack of energy or lack of interest in doing activities. For example, he actively sought out a restaurant for lunch on the day of the evaluation by asking questions and walked a small number of blocks to find one that interested him. Any depression he might have is certainly not so severe as to cause neurocognitive deficits.

There is a possibility he suffers from an anxiety disorder, although the anxiety scale was one of only two or three scales that were not elevated to significant levels on the MMPI-2. He demonstrated a "panic-like" episode during testing that appeared "put on" rather than legitimate panic, although it could have theoretically been an anxiety manifestation. Neither he nor his wife noted panic disorder symptoms, and he said he never experienced an event like it before. There was really very little suggestion of anxiety disorder when discussing his daily routine and recent symptoms.

Given available information and current test results, malingering must be seriously considered. It should always be ruled out in the medicolegal context, particularly when there is potential for substantial secondary gain, marked discrepancy between claimed disability and objective test findings, and lack of cooperation during diagnostic testing. Considering Slick et al. (1999) classification criteria for "possible," "probable," and "definite" malingering of neurocognitive dysfunction is helpful. Mr. Singer's performance meets the criteria for probable malingered neurocognitive dysfunction because his evaluation occurred in the context of substantial secondary gain. By continuing to receive medical disability such that he can continue his current leisure-filled lifestyle, there exists probable response bias defined as positive performance on one or more well-validated psychometric tests designed to measure exaggeration or fabrication of cognitive deficits (he was positive on two), discrepancy between test data and known patterns of brain functioning, discrepancy between test data and reliable collateral reports (in this instance his severely impaired performance on the CARB and WMT in light of his ability to pay the bills, prepare taxes, and monitor their investments), and discrepancy between test data and documented background history (in the nature of his alleged brain injury during medical procedures). Only two or more of the criteria are needed, and his performance meets four of six possible criteria (see Table 3, p. 209). Given this information, it appears that Mr. Singer is malingering neurocognitive dysfunction.

The presence of malingering does not automatically rule out the presence of sincere neurocognitive deficits. Mr. Singer may have some very mild cognitive difficulties. He may not be functioning at the same level of cognitive ability as he was prior to the transplantation. This would not be surprising given his historically superior intellectual ability. It is impossible to determine his true level of functioning due to invalid test results. Given his test results and reported daily and weekly activities, there is nothing, from a neurocognitive perspective, limiting his ability to return to a productive work setting.

Example Two – Child Custody Case

Mrs. Diaz is a 29-year-old Caucasian woman who was ordered by the court to undergo a psychological evaluation. She had gone to court because of a dispute with her ex-husband about his visitation with their 6-year-old son. Mrs. Diaz had previously been awarded custody of the boy. She had a college education, was of average intelligence, and would likely be considered middle-class, in terms of SES. She worked in a secretarial position. She was not suspected of child abuse or neglect. She was cooperative during the interview and testing. Because the referral question was so narrow, testing was limited to the MMPI-2, the MCSDS, and the PDS. The scores on these measures are presented in Table 4 (p. 215).

TABLE 4: Test Results for Example 2, Administration 1

MMPI-2	Raw	T
VRIN	6	57
L	7	67
F	2	44
K	22	65
Fb	1	46
F(p)	0	41
Sd	20	74
Mp	15	70
S	30	55
SD	29	
Tt	14	
Od	16	
O-S	-10	
MCSDS		
Total Score	23	

PDS	Raw	T
IM	15	73
SDE	3	53
Total	18	76

Looking first at VRIN, it can be seen that Mrs. Diaz did not respond in a random fashion to the MMPI-2. On the traditional validity scales, there appeared to be some areas for concern. Her L and K scale scores were slightly elevated, and F was very low, which raised a concern about possible defensive responding. The high L score was not the result of low education or SES, and may suggest that Mrs. Diaz was attempting to deny that she is susceptible to any common human difficulties. She may have difficulty dealing with stress (it is likely that this court-ordered evaluation was stressful), or be inflexible in her approach to problem solving. The K score suggested that she was trying to deny having any vulnerabilities and present herself as having a "stiff upper lip." Taken together, the moderately high L and K and the low F suggested that she was faking-good, at least to an extent, and that this denial may have been partially intentional (IM) and partially unintentional (SDE). None of the clinical scales were elevated above a T-score of 65, which is not surprising considering her negative history of mental health problems. Her Mean Elevation was 45.6, just into the normal range.

To further understand the mild elevations on L and K, it is important to look at the other scales measuring socially desirable responding on the MMPI-2 as well as the PDS and MCSDS. First of all, on the MMPI-2, the scales that tend to be better at measuring IM, L, Mp, and Sd, were all slightly elevated. The scores typically measuring more of a SDE style of responding, K, SD, and S, were not clearly elevated. SD and S were just below the cut offs suggesting socially desirable responding and K was in an area suggesting possibly overly positive responding, but it was not elevated to an extent that this would clearly be the case. Other scales of interest on the MMPI-2 included the Od, scale which was just below the cut off, and the Tt scale, which was right at the cut off, suggesting overly positive responding. The O-S index was well below the suggested cut off for social desirability.

On the MCSDS, Mrs. Diaz obtained a fairly high score. Remember that in Andrews and Meyer's (2003) study of forensic norms on the MCSDS, the group with the highest mean score (22.46) was the group being evaluated for access of possible custody of a child, who were not suspected of abuse or neglect of a child. Mrs. Diaz's score is very consistent with the average score of individuals in a situation similar to hers. On the PDS, Mrs. Diaz obtained an IM score significantly above average; the SDE score is only slightly above average and not a reason for concern. Remember that Paulhus (1998) suggested that if the IM score is high and the SDE score is low, this is a healthy profile, indicating that the individual is aware of her own faults, but that this likely indicates some level of overly positive self-presentation. Mrs. Diaz was likely influenced by the circumstances of her evaluation to present herself in a socially desirable way.

Mrs. Diaz completed the MMPI-2, MCSDS, and PDS under difficult circumstances. A great deal of ambiguity surrounded the purpose of the testing, with the judge's referral being only for a "psychological evaluation." Even when the examiner attempted to obtain more clarification on the referral question, nothing more specific than this was provided. There was no indication in the referral that the judge wished for the child to be evaluated. With the ambiguous nature of the assessment, Mrs. Diaz was clearly anxious about what the results would be used for. She was not sure whether her ex-husband was going to sue her for custody, or if his visitation would be the only matter under consideration in the court proceedings.

Mrs. Diaz appeared quite anxious during clinical interviews. However, she seemed quite candid about her relationship with her ex-husband and the difficulties leading up to the current circumstances. She did not appear to be trying to gloss over her role in her divorce or the conflicts she had with her ex-husband. Because of her obvious anxiety about the situation, and the inconsistency between her somewhat elevated scores suggestive of impression management and her relative frankness during interviews, the examiner spoke with her about the first MMPI-2, MCSDS, and PDS she completed and what the results suggested. She was told that her reaction to the testing was understandable, given her situation, and she was offered an opportunity to take the tests again. This second set of scores is presented in Table 5 (p. 218).

Mrs. Diaz's second MMPI-2 appeared to be less problematic upon examination of the validity scales. Her L scale score decreased to within the normal range and her K scale score decreased slightly. Most of her scores on other measures of social desirability decreased somewhat. In fact, the only score that remained obviously above the cut off, suggestive of self-favorable responding, was the Sd score. Her clinical scale scores remained in the normal range and her ME increased to 48.2, still within the normal range. Her scores on the MCSDS and PDS decreased as well and no longer appeared nearly as suggestive of intentional socially desirable responding. Her IM score on the PDS decreased significantly while her SDE score remained in the acceptable range. She did seem to have made an effort to respond as honestly as possible, based on conversations with her both before and after the testing.

In reporting the results of the testing to the court, the examiner did make note of the first set of testing results by stating that it was believed

TABLE 5: Test Results for Example 2, Administration 2

MMPI-2	Raw	T
VRIN	5	52
L	5	57
F	2	44
K	20	61
Fb	1	46
F(p)	0	41
Sd	19	71
Mp	12	61
S	28	53
SD	27	
Tt	13	
Od	13	
O-S	-10	
MCSDS		
Total Score	19	

PDS	Raw	T
IM	11	62
SDE	3	53
Total	14	65

that the ambiguity of the situation had contributed to Mrs. Diaz's anxiety and at least partially led to the overly positive presentation in the first tests. The results of the second test were presented and interpreted as being valid and suggestive of a generally well-adjusted individual, who was under stress, and perhaps having some difficulty dealing with it, and as a result responding in a manner that suggested she did not want to admit to any vulnerabilities or difficulties.

Example Three – Correctional Treatment Setting

Inmate Rinker presented at the prison psychology department complaining of anxiety. He had been seen by the medical department after reporting he was in need of treatment for anxiety and depression. The basic medical workup done at intake had shown no physiological abnormalities, and the physician's assistant (PA) referred the inmate to the psychologist to determine whether he suffered from a mental disorder, and whether he should be provided with psychotropic medication.

Prison records, including a report written by a member of the probation department before sentencing, were reviewed. Inmate Rinker was serving 10 years for a drug-related offense, and had been incarcerated approximately 4 months at the time he approached staff indicating he was experiencing stress and depression.

Interviews with unit officers revealed the inmate to have adjusted appropriately. He was enrolled in mandatory GED classes and was working on the carpentry detail. His supervisor described him as fairly lazy, but noted that as long he monitored the inmate closely, his work was good. Disciplinary documentation showed that during the brief time the inmate had been in custody, he had been caught in possession of marijuana and was suspected of being drunk on more than one occasion.

The report from the probation department indicated that the inmate had experienced a rough childhood and at one point, had been placed in a special school for youth with behavioral issues. He had several juvenile arrests for minor infractions, including possession of marijuana. Records also revealed a significant substance abuse history, including hallucinogens, opiates, and narcotics. While at the county jail awaiting sentencing, the inmate had been prescribed trazodone for sleep problems by a consulting physician.

After reviewing these records, the psychologist conducted a clinical interview with inmate Rinker, who indicated he was "bipolar." He stated his moods were constantly shifting and mentioned that he had gotten medication for his problems when in the county jail. When asked to elaborate on his symptoms of bipolar disorder, inmate Rinker again stated that his moods shifted rapidly. When questioned about the frequency of these mood shifts, he stated that his moods went up and down several times per day. He also stated that he felt nervous and stressed all the time and could not concentrate enough to read a book. He described symptoms consistent with panic attacks, such as heart palpitations and shortness of breath. He also reported that he sometimes thought he heard crying babies. He asked if he could get "something" to help him sleep. The psychologist began to explain some relaxation techniques that are often found helpful with individuals who have sleep difficulties. Inmate Rinker quickly stated he was not capable of attempting relaxation exercises due to his concentration problems and jumpiness. He professed the belief that a stronger dosage of the same medication he was given in the past would likely help him deal with his current difficulties.

During the interview, inmate Rinker presented several behavioral cues that suggested he was being less than truthful about his reported difficulties. On several occasions he appeared to be attempting to squelch facial expressions suggestive of anger. This was particularly the case when he was asked to elaborate on the symptoms he was reporting. Further, inmate Rinker displayed many pauses in his speech when he was asked to provide more details about his difficulty. Of course, inmate Rinker's report of his symptoms was questionable as well. He reported that he had bipolar disorder, but did not describe true symptoms of this disorder when asked to elaborate on his difficulties. As was suggested in Chapter 1, inmate Rinker was not provided with a checklist of symptoms during the interview that may have provided him with enough information to convincingly describe symptoms of a mood disorder.

Based on the interview, the TMS was scored, and a significant elevation was noted. At this point, the psychologist hypothesized the inmate could be malingering, but wanted to further investigate the veracity of his claims, as he had reported some possibly legitimate anxiety symptoms.

Inmate Rinker was administered the SIRS. He obtained three scale elevations in probable range: Blatant Symptoms, Subtle Symptoms, and Selectivity of Symptoms. His total score on the instrument was 82. Scoring criteria indicate that three or more scales in the probable range are suggestive of malingering. Total scores greater than 76 on the instrument also provide evidence of response bias. The presence of an external motivation for feigning psychological symptoms was present in inmate Rinker's repeated requests for medication. Therefore, malingering seemed likely.

At this point, the psychologist decided that further testing was unlikely to produce valid profiles or information useful in answering the referral question. The psychologist concluded that while the inmate might be having some minor stress related to adjustment to incarceration, his symptoms could easily be treated through behavioral interventions and supportive therapy. Those options were offered to inmate Rinker, who promptly declined. The inmate did not meet criteria for a mood disorder. His presentation was not consistent with his reports, and his scores on the two measures of malingering, in combination with his external motive, suggested he was engaging in dissimulation. Based on the inmate's history of drug abuse and the information collected during interviews and testing, the psychologist concluded that the inmate was most likely seeking medication for abusive purposes and was exaggerating his level of distress. He was not referred back to medical staff for psychotropic treatment of mental disorder.

SUMMARY

As can be seen from the examples given, there are many different sources of information present in an evaluation setting. It is important to pay attention to each of these sources of information, as the Multiple Data Sources Model suggests. In each of the cases described, interview and test information were combined and compared. It is always important to note whether the individual's presentation both in and out of the interview situation is consistent with the symptoms being reported, or lack thereof. In the first example, Mr. Singer's ability to manage his tasks of daily living was clearly inconsistent with the extreme level of impairment he displayed on some of the assessment measures. In the second example, Mrs. Diaz appeared much more frank and open in interviews than she did in her testing. In the third example, inmate Rinker presented with some behavioral cues suggestive of possible deception. He reported symptoms that were not consistent with genuine mental illness, his records showed no clear history of mental illness, and his behaviors (i.e., declining therapy, refusing to try other methods for improving sleep) were not consistent with those of someone seeking help for a problem as much as with someone seeking medication.

Hopefully, these examples will provide some guides on how to gather and integrate information in an assessment when deception is suspected. It is important to note here that training and supervision are needed in order for an individual to be qualified to conduct many of the types of evaluations discussed in this book. This volume is intended for an audience of psychologists, and therefore those reading it are very familiar with various assessment techniques and interpretive strategies. The information presented here is intended to expand upon those skills to improve the ability to assess deception in various settings. However, this book will not make it possible for someone to conduct forensic or neuropsychological assessments if he or she has not obtained sufficient training in such.

REFERENCES

Adelson, R. (2004). Detecting deception. *Monitor on Psychology, 35*(7), 70-73.

Allen, L. M., Conder, R. L., Green, P., & Cox, D. R. (1997). *CARB '97: Manual for the Computerized Assessment of Response Bias.* Durham, NC: CogniSyst, Inc.

Allen, L. M., Iverson, G. L., & Green, P. (2002). Computerized Assessment of Response Bias in forensic neuropsychology. In J. Hom & R. L. Denney (Eds.), *Detection of Response Bias in Forensic Neuropsychology* (pp. 205-225). West Hazleton, PA: Haworth.

Alterman, A. I., Rutherford, M. J., Cacciola, J. S., & Boardman, C. R. (1998). Prediction of 7 months methadone maintenance treatment response by four measures of antisociality [Abstract]. *Drug and Alcohol Dependence, 49*, 217-223.

American Psychiatric Association. (1994). *Diagnostic and Statistical Manual of Mental Disorders* (4th ed.). Washington, DC: Author.

American Psychiatric Association. (2000). *Diagnostic and Statistical Manual of Mental Disorders* (4th ed. text revision). Washington, DC: Author.

American Psychological Association. (2002). *Ethical Principles of Psychologists and Code of Conduct.* Washington, DC: Author.

Andrews P., & Meyer, R. G. (2003). Marlowe-Crowne Social Desirability Scale and Short Form C: Forensic norms. *Journal of Clinical Psychology, 59*, 483-492.

Arbisi, P. A., & Ben-Porath, Y. S. (1995). An MMPI-2 infrequent response scale for use with psychopathological populations: The Infrequency-Psychopathology Scale, F(p). *Psychological Assessment, 7*, 87-102.

Arbisi, P. A., & Ben-Porath, Y. S. (1998). The ability of Minnesota Multiphasic Personality Inventory-2 validity scales to detect fake-bad responses in psychiatric inpatients. *Psychological Assessment, 10*, 221-228.

Archer, R. P. (1992). *MMPI-A: Assessing Adolescent Psychopathology.* Hillsdale, NJ: Erlbaum.

Archer, R. P., Fontaine, J., & McCrae, R. R. (1998). Effects of two MMPI-2 validity scales on basic scale relations to external criteria. *Journal of Personality Assessment, 70*, 87-102.

Ardolf, B., Denney, R. L., & Houston, C. (2004, November). *Base Rate of Negative Response Bias Among Criminal Defendants Referred for Neuropsychological Evaluation.* Poster presented at the 24th annual conference of the National Academy of Neuropsychology, Seattle, WA.

Aronow, E., Reznikoff, M., & Moreland, K. (1994). *The Rorschach Technique: Perceptual Basis, Content Interpretation, and Applications.* Boston: Allyn & Bacon.

Ashendorf, L., Constantinou, M., & McCaffrey, R. J. (2004). The effect of depression and anxiety on the TOMM in community-dwelling older adults. *Archives of Clinical Neuropsychology, 19*, 125-130.

Atkins, D. G. (1999). Validity of the Personality Assessment Inventory for detecting malingering of psychosis in a prison population (Doctoral dissertation, Fielding Graduate University). *Dissertation Abstracts International 60* (4-B), 1839.

Baer, R. A., Wetter, M. W., Nichols, D. S., Green, R., & Berry, D. T. R. (1995). Sensitivity of MMPI-2 validity scales to underreporting of symptoms. *Psychological Assessment, 7*, 419-423.

Bagby, M. R., Nicholson, R. A., & Buis, T. (1998). Utility of the Deceptive-Subtle items in the detection of malingering. *Journal of Personality Assessment, 70*, 405-415.

Bagby, M. R., Nicholson, R. A., Buis, T., Radavanavic, H., & Fidler, B. J. (1999). Defensive responding on the MMPI-2 in family custody and access evaluations. *Psychological Assessment, 11*, 24-28.

Bagby, M. R., Rogers, R., & Buis, T. (1994). Detecting malingered and defensive responding on the MMPI-2 in a forensic inpatient sample. *Journal of Personality Assessment, 62*, 191-203.

Bagby, M. R., Rogers, R., Nicholson, R. A., Buis, T., Seeman, M. V., & Rector, N. A. (1997). Effectiveness of the MMPI-2 validity indicators in the detection of defensive responding in clinical and nonclinical samples. *Psychological Assessment, 9*, 406-413.

Ballard, R. (1992). Short forms of the Marlowe-Crowne Social Desirability Scale. *Psychological Reports, 71*, 1155-1160.

Ballard, R., Crino, M. D., & Rubenfeld, S. (1988). Social desirability response bias and the Marlowe-Crowne Social Desirability Scale. *Psychological Reports, 63*, 227-237.

Barger, S. D. (2002). The Marlowe-Crowne affair: Short forms, psychometric structure, and social desirability. *Journal of Personality Assessment, 79*, 286-305.

Bartol, C., & Bartol, A. (2004). *Psychology and Law*. Belmont, CA: Thomson/Wadsworth.

Beaber, R. J., Marston, A., Michelli, J., & Mills, M. (1985). A brief test for measuring malingering in schizophrenic individuals. *American Journal of Psychiatry, 142*(12), 1478-1481.

Beetar, J., & Williams, J. (1995). Malingering response styles on the Memory Assessment Scales and symptom validity tests. *Archives of Clinical Neuropsychology, 10*, 57-72.

Beretvas, S. N., Meyers, J. L., & Leite, W. L. (2002). A reliability generalization study of the Marlowe-Crowne Social Desirability Scale. *Educational and Psychological Measurement, 62*, 570-589.

Berry, D. T. R., Adams, J. J., Clark, C. D., Thacker, S. R., Burger, T. L., Wetter, M. W., Baer, R. A., & Borden, J. W. (1996). Detection of a cry for help on the MMPI-2: An analog investigation. *Journal of Personality Assessment, 67*, 26-36.

Berry, D. T. R., Bagby, M. R., Smerz, J., Rinaldo, J. C., Caldwell-Andrews, A., & Baer, R. A. (2001). Effectiveness of NEO-PI-R Research Validity Scales for discriminating analog malingering and genuine psychopathology. *Journal of Personality Assessment, 76*(3), 496-516.

Bianchi v. Blodgett, No. 93-35524 (U. S. Ct. of Appeals for the 9th Cir., May 6, 1979).

Bianchini, K. J., Greve, K. W., & Love, J. M. (2003). Definite malingered neurocognitive dysfunction in moderate/severe traumatic brain injury. *Clinical Neuropsychologist, 17*, 574-580.

Binder, L. M. (1990). Malingering following minor head trauma. *Clinical Neuropsychologist, 4*, 25-36.

Binder, L. M. (1993). An abbreviated form of the Portland Digit Recognition Test. *Clinical Neuropsychologist, 7*, 104-107.

Binder, L. M. (2002). The Portland Digit Recognition Test: A review of validation data and clinical use. In J. Hom & R. L. Denney (Eds.), *Detection of Response Bias in Forensic Neuropsychology* (pp. 27-41). West Hazleton, PA: Haworth.

Binder, L. M., & Kelly, M. P. (1996). Portland Digit Recognition Test performance by brain dysfunction patients without financial incentives. *Assessment, 3*(4), 403-409.

Binder, L. M., & Willis, S. C. (1991). Assessment of motivation after financially compensable minor head trauma. *Psychological Assessment, 3,* 141-147.

Binet, A., & Fere, C. (1888). *Animal Magnetism.* New York: Appleton.

Blum, G. S., & Graef, J. R. (1971). The detection over time of subjects simulating hypnosis. *International Journal of Clinical and Experimental Hypnosis, 19,* 211-224.

Boccaccini, M. T., & Brodsky, S. L. (1999). Diagnostic test usage in emotional injury cases. *Professional Psychology: Research and Practice, 30*(3), 253-259.

Boone, D. (1994). Reliability of the MMPI-2 subtle and obvious scales with psychiatric inpatients. *Journal of Personality Assessment, 62,* 346-351.

Boone, K. B., & Lu, P. H. (1999). Impact of somatoform symptomatology on credibility of cognitive performance. *Clinical Neuropsychologist, 13,* 414-419.

Boone, K. B., Salazar, X., Lu, P., Waner-Chacon, K., & Razani, J. (2002). The Rey 15-Item Recognition Trial: A technique to enhance sensitivity of the Rey 15-Item Memorization Test. *Journal of Clinical and Experimental Neuropsychology, 24,* 561-573.

Boyd, A. R. (2003). Psychopathy and sex offender treatment: PCL-R total and factor scores and their relationship to treatment completion and admission of offense behavior (Doctoral dissertation, University of Louisville, 2003). *Dissertation Abstracts International, 64* (5-B), 2379.

Brady, J. P., & Lind, D. L. (1961). Experimental analysis of hysterical blindness. *Archives of General Psychiatry, 4,* 331-339.

Braginsky, B. M., & Braginsky, D. D. (1967). Schizophrenic patients in the psychiatric interview: An experimental study of their effectiveness at manipulation. *Journal of Consulting Psychology, 31,* 543-547.

Brandt, J. R., Kennedy, W. A., Patrick, C. J., & Curtin, J. J. (1997). Assessment of psychopathy in a population of incarcerated adolescent offenders. *Psychological Assessment, 9,* 429-435.

Brown, L., Sherbenou, R. J., & Johnsen, S. K. (1982). *Test of Nonverbal Intelligence: A Language Free Measure of Cognitive Ability.* Los Angeles: Western Psychological Services.

Bruck, M., & Ceci, S. J. (2002). Reliability and suggestibility of children's statements: From science to practice. In D. H. Schetky & E. P. Benedek (Eds.), *Principles and Practice of Child and Adolescent Forensic Psychiatry* (pp. 137-149). Arlington, VA: American Psychiatric Publishing.

Butcher, J. N., Arbisi, P. A., Atlis, M. M., & McNulty, J. L. (2003). The construct validity of the Lees-Haley Fake Bad Scale: Does this scale measure somatic malingering and feigned emotional distress? *Archives of Clinical Neuropsychology, 18*, 473-485.

Butcher, J. N., Graham, J., Dahlstrom, W., Tellegen, A., & Kaemmer, B. (1989). *Minnesota Multiphasic Personality Inventory-2: Manual for Administration and Scoring.* Minneapolis: University of Minnesota Press.

Butcher, J. N., & Han, K. (1995). Development of an MMPI-2 scale to assess the presentation of self in a superlative manner: The S scale. In J. N. Butcher & C. D. Spielberger (Eds.), *Advances in Personality Assessment* (Vol. 10, pp. 25-50). Hillsdale, NJ: Erlbaum.

Butcher, J. N., & Williams, C. L. (2000). *Essentials of MMPI-2 and MMPI-A Interpretation* (2nd ed.). Minneapolis: University of Minnesota Press.

Butcher, J. N., Williams, C. L., Graham, J. R., Archer, R., Tellegen, A., Ben-Porath, Y. S., & Kaemmer, B. (1992). *MMPI-A Manual for Administration, Scoring, and Interpretation.* Minneapolis: University of Minnesota Press.

Cacciola, J. S., Rutherford, M. J., & Alterman, A. I. (1990, June). *Use of the Psychopathy Checklist With Opiate Addicts.* Paper presented to the Committee on Problems in Drug Dependence, National Drug Administration, Richmond, VA.

Caine, S. L., Kinder, B. N., & Frueh, B. (1995). Rorschach susceptibility to malingered depressive disorders in adult females. In J. N. Butcher & C. D. Spielberger (Eds.), *Advances in Personality Assessment* (Vol. 10, pp. 165-174). Hillsdale, NJ: Erlbaum.

Caldwell, A. (1988). *MMPI Supplemental Scale Manual.* Los Angeles: Caldwell Report.

Caldwell-Andrews, A., Baer, R. A., & Berry, D. T. (2000). Effects of response sets on NEO-PI-R scores and their relations to external criteria. *Journal of Personality Assessment, 74*, 472-488.

Carp, A. L., & Shavzin, A. R. (1950). The susceptibility to falsification of the Rorschach psychodiagnostic technique. *Journal of Consulting Psychology, 14*, 230-233.

Cashel, M. L., Rogers, R., Sewell, K., & Martin-Cannici, C. (1995). The Personality Assessment Inventory (PAI) and the detection of defensiveness. *Assessment, 2*, 333-342.

Chankin, L. B. (2003). A youthful offender typology based on the Personality Assessment Inventory (Doctoral dissertation). *Dissertation Abstracts International, 63* (8-B), 3907.

Cima, M., Merckelbach, H., Hijman, H., Knauer, E., & Hollnack, S. (2002). I can't remember your honor: Offenders who claim amnesia. *German Journal of Psychiatry, 5*, 24-34.

Cima, M., Merckelbach, H., & Hollnack, S. (2003). Characteristics of psychiatric prison inmates who claim amnesia. *Personality and Individual Differences, 35*, 373-380.

Clark, B. K. (2002). Developmental aspects of memory in children. In D. H. Schetky & E. P. Benedek (Eds.), *Principles and Practice of Child and Adolescent Forensic Psychiatry* (pp. 134-149). Arlington, VA: American Psychiatric Publishing.

Clark, C. R. (1997). Sociopathy, malingering, and defensiveness. In R. Rogers (Ed.), *Clinical Assessment of Malingering and Deception* (2nd ed., pp. 68-84). New York: Guilford.

Cleckley, H. (1976). *The Mask of Sanity* (5th ed.). St. Louis, MO: Mosby.

Clifton, C. (2002). *Detecting Deception: Winning the Polygraph Game.* Boulder, CO: Paladin Press.

Cofer, C. N., Chance, J., & Judson, A. J. (1949). A study of malingering on the MMPI. *Journal of Psychology, 27*, 491-499.

Cogburn, R. A. K. (1993). A study of psychopathy and its relation to success in interpersonal deception (Doctoral dissertation). *Dissertation Abstracts International, 54*, 2191-B.

Cohn, M. G. (1995). Epidemiology of malingering strategies (Doctoral dissertation, University of Tulsa, 1990). *Dissertation Abstracts International, 55* (12-B), 5562.

Colwell, K., Hiscock-Anisman, C., Memon, A., Young, R., & Yaeger, H. (2002, March). *Strategies of Impression Management Among Deceivers and Truth-Tellers: How Liars Attempt to Convince.* Poster session presented at the annual meeting of the American Psychology-Law Society, Austin, TX.

Committee on Ethical Guidelines for Forensic Psychologists. (1991). Specialty guidelines for forensic psychologists. *Law and Human Behavior, 15*, 655-665.

Conkey, V. (1999). Determining the sensitivity of the MMPI-A to random responding and malingering in adolescents (Doctoral dissertation, Ohio University). *Dissertation Abstracts International, 60*, 3608.

Connell, D. K. (1991). *The SIRS and the M Test: The Differential Validity and Utility of Two Instruments Designed to Detect Malingered Psychosis in a Correctional Sample.* Unpublished doctoral dissertation, University of Louisville.

Cooke, D. J., & Michie, C. (1997). An Item Response Theory evaluation of the Hare Psychopathy Checklist. *Psychological Assessment, 9,* 3-14.

Cooke, D. J., & Michie, C. (2001). Refining the construct of psychopathy: Towards a hierarchical model. *Psychological Assessment, 13,* 171-188.

Cornell, D. G., & Hawk, G. L. (1989). Clinical presentation of malingerers diagnosed by experienced forensic psychologists. *Law and Human Behavior, 13,* 357-383.

Costa, P. T., & McCrae, R. R. (1989). *NEO PI/FFI Manual Supplement.* Odessa, FL: Psychological Assessment Resources.

Costa, P. T., & McCrae, R. R. (1992). *Professional Manual for the Revised NEO Personality Inventory (NEO PI-R) and NEO Five-Factor Inventory.* Odessa, FL: Psychological Assessment Resources.

Costa, P. T., McCrae, R. R., & Dye, D. A. (1991). Facet scales for Agreeableness and Conscientiousness: A revision of the NEO Personality Inventory. *Personality and Individual Differences, 12,* 887-898.

Craig, R. J. (1993). *The Millon Clinical Multiaxial Inventory: A Clinical Research Information Synthesis.* Hillsdale, NJ: Erlbaum.

Craig, R. J. (1997). A selected review of the MCMI empirical literature. In T. Millon (Ed.), *The Millon Inventories: Clinical and Personality Assessment* (pp. 303-326). New York: Guilford.

Craig, R. J. (1999). Essentials of MCMI-III assessment. In S. Strack (Ed.), *Essentials of Millon Inventories Assessment* (pp. 1-50). New York: Wiley.

Creevy, C., Hubbard, K. L., & Zapf, P. A. (2004, March). *A Survey of Attitudes and Practices Regarding Malingering.* Paper presented at the annual meeting of the American Psychology-Law Society, Scottsdale, Arizona.

Cronbach, L. (1949). Statistical methods applied to Rorschach scores. *Psychological Bulletin, 46,* 393-429.

Crowne, D. P., & Marlowe, D. (1960). A new scale of social desirability independent of psychopathology. *Journal of Consulting Psychology, 24,* 349-354.

Daubert v. Merrill Dow Pharmaceuticals, Inc., 113 S.Ct. 2786 (1993).

Dawes, R. M. (1994). *House of Cards: Psychology and Psychotherapy Built on Myth.* New York: Free Press.

Delain, S. L., Stafford, K. P., & Ben-Porath, Y. (2003). Use of the TOMM in a criminal court forensic assessment setting. *Assessment, 10,* 370-381.

Denney, R. L. (1996). Symptom Validity Testing of remote memory in a criminal forensic setting. *Archives of Clinical Neuropsychology, 11,* 589-603.

Denney, R. L. (1997, November). *Critical Issues in Criminal Forensic Neuropsychology: Competency to Stand Trial and Sanity Evaluations.* Two hour presentation at the 17th annual convention of the National Academy of Neuropsychology, Las Vegas, NV.

Denney, R. L. (1999). A brief Symptom Validity Testing procedure for Logical Memory of the Wechsler Memory Scale-Revised which can demonstrate verbal memory in the face of claimed disability. *Journal of Forensic Neuropsychology, 1*(1), 5-26.

Denney, R. L., & Scully, B. M. (1996). Exaggeration of neuropsychological impairment in Pick's Disease: A case study [Abstract]. *Archives of Clinical Neuropsychology, 11*(5), 382.

Derogatis, L. R. (1994). *Symptom Checklist-90-R (SCL-90-R): Administration, Scoring, and Procedures Manual.* Minneapolis, MN: National Computer Systems.

Edens, J. F., Buffington, J. K., & Tomicic, T. L. (2000). An investigation of the relationship between psychopathic traits and malingering on the Psychopathic Personality Inventory. *Assessment, 7,* 281-296.

Edens, J. F., Buffington, J. K., Tomicic, T. L., & Riley, B. D. (2001). Effects of positive impression management on the Psychopathic Personality Inventory. *Law and Human Behavior, 25,* 235-256.

Edens, J. F., Cruise, K. R., & Buffington-Vollum, J. K. (2001). Forensic and correctional applications of the Personality Assessment Inventory. *Behavioral Sciences and the Law, 19*(4), 519-543.

Edens, J. F., Otto, R. K., & Dwyer, T. (1999). Utility of the Structured Inventory of Malingered Symptomatology in identifying persons motivated to malinger psychopathology. *Journal of the American Academy of Psychiatry and the Law, 27*(3), 387-396.

Edwards, A. L. (1957). *The Social Desirability Variable in Personality Assessment and Research.* New York: Dryden Press.

Ekman, P. (1989). Why lies fail and what behaviors betray a lie. In J. C. Yuille (Ed.), *Credibility Assessment. NATO Advanced Science Institute Series. Series D: Behavioural and Social Sciences* (Vol 47, pp. 71-81). Dordrecht, The Netherlands: Kluwer Academic Publishers.

Ekman, P. (1992). *Telling Lies: Clues to Deceit in the Marketplace, Politics, and Marriage.* New York: W. W. Norton.

Ekman, P. (2003). *Emotions Revealed: Recognizing Faces and Feelings to Improve Communication and Emotional Life*. New York: Owl Books.

Ekman, P., & Friesen, W. V. (1982). Felt, false, and miserable smiles. *Journal of Nonverbal Behavior, 6*(4), 238-252.

Ekman, P., Friesen, W. V., & O'Sullivan, M. (1997). Smiles when lying. In P. Ekman & E. L. Rosenberg (Eds.), *What the Face Reveals: Basic and Applied Studies of Spontaneous Expression Using the Facial Action Coding System (FACS)* (pp. 201-214). New York: Oxford University Press.

Elhai, J. D., Naifeh, J. A., Zucker, I. S., Gold, S. N., Deitsch, S. E., & Frueh, B. C. (2004). Discriminating malingered from genuine civilian posttraumatic stress disorder: A validation of three MMPI-2 infrequency scales (F, Fp, and Fptsd). *Assessment, 11*, 139-144.

Elhai, J. D., Ruggiero, K. J., Frueh, B. C., Beckham, J. C., & Gold, P. B. (2002). The Infrequency-Posttraumatic Stress Disorder Scale (Fptsd) for the MMPI-2: Development and initial validation with veterans presenting with combat-related PTSD. *Journal of Personality Assessment, 79*, 531-549.

Emery, C. (1998). *Secret, Don't Tell: The Encyclopedia of Hypnotism*. Clare, MI: Acorn Hill Press.

Estabrooks, G. H., & Lockridge, R. (1957). *Hypnotism* (3rd ed.). New York: E. P. Dutton.

Exner, J. (1974). *The Rorschach: A Comprehensive System: Volume 1*. New York: Wiley.

Fairman, J. C., Denney, R. L., & Halfaker, D. A. (2003, October). *Evaluation of Negative Response Bias on the WAIS-III*. Paper presented at the 23rd annual conference of the National Academy of Neuropsychology, Dallas, TX.

Faust, D., & Ackley, M. A. (1998). Did you think it was going to be this easy? Some methodological suggestions for the investigation and development of malingering detection techniques. In C. R. Reynolds, (Ed.), *Detection of Malingering During Head Injury Litigation* (pp. 261-286). New York: Springer.

Faust, D., Hart, K., & Guilmette, T. J. (1988). Pediatric malingering: The capacity of children to fake believable deficits on neuropsychological testing. *Journal of Consulting and Clinical Psychology, 56*, 578-582.

Faust, D., Hart, K., Guilmette, T. J., & Arkes, H. R. (1988). Neuropsychologists' capacity to detect adolescent malingerers. *Professional Psychology: Research and Practice, 19*, 508-515.

Fautek, P. K. (1995). Detecting the malingering of psychosis in offenders: No easy solutions. *Criminal Justice and Behavior, 22*(1), 3-19.

Federal Bureau of Investigation. (1993). *Uniform Crime Reports: 1993.* Washington, DC: U. S. Department of Justice.

Fivush, R., & Shukat, J. R. (1995). Content, consistency, and coherence of early autobiographical recall. In M. S. Zaragoza, J. R. Graham, G. C. N. Hall, R. Hirschman, & Y. S. Ben-Porath (Eds.), *Memory and Testimony in the Child Witness. Applied Psychology: Individual, Social, and Community Issues* (Vol. 1, pp. 5-23). Thousand Oaks, CA: Sage.

Ford, C. V., King, B. H., & Hollender, M. H. (1988). Lies and liars: Psychiatric aspects of prevarication. *American Journal of Psychiatry, 145,* 554-562.

Forrest, D. (1999). *The Evolution of Hypnosis.* Farfar, Scotland: Black Ace Books.

Forth, A. E., Brown, S. L., Hart, S. D., & Hare, R. D. (1996). The assessment of psychopathy in male and female noncriminals: Reliability and validity. *Personality and Individual Differences, 20,* 531-543.

Forth, A. E., & Burke, H. C. (1998). Psychopathy in adolescence: Assessment, violence, and developmental precursors. In D. J. Cooke, A. E. Forth, & R. D. Hare (Eds.), *Psychopathy: Theory, Research, and Implications for Society* (pp. 205-229). Dordrecht, The Netherlands: Kluwer Academic Publishers.

Forth, A. E., Hart, S. D., & Hare, R. D. (1990). Assessment of psychopathy in male young offenders. *Psychological Assessment: A Journal of Consulting and Clinical Psychology, 2,* 342-344.

Forth, A. E., Kosson, D. S., & Hare, R. D. (1994). *The Psychopathy Checklist: Youth Version.* Unpublished test manual, Carleton University, Ottawa, Ontario.

Fosberg, I. A. (1938). Rorschach reactions under varied instructions. *Rorschach Research Exchange, 3,* 12-30.

Fosberg, I. A. (1941). An experimental study of the reliability of the Rorschach psychodiagnostic technique. *Rorschach Research Exchange, 5,* 72-84.

Fox, D. D., Gerson, A., & Lees-Haley, P. R. (1995). Interrelationship of MMPI-2 validity scales in personal injury claims. *Journal of Clinical Psychology, 51,* 42-47.

Frank, L. K. (1939). Projective methods for the study of personality. *Journal of Psychology, 8,* 389-413.

Frank, M. G., & Ekman, P. (2004). Appearing truthful generalizes across different deception situations [Electronic version]. *Journal of Personality and Social Psychology, 86,* 486-495.

Franzen, M. D., & Marten, N. (1996). Do people with knowledge fake better? *Applied Neuropsychology, 3*, 82-85.

Frederick, R. I. (2002). Review of the Validity Indicator Profile. In J. Hom & R. L. Denney (Eds.), *Detection of Response Bias in Forensic Neuropsychology* (pp. 125-145). Binghamton, NY: Haworth.

Frederick, R. I. (2003). *Validity Indicator Profile Manual*. Minnetonka, MN: NCA Assessments.

Frederick, R. I., Carter, M., & Powel, J. (1995). Adapting symptom validity testing to evaluate suspicious complaints of amnesia in medicolegal evaluations. *The Bulletin of the American Academy of Psychiatry and the Law, 23*(2), 227-233.

Frederick, R. I., & Denney, R. L. (1998). Minding your "ps and qs" when using forced-choice recognition tests. *Clinical Neuropsychologist, 12*, 193-205.

Frederick, R. I., Sarfaty, S. D., Johnston, D., & Powel, J. (1994). Validation of a detector of response bias on a forced-choice test of nonverbal ability. *Neuropsychology, 8*(1), 118-125.

Friedman, A. F., Lewak, R., Nichols, D. S., & Webb, J. T. (2001). *Psychological Assessment With the MMPI-2*. Mahwah, NJ: Erlbaum.

Frueh, B. P., & Kinder, B. N. (1994). The susceptibility of the Rorschach Inkblot Test to malingering of combat-related PTSD. *Journal of Personality Assessment, 62*, 280-298.

Frye v. United States, 298 F. 1013, 34 A.L.R. 145 (D.C. Cir. 1923).

Gacono, C. B. (1998). The use of the Psychopathy Checklist-Revised (PCL-R) and Rorschach in treatment planning with antisocial personality disordered patients. *International Journal of Offender Therapy and Comparative Psychology, 42*, 49-64.

Gacono, C. B. (2000). Suggestions for the institutional implementation and use of the Psychopathy Checklists. In C. B. Gacono (Ed.), *The Clinical and Forensic Assessment of Psychopathy: A Practitioner's Guide*. Hillsdale, NJ: Erlbaum.

Gacono, C. B., & Hare, R. D. (2000). PCL-R Clinical and Forensic Interview Schedule, Appendix A. In C. B. Gacono (Ed.), *The Clinical and Forensic Assessment of Psychopathy: A Practitioner's Guide* (p. 409). Hillsdale, NJ: Erlbaum.

Gacono, C. B., & Hutton, H. E. (1994). Suggestions for the clinical and forensic use of the Hare Psychopathy Checklist-Revised. *International Journal of Law and Psychiatry, 17*, 303-317.

Gacono, C. B., & Meloy, J. R. (1994). *The Rorschach Assessment of Aggressive and Psychopathic Personalities*. Hillsdale, NJ: Erlbaum.

Gacono, C. B., Meloy, J. R., Sheppard, K., Speth, E., & Roske, A. (1995). A clinical investigation of malingering and psychopathy in hospitalized insanity acquittees [Abstract]. *Bulletin of the American Academy of Psychiatry and the Law, 23*, 387-397.

Gacono, C. B., Meloy, J. R., Speth, E., & Roske, A. (1997). Above the law: Escapee from a maximum security forensic hospital and psychopathy. *Bulletin of the American Academy of Psychiatry and the Law, 25*, 547-550.

Gacono, C. B., Nieberding, R. J., Owen, A., Rubel, J., & Bodholdt, R. (2000). Treating Conduct Disorder, Antisocial, and Psychopathic Personalities. In J. Ashford, B. Sales, & W. Reid (Eds.), *Treating Adult and Juvenile Offenders With Special Needs* (pp. 99-129). Washington, DC: American Psychological Association.

Gaies, L. A. (1993). *Malingering of Depression on the Personality Assessment Inventory.* Unpublished doctoral dissertation, University of South Florida, Tampa.

Ganellen, R. J., Wasyliw, O. E., Haywood, T. W., & Grossman, L. S. (1996). Can psychosis be malingered? An empirical study. *Journal of Personality Assessment, 66*(1), 65-80.

Garb, H. W. (1999). Call for a moratorium on the use of the Rorschach inkblot test in clinical and forensic settings. *Assessment, 6*, 313-315.

Gillis, J. R., Rogers, R., & Bagby, R. M. (1991). Validity of the M Test: Simulation design and natural-group approaches. *Journal of Personality Assessment, 57*(1), 130-140.

Goebel, R. (1983). Detection of faking on the Halstead-Reitan Neuropsychological Test Battery. *Journal of Clinical Psychology, 39*, 731-742.

Good, R. (1942). Malingering. *British Medical Journal, 2*, 358-362.

Gothard, S. (1993). Detection of malingering in mental competency evaluations (Doctoral dissertation). *Dissertation Abstracts International, 55*(2-B), 591.

Gough, H. G. (1947). Simulated patterns on the MMPI. *Journal of Abnormal and Social Psychology, 42*, 215-225.

Gough, H. G. (1950). The F minus K Dissimulation index for the Minnesota Multiphasic Personality Inventory. *Journal of Consulting Psychology, 14*, 408-413.

Gough, H. G. (1954). Some common misconceptions about neuroticism. *Journal of Consulting Psychology, 18*, 287-292.

Gough, H. G. (1957). *The California Psychological Inventory Manual.* Palo Alto, CA: Consulting Psychologists Press.

Gouvier, W. D., Hayes, J. S., & Smiroldo, B. B. (1998). The significance of base rates, test sensitivity, test specificity, and subjects' knowledge of symptoms in assessing TBI sequelae and malingering. In C. R. Reynolds (Ed.), *Detection of Malingering During Head Injury Litigation* (pp. 55-79). New York: Plenum.

Gray, N. S., Snowden, R. J., MacCulloch, S., Phillips, H., Taylor, J., & MacCulloch, M. J. (2004). Relative efficacy of criminological, clinical, and personality measures of future risk of offending in mentally disordered offenders: A comparative study of HCR-20, PCL:SV, and OGRS. *Journal of Consulting and Clinical Psychology, 72*, 523-530.

Green, P., Allen, L. M., & Astner, K. (1996). *The Word Memory Test: A User's Guide to the Oral and Computer-Administered Forms, U. S. Version 1.1.* Durham, NC: CogniSyst, Inc.

Green, P., Lees-Haley, P. R., & Allen, L. M. (2002). The Word Memory Test and the validity of neuropsychological test scores. In J. Hom & R. L. Denney (Eds.), *Detection of Response Bias in Forensic Neuropsychology* (pp. 97-124). Binghamton, NY: Haworth.

Greiffenstein, M. F., Baker, W. J., & Gola, T. (1994). Validation of malingered amnesia measures with a large clinical sample. *Psychological Assessment, 6*, 218-224.

Greiffenstein, M. F., Gola, T., & Baker, W. J. (1995). MMPI-2 validity scales versus domain specific measures in detection of factitious traumatic brain injury. *The Clinical Neuropsychologist, 9*, 230-240.

Greve, K. W., & Bianchini, K. J. (2004). Response to Butcher et al., The construct validity of the Lees-Haley Fake-Bad Scale [Letter to the Editor]. *Archives of Clinical Neuropsychology, 19*, 337-339.

Greve, K. W., Bianchini, K. J., Mathias, C. W., Houston, R. J., & Crouch, J. A. (2002). Detecting malingered performance with the Wisconsin Card Sorting Test: A preliminary investigation in traumatic brain injury. *Clinical Neuropsychologist, 16*, 179-191.

Griffin, G., Normington, J., May, R., & Glassmire, D. (1996). Assessing dissimulation among Social Security disability income claimants. *Journal of Consulting and Clinical Psychology, 64*, 1425-1430.

Grisso, T. (1986). *Evaluating Competencies: Forensic Assessments and Instruments.* New York: Plenum.

Grisso, T. (2003). *Evaluating Competencies: Forensic Assessments and Instruments* (2nd ed.). New York: Plenum.

Grote, C. L., Kooker, E. K., Garron, D. C., Nyenhuis, D. L., Smith, C. A., & Mattingly, M. L. (2000). Performance of compensation seeking and non-compensation seeking samples on the Victoria Symptom Validity Test: Cross validation and extension of a standardized study. *Journal of Clinical and Experimental Neuropsychology, 22*(6), 709-719.

Guy, L. S., Edens, J. F., Otto, R. K., Poythress, N. G., Buffington, J. K., & Tomicic, T. L. (2000, March). *Factors Differentiating Successful Versus Unsuccessful Malingerers.* Poster session presented at the biennial meeting of the American-Psychology Law Society, New Orleans, LA.

Gynther, M. D., Altman, H., & Sletten, I. W. (1973). Replicated correlates of MMPI two-point code types: The Missouri actuarial system. *Journal of Clinical Psychology, 29,* 263-289.

Hager, J. C., & Ekman, P. (1997). The asymmetry of facial actions is inconsistent with models of hemispheric specialization. In P. Ekman & E. L. Rosenberg (Eds.), *What the Face Reveals: Basic and Applied Studies of Spontaneous Expression Using the Facial Action Coding System (FACS)* (pp. 40-57). New York: Oxford University Press.

Hall, H., & Pritchard, D. (1996). *Detecting Malingering and Deception: Forensic Distortion Analysis.* Delray Beach, FL: St. Lucie Press.

Hall, J. R., Benning, S. D., & Patrick, C. J. (2004). Criterion-related validity of the three-factor model of psychopathy: Personality, behavior, and adaptive functioning. *Assessment, 11,* 4-16.

Hamilton, J. C., Deemer, H. N., & Janata, J. W. (2003). Feeling sad but looking good: Sick role features that lead to favorable interpersonal judgments. *Journal of Social and Clinical Psychology, 22,* 253-274.

Hamsher, J. H., & Farina, A. (1967). "Openness" as a dimension of projective test responses. *Journal of Consulting Psychology, 31,* 525-528.

Hankins, G. C., Barnard, G. W., & Robbins, L. (1993). The validity of the M Test in a residential forensic facility. *Bulletin of the American Academy of Psychiatry and the Law, 21*(1), 111-121.

Hanley, C. (1957). Deriving a measure of test-taking defensiveness. *Journal of Consulting Psychology, 21,* 391-397.

Hare, R. D. (1980). A research scale for the assessment of psychopathy in criminal populations. *Personality and Individual Differences, 1,* 111-117.

Hare, R. D. (1985). Comparison of procedures for the assessment of psychopathy. *Journal of Consulting and Clinical Psychology, 53,* 7-16.

Hare, R. D. (1991). *Manual for the Hare Psychopathy Checklist-Revised.* North Tonawanda, NY: Multi-Health Systems.

Hare, R. D. (1996). Psychopathy: A clinical construct whose time has come. *Criminal Justice and Behavior, 23,* 25-54.

Hare, R. D. (1998a). The Hare PCL-R: Some issues concerning its use and misuse. *Legal and Criminological Psychology, 3,* 99-119.

Hare, R. D. (1998b). Psychopaths and their nature: Implications for the mental health and criminal justice systems. In T. Millon, E. Simonson, M. Birket-Smith, & R. D. Davis (Eds.), *Psychopathy: Antisocial, Criminal, and Violent Behavior* (pp. 188-212). New York: Guilford.

Hare, R. D. (2003). *The Hare Psychopathy Checklist–Revised* (2nd ed.). Toronto: Multi-Health Systems.

Hare, R. D., & Forth, A. E. (1998, December). *Training in the Use of the Psychopathy Checklist-Revised*. Training session for the Sex Offender Risk Assessment certification, Lexington, KY.

Hare, R. D., Harpur, T. J., Hakstian, A. R., Forth, A. E., Hart, S. D., & Newman, J. P. (1990). The Revised Psychopathy Checklist: Reliability and factor structure. *Psychological Assessment: A Journal of Consulting and Clinical Psychology, 2*, 338-341.

Hare, R. D., & Neumann, C. C. (2005). Structural models of psychopathy. *Current Psychiatric Reports, 7*, 57-64.

Harpur, T. J., Hakstian, A. R., & Hare, R. D. (1988). Factor structure of the Psychopathy Checklist. *Journal of Consulting and Clinical Psychology, 56*, 741-747.

Harris, M. R., & Resnick, P. J. (2003). Suspected malingering: Guidelines for clinicians [Electronic version]. *Psychiatric Times, XX*(13).

Hart, S. D. (2000, March). *Assessing Psychopathy: An Overview of the Hare Scales*. Workshop given at the American Academy of Forensic Psychology Workshop Series, New Orleans, LA.

Hart, S. D., Cox, D. E., & Hare, R. D. (1995). *Manual for the Hare Psychopathy Checklist-Revised: Screening Version (PCL:SV)*. Toronto: Multi-Health Systems.

Hart, S. D., & Hare R. D. (1997). Psychopathy: Assessment and association with criminal conduct. In D. M. Stoff, J. Breiling, & J. D. Maser (Eds.), *Handbook of Antisocial Behaviors* (pp. 22-35). New York: Wiley.

Hart, S. D., Hare, R. D., & Forth, A. E. (1994). Psychopathy as a risk marker for violence: Development and validation of a screening version of the Revised Psychopathy Checklist. In J. Monahan & H. Steadman (Eds.), *Violence and Mental Disorder: Developments In Risk Assessment* (pp. 81-98). Chicago: University of Chicago Press.

Hartman, D. E. (2002). The unexamined lie is a lie worth fibbing: Neuropsychological malingering and the Word Memory Test. *Archives of Clinical Neuropsychology, 17*, 709-714.

Haskett, J. (1995). *Tehachapi Malingering Scale: Research Revision No. 5 Manual*. Modesto, CA: Logocraft.

Hathaway, S. R., & McKinley, J. C. (1940). A multiphasic personality schedule (Minnesota): I. Construction of the schedule. *Journal of Psychology, 10,* 249-254.

Hawk, G. L., & Cornell, D. G. (1989). MMPI profiles of malingerers diagnosed in pretrial evaluations. *Journal of Clinical Psychology, 45,* 673-678.

Hayes, J. S., Hale, D. B., & Gouvier, W. D. (1998). Malingering detection in a mentally retarded forensic population. *Applied Neuropsychology, 5,* 33-36.

Heaton, R. K., Smith, H. H., Lehman, R. A. W., & Vogt, A. T. (1978). Prospects for faking believable deficits on neuropsychological testing. *Journal of Consulting and Clinical Psychology, 46*(5), 802-900.

Heilbrun, K. (1992). The role of psychological testing in forensic assessment. *Law and Human Behavior, 16,* 257-272.

Heinze, M. C. (1999). "Yet there's a method to his madness . . . ": Dimensions of deception and dangerousness. *Aggression and Violent Behavior, 4*(4), 387-412.

Helmes, E., & Holden, R. R. (2003). The construct of social desirability: One or two dimensions? *Personality and Individual Differences, 34,* 1015-1023.

Hemphill, J. F., & Hare, R. D. (2004). *The Self-Report Psychopathy Scale-II (SRP-II).* Unpublished manuscript.

Hemphill, J. F., Hare, R. D., & Wong, S. (1998). Psychopathy and recidivism: A review. *Legal and Criminological Psychology, 3,* 137-170.

Hiscock, M., & Hiscock, C. K. (1989). Refining the forced-choice method for the detection of malingering. *Journal of Clinical and Experimental Neuropsychology, 11,* 967-974.

Hoekstra, W. R. (2000). Utility of the Personality Assessment Inventory in adolescents: Discrimination ability with violent versus nonviolent offending incarcerated juveniles (Doctoral dissertation). *Dissertation Abstracts International, 60* (8-B), 4226.

Holden, R. R., Book, A. S., Edwards, M. J., Wasylkiw, L., & Starzyk, K. B. (2003). Experimental faking in self-reported psychopathology: Unidimensional or multidimensional? *Personality and Individual Differences, 35,* 1107-1117.

Hollrah, J. L., Schlottmann, R. S., Scott, A. B., & Brunetti, D. G. (1995). Validity of the MMPI subtle items. *Journal of Personality Assessment, 65,* 278-299.

Hom, J., & Denney, R. L. (2002). Preface. In J. Hom & R. L. Denney (Eds.), *Detection of Response Bias in Forensic Neuropsychology* (pp. xi-xvi). Binghamton, NY: Haworth.

Honts, C., & Raskin, D. (2004, March). *Polygraph Critics Advocate Convicting the Innocent.* Paper presented at the meeting of the American Psychology-Law Society, Scottsdale, AZ.

Iverson, G. (1995). Qualitative aspects of malingered memory deficits. *Brain Injury, 9,* 35-40.

Kennedy, J., & Coe, W. C. (1994). Nonverbal signs of deception during posthypnotic amnesia. *International Journal of Clinical and Experimental Hypnosis, 42,* 13-19.

Killgore, W. D., & DellaPietra, L. (2000). Using the WMS-III to detect malingering: Empirical validation of the Rarely Missed Index (RMI). *Journal of Clinical and Experimental Neuropsychology, 22,* 761-771.

Kinnument, T., Zamansky, H. S., & Block, M. (1994). Is the hypnotized subject lying? *Journal of Abnormal Psychology, 103*(2), 184-191.

Kirsch, I., Silva, C. E., Carone, J. E., Johnston, J. D., & Simon, B. (1989). The Surreptitious Observation design. *Journal of Abnormal Psychology, 98*(2), 132-136.

Knight, S., & Meyer, R. (2005). *Attitudes and Beliefs Toward Forensic Hypnosis in an Expert Sample.* Manuscript submitted for publication.

Knight, S., & Meyer, R. (in press). *Forensic Hypnosis.* Sarasota, FL: Professional Resource Press.

Kopelman, M. D. (1987). Crime and amnesia: A review. *Behavioral Sciences and the Law, 5,* 323-342.

Kosson, D. S., Smith, S. S., & Newman, J. P. (1990). Evaluating the construct validity of psychopathy in black and white male inmates: Three preliminary studies. *Journal of Abnormal Psychology, 99,* 250-259.

Krahn, L. E., Li, H., & O'Connor, M. K. (2003). Patients who strive to be ill: Factitious disorder with physical symptoms. *American Journal of Psychiatry, 160,* 1163-1168.

Kumho Tire Co. v. Carmichael, 526 U.S. 137 (1999).

Kurtz, R., & Meyer, R. G. (1994, March). *Vulnerability of the MMPI-2, M Test, and SIRS to Different Strategies of Malingering Psychosis.* Paper presented at the meeting of the American Psychology-Law Society, Santa Fe, NM.

Labarge, A. S., McCaffrey, R. J., & Brown, T. A. (2003). Neuro-psychologists' abilities to determine the predictive value of diagnostic tests. *Archives of Clinical Neuropsychology, 18,* 165-175.

Lachar, D. (1974). *The MMPI: Clinical Assessment and Automated Interpretation.* Los Angeles: Western Psychological Services.

Lacy, J. H. (1993). Self-damaging and addictive behavior in bulimia nervosa. *British Journal of Psychiatry, 163,* 190-194.

Lamb, H. R., & Weinberger, L. E. (1998). Persons with severe mental illness in jails and prisons: A review. *Psychiatric Services, 49*, 483-492.

Langeluddecke, P. M., & Lucas, S. K. (2003). Quantitative measures of memory malingering on the Wechsler Memory Scale–Third Edition in mild head injury litigants. *Archives of Clinical Neuropsychology, 18*, 181-197.

Lanyon , R. I., & Goodstein, L. D. (1997). *Personality Assessment: Third Edition*. New York: Wiley.

Larrabee, G. J. (1997). Neuropsychological outcome, post concussion symptoms, and forensic considerations in mild closed head trauma. *Seminars in Clinical Neuropsychiatry, 2*, 196-206.

Larrabee, G. J. (1998). Somatic malingering on the MMPI and MMPI-2 in personal injury litigants. *The Clinical Neuropsychologist, 12*, 179-188.

Larrabee, G. J. (2000). Forensic neuropsychological assessment. In R. D. Vanderploeg (Ed.), *Clinician's Guide to Neuropsychological Assessment* (2nd ed., pp. 301-335). Hillsdale, NJ: Erlbaum.

Larrabee, G. J. (2002, April). *Identification of Personal Injury Malingerers Using the MMPI-2 and Patterns of Atypical Neuropsychological Test Performance*. Paper presented at the 12th annual Nelson Butter's West Coast Neuropsychology Conference, San Diego, CA.

Larrabee, G. J. (2003a). Detection of malingering using neuropsychologically atypical performance patterns on standard neuropsychological tests. *Clinical Neuropsychologist, 17*, 410-425.

Larrabee, G. J. (2003b). Detection of symptom exaggeration with the MMPI-2 in litigants with malingered neurocognitive dysfunction. *Clinical Neuropsychologist, 17*, 54-68.

Larrabee, G. J. (2003c). Exaggerated MMPI-2 symptom report in personal injury litigants with malingered neurocognitive deficit. *Archives of Clinical Neuropsychology, 18*, 673-686.

Larrabee, G. J. (2003d). Exaggerated pain report in litigants with malingered neurocognitive dysfunction. *Clinical Neuropsychologist, 17*, 395-401.

Lees-Haley, P. R. (1991). Ego strength denial on the MMPI-2 as a clue to simulation of personal injury in vocational neuropsychological and emotional distress evaluations. *Perceptual and Motor Skills, 72*, 815-819.

Lees-Haley, P. R. (1997). Attorneys influence expert evidence in forensic psychological and neuropsychological cases. *Assessment, 4*, 321-324.

Lees-Haley, P. R., Dunn, J. T., & Betz, B. P. (1999). Test review: The Victoria Symptom Validity Test. *American Psychology-Law Society News, Fall*, 12-16.

Lees-Haley, P. R., English, L. T., & Glenn, W. J. (1991). A Fake Bad Scale on the MMPI-2 for personal injury claimants. *Psychological Reports, 68*, 203-210.

Lees-Haley, P. R., & Fox, D. D. (2004). Commentary on Butcher, Arbisi, Atlis, and McNulty (2003) on the Fake Bad Scale. *Archives of Clinical Neuropsychology, 19*, 333-336.

Lees-Haley, P. R., Iverson, G. L., Lange, R. T., Fox, D. D., & Allen, L. M. (2002). Malingering in forensic neuropsychology: *Daubert* and the MMPI-2. In J. Hom & R. L. Denney (Eds.), *Detection of Response Bias in Forensic Neuropsychology* (pp. 167-203). Binghamton, NY: Haworth.

Lewak, R., & Meloy, J. R. (March, 2000). *Forensic Case Analysis Using the MMPI-2 and Rorschach.* Workshop given at the American Academy of Forensic Psychology Workshop Series, New Orleans, LA.

Lewis, J. L., Simcox, A. M., & Berry, D. T. R. (2002). Screening for feigned psychiatric symptoms in a forensic sample by using the MMPI-2 and Structured Inventory of Malingered Symptomatology. *Psychological Assessment, 14*, 170-176.

Lewis, M. (1993). The development of deception. In M. Lewis & C. Saarni (Eds.), *Lying and Deception in Everyday Life* (pp. 90-105). New York: Guilford.

Leyra v. Denno, 347 U.S. 556, 74 S.Ct. 716, 98 L.Ed. 948 (1954).

Lezak, M. D. (1995). *Neuropsychological Assessment* (3rd ed.). New York: Oxford University Press.

Lilienfeld, S. O., & Andrews, B. P. (1996). Development and preliminary studies of a self-report measure of psychopathic personality traits in noncriminal populations. *Journal of Personality Assessment, 66*, 488-524.

Lim, J., & Butcher, J. N. (1996). Detection of faking on the MMPI-2: Differentiation among faking-bad, denial and claiming extreme virtue. *Journal of Personality Assessment, 67*, 1-25.

Loevinger, J. (1957). Objective tests as instruments of psychological theory. *Psychological Reports, 3*, 635-694.

Louth, S. M., Williamson, S., Alpert, M., Pouget, E. R., & Hare, R. D. (1998). Acoustic distinctions in the speech of male psychopaths. *Journal of Psycholinguistic Research, 27*, 375-384.

Mann, S., Vrij, A., & Bull, R. (2004). Detecting true lies: Police officers' ability to detect suspects' lies. *Journal of Applied Psychology, 89*, 137-149.

Martin, D. J., & Lynn, S. J. (1996). The hypnotic simulation index: Successful discrimination of real versus simulating participants. *The International Journal of Clinical and Experimental Hypnosis, 44*(4), 338-353.

McCann, J. T. (1998a). Defending the Rorschach in court: An analysis of admissibility using legal and professional standards. *Journal of Personality Assessment, 70*(1), 125-144.

McCann, J. T. (1998b). *Malingering and Deception in Adolescents.* Washington, DC: American Psychological Association.

McCrae, R. R., & Costa, P. T. (1983). Social desirability scales: More substance than style. *Journal of Consulting and Clinical Psychology, 51*, 882-888.

McKinzey, R. K., Prieler, J., & Raven, J. (2003). Detection of children's malingering on Raven's Standard Progressive Matrices. *British Journal of Clinical Psychology, 42*, 95-99.

McLearen, A. M., Pietz, C. A., & Denney, R. L. (2004). Evaluation of psychological damages. In W. O'Donoghue & E. Levensky (Eds.), *Handbook of Forensic Psychology: A Resource for Mental Health and Legal Professionals* (pp. 267-299). San Diego, CA: Elsevier Academic Press.

McLearen, A. M., & Zapf, P. A. (2002, August). *Utility of Routine Malingering Assessment in Jails.* Poster presented at the annual conference of the American Psychological Association, Chicago, IL.

McLearen, A. M., Zapf, P. A., & Clements, C. B. (2004, March). *Malingering in Jails: Factors Analysis of Lower Threshold Symptom Exaggeration.* Paper presented at the annual conference of the American Psychology-Law Society, Scottsdale, AZ.

Meehl, P. E., & Hathaway, S. R. (1946). The K factor as a suppressor variable in the MMPI. *Journal of Applied Psychology, 30*, 525-564.

Meloy, J. R., & Gacono, C. B. (1992). The aggression response and the Rorschach. *Journal of Clinical Psychology, 48*, 104-114.

Meloy, J. R., & Gacono, C. B. (1995). Assessing the psychopathic personality. In J. N. Butcher (Ed.), *Clinical Personality Assessment* (pp. 410-422). New York: Oxford University Press.

Melton, G. B., Petrila, J., Poythress, N. G., & Slobogin, C. (1997). *Psychological Evaluations for the Courts: A Handbook for Mental Health Professionals and Lawyers* (2nd ed.). New York: Guilford.

Merckelbach, H., Hauer, B., & Rassin, E. (2002). Symptom Validity Testing of feigned dissociative amnesia: A simulation study. *Psychology, Crime and Law, 8*, 311-318.

Meyer, R. G. (1992). *Practical Clinical Hypnosis: Techniques and Applications*. New York: Lexington Books.

Meyer, R. G., & Weaver, C. M. (2007). *The Clinician's Handbook: Integrated Diagnostics, Assessment, and Intervention in Adult and Adolescent Psychopathology* (5th ed.). Long Grove, IL: Waveland.

Meyers, J. E., Galinsky, A. M., & Volbrecht, M. (1999). Malingering and mild brain injury: How low is too low. *Applied Neuropsychology, 6*, 208-216.

Meyers, J. E., & Volbrecht, M. (1998). Validation of Reliable Digits for detection of malingering. *Assessment, 5*, 301-305.

Meyers, J. E., & Volbrecht, M. (2003). A validation of multiple malingering detection methods in a large clinical sample. *Archives of Clinical Neuropsychology, 18*, 261-276.

Miller, H. A. (2001). *M-FAST: Miller Forensic Assessment of Symptoms Test Professional Manual*. Odessa, FL: Psychological Assessment Resources.

Miller, R. D. (2003). People v. Palmer: Amnesia and competency to proceed revisited. *The Journal of Psychiatry and Law, 31*, 165-185.

Millis, S. R. (1992). The Recognition Memory Test in the detection of malingered and exaggerated memory deficits. *Clinical Neuropsychologist, 6*, 406-414.

Millis, S. R. (2002). Warrington's Recognition Memory Test in the detection of response bias. In J. Hom & R. L. Denney (Eds.), *Detection of Response Bias in Forensic Neuropsychology* (pp. 147-166). Binghamton, NY: Haworth.

Millis, S. R. (2004). Evaluation of malingered neurocognitive disorders. In M. Rizzo & P. J. Eslinger (Eds.), *Principles and Practice of Behavioral Neurology and Neuropsychology* (pp. 1077-1089). Philadelphia: Saunders.

Millis, S. R., Putnam, S. H., & Adams, K. M. (1995, March). *Neuropsychological Malingering and the MMPI-2: Old and New Indicators*. Paper presented at the 30th annual symposium on Recent Developments in the Use of the MMPI, MMPI-2, and MMPI-A, St. Petersburg, FL.

Millis, S. R., Putnam, S. H., Adams, K. M., & Ricker, J. H. (1995). The California Verbal Learning Test in the detection of incomplete effort in neuropsychological evaluation. *Psychological Assessment, 7*(4), 463-471.

Millon, T. (1987). *Millon Clinical Multiaxial Inventory – II Manual* (2nd ed.). Minneapolis, MN: National Computer Systems.

Millon, T. (1993). *The Millon Adolescent Clinical Inventory Manual*. Minneapolis, MN: National Computer Systems.

Millon, T., Millon, C., & Davis, R. (1994). *The MCMI-III Manual*. Minneapolis, MN: NCS Assessments.

Minor, H. I., Hartmann, D. J., & Terry, S. (1997). Predictors of juvenile court actions and recidivism. *Crime and Delinquency, 43*(3), 328-344.

Mittenberg, W., Aguila-Puentes, G., Patton, C., Canyock, E. M., & Heilbronner, R. (2002). Neuropsychological profiling of symptom exaggeration and malingering. In J. Hom & R. L. Denney (Eds.), *Detection of Response Bias in Forensic Neuropsychology* (pp. 227-240). Binghamton, NY: Haworth.

Mittenberg, W., Patton, C., Canyock, E. M., & Condit, D. C. (2002). A national survey of symptom exaggeration and malingering base rates. *Journal of the International Neuropsychological Society, 8*(2), 247.

Moffit, T. E. (1993). Adolescence-limited and life-course-persistent antisocial behavior: A developmental typology. *Psychological Review, 106*, 674-701.

Moore, M., Braga, A., & Petrie, C. (2002). *The Truth About Lie Detection: An Assessment of the Polygraph*. Washington, DC: National Academy Press.

Morey, L. C. (1991). *Personality Assessment Inventory Professional Manual*. Odessa, FL: Psychological Assessment Resources.

Morey, L. C. (1993, August). *Defensiveness and Malingering Indices for the PAI*. Paper presented at the 101st annual meeting of the American Psychological Association, Toronto, Canada.

Morey, L. C. (1996). *An Interpretive Guide to the Personality Assessment Inventory*. Odessa, FL: Psychological Assessment Resources.

Morey, L. C. (1998). Teaching and learning the Personality Assessment Inventory (PAI). In L. Handler & M. J. Hilsenroth (Eds.), *Teaching and Learning Personality Assessment: The LEA Series in Personality and Clinical Psychology* (pp. 191-214). Mahwah, NJ: Erlbaum.

Mrad, D. (1996, September). *Criminal Responsibility Evaluations*. Paper presented at the Issues in Forensic Assessment Symposium, Federal Bureau of Prisons, Atlanta, GA.

National Research Council. (2003). *The Polygraph and Lie Detection* [Committee to Review the Scientific Evidence on the Polygraph. Division of Behavioral and Social Sciences and Education]. Washington, DC: The National Academies Press.

Nelson, S. E. (1952). The development of an indirect, objective measure of social status and its relationship to certain psychiatric syndromes (Doctoral dissertation). *Dissertation Abstracts, 12*, 782.

Netter, B. E. C., & Viglione, D. J., Jr. (1994). An empirical study of malingering schizophrenia on the Rorschach. *Journal of Personality Assessment, 62*(1), 45-57.

Nicholson, R. A. (1999). Forensic assessment. In R. Roesch & S. D. Hart (Eds.), *Psychology and Law: The State of the Discipline* (pp. 122-175). Dordrecht, The Netherlands: Kluwer Academic Publishers.

Nicholson, R. A., & Norwood, S. (2000). The quality of forensic psychological assessment, reports, and testimony: Acknowledging the gap between promise and practice. *Law and Human Behavior, 24,* 9-44.

Nies, K. J., & Sweet, J. J. (1994). Neuropsychological assessment and malingering: A critical review of past and present strategies. *Archives of Clinical Neuropsychology, 9,* 501-552.

Norris, M. P., & May, M. C. (1998). Screening for malingering in a correctional setting. *Law and Human Behavior, 22*(3), 315-323.

Office of Technology Assessment, United States Congress. (1983). *Scientific Validity of Polygraph Testing: A Research Review and Evaluation.* Washington, DC: U.S. Government Printing Office.

Oldershaw, L., & Bagby, M. R. (1997). Children and deception. In R. Rogers (Ed.), *Clinical Assessment of Malingering and Deception* (2nd ed., pp. 153-166). New York: Guilford.

Orne, M. T. (1971). The simulation of hypnosis. *The International Journal of Clinical and Experimental Hypnosis, 19*(4), 183-210.

Orne, M. T. (1972). Can a hypnotized subject be compelled to carry out otherwise unacceptable behavior? *International Journal of Clinical and Experimental Hypnosis, 20,* 101-117.

Osberg, T. M., & Harrigan, P. (1999). Comparative validity of the MMPI-2 Wiener-Harmon Subtle-Obvious scales in male prison inmates. *Journal of Personality Assessment, 72,* 36-48.

Overall, J. E., & Gorham, D. R. (1962). The Brief Psychiatric Rating Scale. *Psychological Reports, 10,* 799-812.

Pankratz, L. (1979). Symptom validity testing and symptom retraining: Procedures for the assessment and treatment of functional sensory deficits. *Journal of Consulting and Clinical Psychology, 47,* 409-410.

Pankratz, L. (1983). A new technique for the assessment and modification of feigned memory deficit. *Perceptual and Motor Skills, 57,* 367-372.

Pankratz, L., & Binder, L. M. (1997). Malingering on intellectual and neuropsychological measures. In R. Rogers (Ed.), *Clinical Assessment of Malingering and Deception* (2nd ed., pp. 223-236). New York: Guilford.

Pankratz, L., Fausti, S. A., & Peed, S. (1975). A forced-choice technique to evaluate deafness in the hysterical or malingering patient. *Journal of Consulting and Clinical Psychology, 43*, 421-422.

Patrick, C. J., Cuthbert, B. N., & Lang, P. J. (1994). Emotion in the criminal psychopath: Fear image processing. *Journal of Abnormal Psychology, 103*, 523-534.

Patrick, C. J. ,& Iacono, W. G. (1989). Psychopathy, threat, and polygraph test accuracy. *Journal of Applied Psychology, 74*, 347-355.

Paulhus, D. L. (1984). Two-component models of socially desirable responding. *Journal of Personality and Social Psychology, 46*, 598-609.

Paulhus, D. L. (1998). *Paulhus Deception Scales (PDS): The Balanced Inventory of Desirable Responding-7*. North Tonawanda, NY: Multi-Health Systems.

Pensa, R., Dorfman, W. I., Gold, S. N., & Schneider, B. (1996). Detection of malingered psychosis with the MMPI-2. *Psychotherapy in Private Practice, 14*(4), 47-63.

People v. Ebanks, 117 Cal. 652 LRA 269, 49 P. 1049 (1897).

People v. John Johnson. American Journal of Insanity, April, 303-346 (1848).

People v. Stow, 49 Cal. 3rd 1136, 265 Cal. Rptr. 111, 783 P.2d 698 (1989).

Perry, G., & Kinder, B. (1990). The susceptibility of the Rorschach to malingering: A critical review. *Journal of Personality Assessment, 54*, 47-57.

Pietz, C., McLearen, A. M., Neller, D., Matthews, B., & Beatty, A. (2004). *Detecting Malingering With the M-FAST in a County Jail: Preliminary Data*. Unpublished manuscript.

Porter, S., & Yuille, J. C. (1995). Credibility assessment of criminal suspects through statement analysis. *Psychology, Crime, and Law, 1*, 319-331.

Power, D. J. (1977). Memory, identification and crime. *Medicine, Science, and the Law, 17*, 132-139.

Poythress, N. G., Edens, J. F., & Watkins, M. M. (2001). The relationship between psychopathic personality features and malingering symptoms of major mental illness. *Law and Human Behavior, 25*, 567-582.

Quinn, K. M. (1991). False and unsubstantiated sexual abuse allegations: Clinical issues. *Child and Youth Services, 15*, 145-157.

Quinsey, V. L., Rice, M. E., & Harris, G. T. (1995). Actuarial prediction of sexual recidivism. *Journal of Interpersonal Violence, 10*, 85-105.

Raven, J. C., Court, J. H., & Raven, J. (1999). *Standard Progressive Matrices*. Oxford: Oxford Psychologists Press.

Reitan, R. M., & Wolfson, D. (2002). Detection of malingering and invalid test results using the Halstead-Reitan Battery. In J. Hom & R. L. Denney (Eds.), *Detection of Response Bias in Forensic Neuropsychology* (pp. 275-314). Binghamton, NY: Haworth.

Resnick, P. J. (1984). The detection of malingered mental illness. *Behavioral Sciences and the Law, 2*(1), 20-38.

Rey, A. (1958). *L'Examen Clinique en Psychologie.* Paris: Presses Universitaires de France.

Reynolds, W. M. (1982). Development of reliable and valid short forms of the Marlowe-Crowne Social Desirability Scale. *Journal of Clinical Psychology, 38,* 119-125.

Rock v. Arkansas, 483 U.S. 44 (1987).

Rogers, R. (1984). Towards an empirical model of malingering and deception. *Behavorial Sciences and the Law, 2,* 93-112.

Rogers, R. (1986). *Conducting Insanity Evaluations.* New York: Van Nostrand Reinhold.

Rogers, R. (1988). Structured interviews and dissimulation. In R. Rogers (Ed.), *Clinical Assessment of Malingering and Deception* (pp. 250-268). New York: Guilford.

Rogers, R. (1990). Development of a new classificatory model of malingering. *Bulletin of the American Academy of Psychiatry and the Law, 18,* 323-333.

Rogers, R. (1992). *Structured Interview of Reported Symptoms.* Odessa, FL: Psychological Assessment Resources.

Rogers, R. (1995). *Diagnostic and Structured Interviewing: A Handbook for Psychologists.* Odessa, FL: Psychological Assessment Resources.

Rogers, R. (1997a). Introduction. In R. Rogers (Ed.), *Clinical Assessment of Malingering and Deception* (2nd ed., pp. 1-19). New York: Guilford.

Rogers, R. (1997b). Structured interviews and dissimulation. In R. Rogers (Ed.), *Clinical Assessment of Malingering and Deception* (2nd ed., pp. 301-327). New York: Guilford.

Rogers, R., Bagby, R. M., & Dickens, S. E. (1992). *Structured Interview of Reported Symptoms: Professional Manual.* Odessa, FL: Psychological Assessment Resources.

Rogers, R., Bagby, R. M., & Gillis, J. R. (1992). Improvements in the M Test as a screening measure for malingering. *Bulletin of the American Academy of Psychiatry and the Law, 20*(1), 101-104.

Rogers, R., Gillis, J. R., Dickens, S. E., & Bagby, R. M. (1991). Standardized assessment of malingering: Validation of the SIRS. *Psychological Assessment: A Journal of Clinical and Consulting Psychology, 3,* 89-96.

Rogers, R., Harrell, E. H., & Liff, C. D. (1993). Feigning neuro-psychological impairments: A critical review of methodological and clinical considerations. *Clinical Psychology Review, 13,* 255-274.

Rogers, R., Hinds, J. D., & Sewell, K. W. (1996). Feigning psychopathology among adolescent offenders: Validation of the SIRS, MMPI-A and SIMS. *Journal of Personality Assessment, 67,* 244-257.

Rogers, R., Ornduff, S. R., & Sewell, K. W. (1993). Feigning specific disorders: A study of the Personality Assessment Inventory (PAI). *Journal of Personality Assessment, 60,* 554-560.

Rogers, R., Sewell, K. W., Cruise, K. R., Wang, E. W., & Ustad, K. L. (1998). The PAI and feigning: A cautionary note on its use in forensic-correctional settings. *Assessment, 5,* 399-405.

Rogers, R., Sewell, K. W., & Goldstein, A. (1994). Explanatory models of malingering: A prototypical analysis. *Law and Human Behavior, 18,* 543-552.

Rogers, R., Sewell, K. W., Martin, M. A., & Vitacco, M. J. (2003). Detection of feigned mental disorders: A meta-analysis of the MMPI-2 and malingering. *Assessment, 10,* 160-177.

Rogers, R., Sewell, K. W., Morey, L. C., & Ustad, K. L. (1996). Detection of feigned mental disorders on the Personality Assessment Inventory: A discriminant analysis. *Journal of Personality Assessment, 67,* 629-640.

Rogers, R., Sewell, K. W., & Salekin, R. T. (1994). A meta-analysis of malingering on the MMPI-2. *Assessment, 1,* 227-237.

Rohling, M. L., Green, P., Allen, L. M., III, & Iverson, G. L. (2002). Depressive symptoms and neurocognitive test scores in patients passing symptom validity tests. *Archives of Clinical Neuropsychology, 17,* 205-222.

Rosenfeld, B., Sands, S. A., & Van Gorp, W. G. (2000). Have we forgotten the base rate problem? Methodological issues in the detection of distortion. *Archives of Clinical Neuropsychology, 15*(4), 349-359.

Ross, S. R., Millis, S. R., Krukowski, R. A., Putnam, S. H., & Adams, K. M. (2004). Detecting incomplete effort on the MMPI-2: An examination of the Fake Bad Scale in mild head injury. *Journal of Clinical and Experimental Neuropsychology, 26,* 115-124.

Rosse, J. G., Stecher, M. D., Miller, J. L., & Levin, R. A. (1998). The impact of response distortion on preemployment personality testing and hiring decisions. *Journal of Applied Psychology, 83*(4), 634-644.

Rowland, L. W. (1939). Will hypnotized persons try to harm themselves or others? *Journal of Abnormal Psychology, 34,* 114-117.

Salekin, R. T. (2000). Test review: The Paulhus Deception Scales. *American Psychology-Law Society News, 20*(3), 8-11.

Salekin, R. T., Rogers, R., & Sewell, K. W. (1997). Construct validity of psychopathy in a female offender sample: A multitrait-multimethod evaluation. *Journal of Abnormal Psychology, 106,* 576-585.

Schinka, J. A., & Borum, R. (1993). Readability of adult psychopathology inventories. *Psychological Assessment, 5*, 384-386.

Schinka, J. A., Kinder, B. N., & Kremer, T. (1997). Research validity scales for the NEO- PI-R: Development and initial validation. *Journal of Personality Assessment, 68*, 127-138.

Schretlen, D. J. (1988). The use of psychological tests to identify malingered symptoms of mental disorder. *Clinical Psychology Review, 8*, 451-476.

Schretlen, D. J. (1997). Dissimulation on the Rorschach and other projective measures. In R. Rogers (Ed.), *Clinical Assessment of Malingering and Deception* (2nd ed., pp. 208-222). New York: Guilford.

Schretlen, D. J., & Arkowitz, H. (1990). A psychological test battery to detect prison inmates who fake insanity or retardation. *Behavioral Sciences and the Law, 8*, 75-84.

Schroeder, M. L., Schroeder, K. G., & Hare, R. D. (1983). Generalizability of a checklist for the assessment of psychopathy. *Journal of Consulting and Clinical Psychology, 51*, 511-516.

Schwartz, S. M., Gramling, S. E., Kerr, K. L., & Morin, C. (1998). Evaluation of intellect and deficit specific information on the ability to fake memory deficits. *International Journal of Law and Psychiatry, 21*(3), 261-272.

Seto, M. C., & Barbaree, H. E. (1999). Psychopathy, treatment behavior, and sex offender recidivism. *Journal of Interpersonal Violence, 14*, 1235-1248.

Seto, M. C., Khattar, N. A., Lalumiere, L. L, & Quinsey, V. L. (1997). Deception and sexual strategy in psychopathy. *Personality and Individual Differences, 22*, 301-307.

Shapiro, D. L. (1993). Detection of malingering and deception. In L. Vandecreek, S. Knapp, & T. L. Jackson (Eds.), *Innovations in Clinical Practice: A Source Book* (Vol. 12, pp. 5-13). Sarasota, FL: Professional Resource Press.

Siegel, S. (1956). *Nonparametric Statistics for the Behavioral Sciences.* New York: McGraw-Hill.

Sierles, F. S. (1984). Correlates of malingering. *Behavioral Sciences and the Law, 2*, 113-118.

Silverton, L., & Gruber, C. (1998). *Malingering Probability Scale Manual.* Los Angeles: Western Psychological Services.

Sinnett, E. R., Holen, M. C., & Albott, W. L. (1999). Profile validity standards for MMPI and MMPI-2 F scales. *Psychological Reports, 84*, 288-290.

Slick, D. J., Hopp, G., Strauss E., & Spellacy, F. J. (1996). Victoria Symptom Validity Test: Efficiency for detecting feigned memory impairment and relationship to neuropsychological tests and MMPI-2 Validity Scales. *Journal of Clinical and Experimental Neuropsychology, 18,* 911-922.

Slick, D. J., Hopp, G., Strauss E., & Thompson, G. B. (1997). *Victoria Symptom Validity Test Professional Manual.* Odessa, FL: Psychological Assessment Resources.

Slick, D. J., Iverson, G. I., & Green, P. (2000). California Verbal Learning Test indicators of suboptimal performance in a sample of head-injury litigants. *Journal of Clinical and Experimental Neuropsychology, 22,* 569-579.

Slick, D. J., Sherman, E. M. S., & Iverson, G. L. (1999). Diagnostic criteria for malingered neurocognitive dysfunction: Proposed standards for clinical practice and research. *Clinical Neuropsychologist, 13,* 545-561.

Smith, G. P. (1997). Assessment of malingering with self-report instruments. In R. Rogers (Ed.), *Clinical Assessment of Malingering and Deception* (2nd ed., pp. 351-370). New York: Guilford.

Smith, G. P., & Borum, R. (1992). Detection of malingering in a forensic sample: A study of the M Test. *Journal of Psychiatry and Law, 20*(4), 505-514.

Smith, G. P., Borum. R., & Schinka, J. A. (1993). Rule-out and rule-in scales for the M Test for malingering: A cross-validation. *Bulletin of the American Academy of Psychiatry and the Law, 21*(1), 107-110.

Smith, G. P., & Burger, G. K. (1997). Detection of malingering: Validation of the Structured Inventory of Malingered Symptomatology (SIMS). *Bulletin of the American Academy of Psychiatry and the Law, 25,* 183-189.

Smith, S. R., & Meyer, R. G. (1987). *Law, Behavior, and Mental Health: Policy and Practice.* New York: New York University Press.

Spanos, N. P., Burgess, D. A., Roncon, V., Wallace-Capretta, S., & Cross, P. (1993) Surreptitiously observed hypnotic responding in simulators and in skill-trained and untrained high hypnotizables. *Journal of Personality and Social Psychology, 65*(2), 392-398.

Spiegel, H., & Spiegel, D. (2004). *Trance and Treatment.* Washington, DC: American Psychiatric Association.

State v. Hurd, 86 N. J. 525, 432 A.2d 86 (1981).

State v. Pusch, 46 N. W.2d 508 (1950).

Steffan, J. S., Clopton, J. R., & Morgan, R. D. (2003). An MMPI-2 scale to detect malingered depression (Md Scale). *Assessment, 10,* 382-392.

Stein, L. A. R., Graham, J. R., & Williams, C. L. (1995). Detecting fake-bad MMPI-A profiles. *Journal of Personality Assessment, 65*, 415-427.

Stober, J. (2001). The Social Desirability Scale-17 (SDS-17): Convergent validity, discriminant validity, and relationship with age. *European Journal of Psychological Assessment, 17*, 222-232.

Storm, J., & Graham, J. R. (2000). Detection of coached general malingering on the MMPI-2. *Psychological Assessment, 12*, 158-165.

Strahan, R., & Gerbasi, K. C. (1972). Short, homogenous versions of the Marlowe-Crowne Social Desirability Scale. *Journal of Clinical Psychology, 28*, 191-193.

Strong, D. R., Greene, R. L., Hoppe, C., Johnston, T., & Oleson, N. (1999). Taxometric analysis of impression management and self-deception on the MMPI-2 in child custody litigants. *Journal of Personality Assessment, 73*, 1-18.

Strong, D. R., Greene, R. L., & Schinka, J. A. (2000). A taxometric analysis of MMPI-2 Infrequency Scales [F and F(p)] in clinical settings. *Psychological Assessment, 12*, 166-173.

Stutts, J. T., Hickey, S. E., & Kasdan, M. L. (2003). Malingering by proxy: A form of pediatric condition falsification. *Journal of Developmental and Behavioral Pediatrics, 24*, 276-278.

Sweet, J. J. (1999). Malingering: Differential diagnosis. In J. J. Sweet (Ed.), *Forensic Neuropsychology: Fundamentals and Practice* (pp. 255-285). Lisse, The Netherlands: Swets & Zeitlinger.

Sweet, J. J., & King, J. H. (2002). Category Test validity indicators: Overview and practice recommendations. In J. Hom & R. L. Denney (Eds.), *Detection of Response Bias in Forensic Neuropsychology* (pp. 241-274). Binghamton, NY: Haworth.

Talwar, V., Lee, K., Bala, N., & Lindsay, R. C. L. (2004). Children's lie-telling to conceal a parent's transgression: Legal implications. *Law and Human Behavior, 28*, 411-435.

Teichner, G., & Wagner, M. T. (2004). The Test of Memory Malingering (TOMM): Normative data from cognitively intact, cognitively impaired, and elderly patients with dementia. *Archives of Clinical Neuropsychology, 19*, 455-464.

Tenhula, W., & Sweet, J. (1996). Double cross-validation of the Booklet Category Test in detecting malingered traumatic brain injury. *Clinical Neuropsychologist, 10*, 104-116.

Teplin, L. A. (1990). Detecting disorder: The treatment of mental illness among jail detainees. *Journal of Consulting and Clinical Psychology, 58*(2), 233-236.

Teplin, L. A. (1994). Psychiatric and substance abuse disorders among male urban jail detainees. *American Journal of Public Health, 84*(2), 290-293.

Thompson, G. B. (2002). The Victoria Symptom Validity Test: An enhanced test of symptom validity. In J. Hom & R. L. Denney (Eds.), *Detection of Response Bias in Forensic Neuropsychology* (pp. 43-67). Binghampton, NY: Haworth.

Tombaugh, T. N. (1996). *The Test of Memory Malingering (TOMM).* Toronto, Canada: Multi-Health Systems.

Tombaugh, T. N. (2002). The Test of Memory Malingering (TOMM) in forensic psychology. In J. Hom & R. L. Denney (Eds.), *Detection of Response Bias in Forensic Neuropsychology* (pp. 69-96). Binghamton, NY: Haworth.

Toupin, J., Mercier, H., Dery, M., Cote, G., & Hodgins, S. (1996). Validity of the PCL-R for adolescents. In D. J. Cooke, A. E. Forth, J. Newman, & R. D. Hare (Eds.), *Issues in Criminological and Legal Psychology: No. 24. International Perspectives on Psychopathy* (pp. 143-145). Leicester, England: British Psychological Society.

Tringone, R. (2002). Essentials of MACI assessment. In S. Strack (Ed.), *Essentials of Millon Inventories Assessment* (2nd ed., pp. 106-174). New York: Wiley.

Trueblood, W., & Schmidt, M. (1993). Malingering and other validity considerations in the neuropsychological evaluation of mild head injury. *Journal of Clinical and Experimental Neuropsychology, 15*(4), 578-590.

Tsushima, W. T., & Tsushima, V. G. (2001). Comparison of the Fake Bad Scale and other MMPI-2 validity scales with personal injury litigants. *Assessment, 8*, 205-212.

U. S. v. Galbreth, 908 F. Supp. 877 (D.N.M. 1995).

U. S. v. Scheffer, 523 U.S. 303 (1998).

Vallabhajosula, B., & van Gorp, W. (2001). Post-Daubert admissibility of scientific evidence on malingering of cognitive deficits. *Journal of the American Academy of Psychiatry and the Law, 29*, 207-215.

Vella-Broderick, D. A., & White, V. (1997). Response set of social desirability in relation to the Mental, Physical, and Spiritual Well-Being Scale. *Psychological Reports, 81*, 127-130.

Verona, E., Patrick, C. J., Curtin, J. J., Bradley, M. M., & Lang, P. (2004). Psychopathy and physiological response to emotionally evocative sounds. *Journal of Abnormal Psychology, 113*, 99-108.

Viglione, D. J., & Landis, P. (1994, March). *The Development of an Objective Test for Malingering*. Paper presented at the biennial meeting of the American Psychology-Law Society, Santa Fe, NM.

Vrij, A. (2000). *Detecting Lies and Deceit: The Psychology of Lying and Implications for Professional Practice*. Chichester, UK: Wiley.

Walters, G. D., White, T. W., & Greene, R. L. (1988). Use of the MMPI to identify malingering and exaggeration of psychiatric symptomatology in male prison inmates. *Journal of Consulting and Clinical Psychology, 56*, 111-117.

Walters, G. L., & Clopton, J. R. (2000). Effect of symptom information and validity scale information on the malingering of depression on the MMPI-2. *Journal of Personality Assessment, 75*, 183-199.

Wang, E. W., Rogers, R., Giles, C. L., Diamond, P. M., Herrington-Wang, L. E., & Taylor, E. L. (1997). A pilot study of the Personality Assessment Inventory (PAI) in corrections: Assessment of malingering, suicide risk, and aggression in male inmates. *Behavioral Sciences and the Law, 15*, 469-482.

Ward, R., Hudson, S. M., & Marshall, W. L. (1995). Cognitive distortions and affective deficits in sex offenders. *Sexual Abuse: A Journal of Research and Treatment, 7*, 67-83.

Warrington, E. K. (1984). *Recognition Memory Test*. Windsor, England: NFER-Nelson.

Wasyliw, O. E., & Grossman, L. S. (1988). The detection of malingering in criminal forensic groups: MMPI validity scales. *Journal of Personality Assessment, 52*, 321-333.

Watkins, J. G. (1984). The Bianchi (L. A. Hillside Strangler) Case: Sociopath or multiple personality disorder? *The International Journal of Clinical and Experimental Hypnosis, 32*(2), 67-101.

Waud, S. P. (1942). Malingering. *Military Surgeon, 91*, 535-538. (Abstract obtained from Psychinfo, 2000, Abstract No. 1943-00917-001).

Weinborn, M., Orr, T., Woods, S. P., Conover, E., & Feix, J. (2003). A validation of the Test of Memory Malingering in a forensic psychiatric setting. *Journal of Clinical and Experimental Neuropsychology, 25*, 979-990.

Wetter, M. W., Baer, R. A., Berry, D. T. R., & Reynolds, S. K. (1994). The effect of symptom information on faking on the MMPI-2. *Assessment, 1*, 199-207.

Wetter, M. W., Baer, R. A., Berry, D. T. R., Smith, G. T., & Larson, L. H. (1992). Sensitivity of MMPI-2 validity scales to random responding and malingering. *Psychological Assessment, 4*, 369-374.

Wetter, M. W., & Corrigan, S. K. (1995). Providing information to clients about psychological tests: A survey of attorneys' and law students' attitudes. *Professional Psychology: Research and Practice, 26*, 474-477.

Widiger, T. A. (2001). The best and the worst of us? *Clinical Psychology: Science and Practice, 8*(3), 374-377.

Wiener, D. N., & Harmon, L. R. (1946). *Subtle and Obvious Keys for the MMPI: Their Development* (VA Advisement Bulletin No. 16). Minneapolis, MN: Regional Veterans Administration Office.

Wiggins, J. S. (1959). Interrelationships among MMPI measures of dissimulation under standard and social desirability instructions. *Journal of Consulting Psychology, 23*, 419-427.

Wilson v. U. S., 391 F.2d 460 (1968).

Wilson, D. J. (2000). *Bureau of Justice Statistics Special Report: Drug Use, Testing, and Treatment In Jails* (NCJ Publication No. 179999). Washington, DC: U. S. Department of Justice.

Wirt, R. D., Lachar, D., Klinedinst, J. K., & Seat, P. D. (1984). *Multidimensional Description of Child Personality: A Manual for the Personality Inventory for Children*. Los Angeles: Western Psychological Services.

Wong, S. (1984). *Criminal and Institutional Behaviors of Psychopaths*. Ottawa, Canada: Ministry of the Solicitor-General of Canada.

Wong, S., & Hare, R. D. (2000). *Program Guidelines for the Institutional Treatment of Violent Psychopathic Offenders*. Unpublished treatment manual.

Wynkoop, T. F., & Denney, R. L. (1999). Exaggeration of neuropsychological deficit in competency to stand trial. *Journal of Forensic Neuropsychology, 1*(2), 29-53.

Wynkoop, T. F., & Denney, R. L. (2001). Test reviews: Computerized Assessment of Response Bias (CARB), Word Memory Test (WMT), and Memory Complaints Inventory (MCI). *Journal of Forensic Neuropsychology, 2*(1) 71-77.

Wynkoop, T. F., & Denney, R. L. (2005). Test review: Green's Word Memory Test (WMT) for Windows. *Journal of Forensic Neuropsychology, 4*, 101-105.

Young, P. C. (1952). Antisocial uses of hypnosis. In L. LeCron (Ed.), *Experimental Hypnosis* (pp. 376-409). New York: Macmillan.

Youngjohn, J. R. (1995) Confirmed attorney coaching prior to neuropsychological evaluation. *Assessment 2*, 279-283.

Youngjohn, J. R., Burrows, L., & Erdal, K. (1995). Brain damage or compensation neurosis? The controversial post-concussion syndrome. *The Clinical Neuropsychologist, 9*(2), 112-123.

Zachary, R. A. (1986). *Shipley Institute of Living Scale Revised Manual.* Los Angeles: Western Psychological Services.

Zani v. State, 767 S. W.2d 825 (Tex. App. - Texarkana 1988).

SUBJECT INDEX

Ability, 133
Ackley, M.A., 114
Acquiescence, 42, 51
Adams, K.M., 110, 131
Adaptational model, 10-11
Adelson, R., 32
Adolescents, 46. *See also* Children
  juveniles and, 162
  perception of, 172
  social norms/values of, 172-173
Adults, 46, 187
African-Americans, 6-7, 195
Age-regression inconsistencies,
  150
Aguila-Puentes, G., 112
Albott, W.L., 64
Allen, L.M., 111, 128
Allison, Ralph, 148
Alterman, A.I., 189
Altman, H., 63-64
American Board of Clinical
  Neuropsychology, 111
American Medical Association,
  136
American Polygraph Association,
  152
American Psychiatric Association
  (APA), 2, 5, 9, 10, 136-137

American Psychological
  Association, 137, 164
American Society of Clinical
  Hypnosis (ASCH), 138,
  144
Ames, Aldrich, 153
Amnesia, 121, 129. *See also* Source
  Amnesia
Andrews, P., 102, 204, 216
Anesthesia, 149-150
Anger, 27, 28
Antisocial Personality Disorder
  (APD), 5, 6, 183, 184, 194
Anxiety, 107
APA. *See* American Psychiatric
  Association
APD. *See* Antisocial Personality
  Disorder
Apprehension, 28
Arbisi, P.A., 63, 73
Archer, R.P., 66, 71
Ardolf, B., 112
Aronow, E., 55
Arons, Harry, 136
ASCH. *See* American Society of
  Clinical Hypnosis
Autonomic nervous system, 27
Axis I diagnosis, 170, 199
Axis II diagnosis, 12

Baer, R.A., 7, 63, 70, 78
Bagby, M.R., 62, 69, 168-169
Bagby, R.M., 198
Baker, W.J., 73, 110, 113
Barber, Theodore, 143
Base rate (BR)
    of MND, 131
    of NRB, 111
BCT. *See* Booklet Category Test
Behavior, 120, 137-140
Behavioral cues
    to detect deception, 21-31, 37-
        39
    nonverbal/physiological, 147-
        148
    observed, 120
Benning, S.D., 186
Ben-Porath, Y.S., 63, 73, 127
Benton Judgment of Line
        Orientation, 128
Benton Visual Form
        Discrimination, 128
Benussi, 151
Berry, D.T.R., 7, 63, 70, 78, 112
Bianchi, Kenneth, 144, 148-150,
        157
Bianchini, K.J., 132
Biased responding, 13
Binder, L.M., 110, 113, 126
Binet, A., 144
Black, Hugo, 141
Blacks, 187
Blinking, 29
Block, M., 147
Blum, G.S., 146
Board of Professional Affairs, 54
Boardman, C.R., 189
Boccaccini, M.T., 55
Body
    language, 24-25, 31, 38
    movements, 27, 31
Bompard, Gabrielle, 139
Booklet Category Test (BCT), 111-
        112, 123

Boone, D., 76
Boone, K.B., 126
Borum, R., 94
Boulch, James, 142
Boyd, A.R., 192
BPRS. *See* Brief Psychiatric Rating
        Scale
BR. *See* Base rate
Braid, James, 135
Brain
    functioning, 120
    wave patterns, 147
Breathing, rapid, 27
Breuer, Josef, 135
Brief Psychiatric Rating Scale
        (BPRS), 71
British Medical Association, 136
Brodsky, S.L., 55
Bruck, M., 171
Brunetti, D.G., 76
Buffington, J.K., 8
Buis, T., 62, 69
Bull, R., 26, 31
Burdock, Ann-Augusta, 140
Burrows, L., 110
Butcher, J.N., 69, 131

Cacciola, J.S., 189
Caldwell, A., 78
California Psychological Inventory
        (CPI), 192
California, Supreme Court of, 60,
        141
California Verbal Learning Tests,
        128
Canyock, E.M., 111, 112
CARB. *See* Computerized
        Assessment of Response
        Bias
Carone, J.E., 146
Carter, M., 130
Category Test, 128
Caucasians, 6
CD. *See* Conduct Disorder

Ceci, S.J., 171
Central Intelligence Agency (CIA),
    153
Central nervous system (CNS), 120
Chakraborty, 69
Chest, heaving, 27
Children, 46. *See also* Adolescents;
    Millon Adolescent Clinical
    Inventory; Minnesota
    Multiphasic Personality
    Inventory for Adolescents;
    Personality Inventory for
    Children; Psychopathy
    Checklist: Youth Version
  assessment strategies for, 163-
    170
  behavior of, 172
  child welfare and, 162
  conclusions/summary on, 180-
    182
  criminal justice system and, 162
  developmental phases of, 165-
    167
  interviewing techniques for,
    171-174
  juveniles and, 162
  malingering/dissimulation in,
    161-182
  managed care and, 162-163
  memory of, 166-167
  motivation of, 168-169
  neurological testing for, 179-180
  parents and, 169
  perception/values of, 172-173
  psychological testing for, 174-
    179, 182
  SIRS for, 173-174
CIA. *See* Central Intelligence
    Agency
Clark, B.K., 166, 172
Clark, C.R., 7, 197, 198, 199
Cleckley, H., 184
Clifton, Charles, 155-156
Clopton, J.R., 74, 76

CNS. *See* Central nervous system
Coe, W.C., 148
Cognitive dysfunctions, 7
Cognitive impairment, 33
Cohn, M.G., 3
Colwell, K., 32
Commonwealth v. Burke, 141
Computerized Assessment of
    Response Bias (CARB)
  performance on, 111, 212, 214
  short-term memory and, 126-
    128, 133
Concentration, 7
Conduct Disorder (CD), 194
Confusion, 7, 94
Connecticut Supreme Court, 144
Conversion disorders, 13, 108, 114
Cooke, D.J., 186
Coping model, 9
Cornell, D.G., 112
Correctional treatment settings,
    219-221
Cote, G., 195
Courts, 8, 129, 156, 157, 167
  hypnosis and, 138-140
  state, 60, 141, 144
CPI. *See* California Psychological
    Inventory
Criminal justice system, 8, 156, 162
Criminological model, 9-10
Cruise, K.R., 48

Das Verbrechen in Hypnose
    (Mayer), 140
*Daubert v. Merrill Dow
    Pharmaceuticals, Inc.,* 126,
    142-143, 157
de Cuvillers, Etienne, 135
Deception. *See also* Malingering
  anecdotal signs of, 145
  assessment models for, 145-146
  basics of, 1-17
  behavioral cues to detect, 21-31,
    37-39

Deception *(Cont'd)*
   case examples of, 208-222
   deliberate, 42
   detection measures/methods for,
      16, 87-106
   general assessment techniques
      for, 15-16, 19-83
   hypnosis and, 143-151
   interview strategies to detect,
      21, 35-39
   precautionary statements and,
      22-23
   psychological tests for, 41
   psychopathy and, 196-202
   response styles with, 41-42
   settings/types of assessments in,
      203-204
   special populations and, 16-17
   spoken words and, 21
   symptom reports and, 33-35
   test selection issues for, 43, 207-
      208
   types of, 23
Declaration of Independence, 135
Deemer, H.N., 12
Defensiveness, 68
Delain, S.L., 127
Delusions, 34, 38
Denial, 9, 68, 216
Denney, R.L., 108, 111, 112-113,
   130
Depression, 59, 75, 107, 111
Depressive disorders, 6
Der Hypnotisme (Moll), 139
Dery, M., 195
Deviant Responding (DR) scale,
   193
DHT. *See* Double Hallucination
   Test
Diagnostic and Statistical Manual
   of Mental Disorders (DSM)
   -*III-R*, 44, 46
   -*IV*, 4, 9, 44, 184
   -*IV-TR*, 170
Dickens, S.E., 198

Digit Memory Test, 109
"Directed Lie Control Question
   Technique," 156
Disabilities, 208-214
Disorientation, 7
Dissimulation, in children, 161-182
Dissimulation Scale (Ds), 74-75
Dissimulation Scale-Revised, 74
Dissimulatory response styles, 180
Distinguished Professional
   Contributions to
   Knowledge, 54
Distress, 28
Dorfman, W.I., 69
Double Hallucination Test (DHT),
   149
DR. *See* Deviant Responding scale
Draw-A-Person Test, 55
Ds. *See* Dissimulation Scale
DSM. *See Diagnostic and*
   Statistical Manual of
   Mental Disorders
du Maurier, George, 138

Eating disorders, 6
Edens, J.F., 8, 198
Education, 7
Edwards, A.L., 77, 102
Ekman, P., 21, 24, 25, 28, 31-32,
   148, 196
Electrodermal skin response (SCR),
   148
Eloise, Michigan, 136
Emery, C., 137
Emotions, 28
   emblems and, 25
   faking, 30
   lies and, 23-24
   timing of, 30
Emotions Revealed: Recognizing
   Faces and Feelings to
   Improve Communication
   and Emotional Life
   (Ekman), 28

Employee Polygraph Protection Act
     (1988), 153
English, L.T., 73
Erdal, K., 110
Erickson, Milton H., 136
Estabrooks, George, 137
*Ethical Principles of Psychologists
     and Code of Conduct*
     (American Psychological
     Association), 164, 181-182
Ethics, 163-165, 181-182
Exaggerated responses, 146
Exner, J., 53, 54
Exner's Comprehensive Scoring
     System, 53
Eyes, 26, 29, 38
Eyrand-Bompard affairs, 139

Facial expressions, 27, 28, 31
     asymmetry of, 29-30, 38
     control of, 27
     timing of, 30
Factitious Disorder (FD), 2, 114,
     204
     descriptive data on, 11-12
     men and, 11-12
     prevalence of, 11-13
     women and, 11-12
Fairman, J.C., 111
Fake Bad Scale (FBS), 73-74, 82,
     207, 212
     correlations of, 132
     performance, 131-132
     usage of, 131
     validity of, 131
Fake-bad responding, 63, 72-79,
     82, 83
Fake-good responding, 14, 60, 61,
     65, 76-79, 104
Faust, D., 114
Fautek, P.K., 55
FBI. *See* Federal Bureau of
     Investigation
FBS. *See* Fake Bad Scale

FCTs. *See* Forced-choice tests
FD. *See* Factitious Disorder
Federal Bureau of Investigation
     (FBI), 153
Federal Rules of Evidence, 157
F-Fb index, 69-70
Fidgeting, 26-27, 38
Finger oscillation test (FOT), 109
Finger Tapping, 128
First International Congress for
     Experimental and Clinical
     Hypnotism, 139
F-K index, 68-69
Fontaine, J., 66, 71
Forced-Choice Test of Nonverbal
     Ability, 109
Forced-choice tests (FCTs), 123,
     130
Ford, C.V., 6
Forehead, 28
Forth, A.E., 194, 195
FOT. *See* Finger oscillation test
Fox, D.D., 132
Fptsd. *See* Infrequency-Post
     Traumatic Stress Disorder
     scale
Frank, M.G., 32
Franzen, M.D., 7
Frederick, R.I., 109, 112, 125, 126,
     130
Freud, Sigmund, 135
Friedman, A.F., 67
Frye v. United States, 142-143,
     151, 157
Fuchs study, 169

Gacono, C.B., 189, 191, 199
GAF. *See* Global Assessment of
     Functioning
Galvanic skin response (GSR), 148
Ganellen, R.J., 56
Garron, D.C., 111
Gillis, J.R., 198
Glenn, W.J., 73

Global Assessment of Functioning
    (GAF), 71
Gola, T., 73, 110, 113
Gold, S.N., 69
Goldstein, A., 9
Goodstein, L.D., 42
Gough, H.G., 74
Gouvier, W.D., 7
Graef, J.R., 146
Graham, J.R., 72, 176
Gramling, S.E., 7
Green, P., 111, 127-128
Green, R., 70, 78
Greene, R.L., 72
Greiffenstein, M.F., 73, 110, 113
Greve, K.W., 132
Grief, 28
Grisso, T., 89
Grossman, L.S., 56
Grote, C.L., 111
Grow, 179
GSR. *See* Galvanic skin response
Guilt, 28
Guy, L.S., 8
Gynther, M.D., 63-64

Hale, D.B., 7
Halfaker, D.A., 111
Hall, H., 145
Hall, J.R., 186
Hallucinations, 149
    auditory, 7, 34, 38
    bizarre, 34
    visual, 34, 38-39
Halstead-Reitan Battery, 128
Hamilton, J.C., 12
Hands, 25, 26
Hanley, C., 77
Hare, R.D., 184, 185, 187-188,
    189, 194, 195
Harrell, E.H., 5, 179
Harris, M.R., 33-34
Hartmann, D.J., 6

Harvard University, 151
Haskett, J., 8
Hauer, B., 130
Hawk, G.L., 112
Hayes, J.S., 7
Haywood, T.W., 56
Head
    injuries, 121
    nodding, 26
Heaton, R.K., 109
Heilbrun, K., 174
Heinze, M.C., 9
Helmes, E., 105
Hickey, J.E., 169
Hinds, J.D., 173, 176-177
Hiscock, C.K., 109
Hiscock Digit Memory Test, 110,
    126
Hiscock, M., 109
Hiscock-Anisman, C., 32
Hodgins, S., 195
Holden, R.R., 105
Holen, M.C., 64
Hollender, M.H., 6
Hollrah, J.L., 76
Hom, J., 108
Honesty, 50-51
Honts, Charles, 154
Houston, C., 112
HSI. *See* Hypnotic Simulation
    Index
Hudson, S.M., 9
Hull, Clark, 136
Hypnosis, 157
    control of behavior by, 137-140
    courts/media and, 138-140
    deception and, 143-151
    deep, 147
    faking, 143-144
    introduction to, 135-137
    malingering and, 143-151
    procedural cues with, 148-149
    in U.S., 136, 140-143

Hypnosis and Sensibility (Hull), 136
Hypnotic analgesia, 147
Hypnotic Simulation Index (HSI), 147
Hypnotic trance, 147-148
Hypochondriasis, 59
Hypomania, 60
Hysteria, 59

Iacono, W.G., 200
ICN. *See* Inconsistency Scale
Identification, 7
Illustrators, 25-26
IM. *See* Impression Management
Impression Management (IM), 13-14, 103, 216
Inconsistency (INC), 52
Inconsistency Scale (ICN), 47-48
INF. *See* Infrequency Scale
Infrequency-Post Traumatic Stress Disorder scale (Fptsd), 75
Infrequency Psychopathology Scale, 72-73, 81-82
Infrequency Scale (INF), 47-48
Insanity defense, 8
Intelligence, 7, 87, 88, 125, 133, 210
Inventory of Problems (IOP), 95, 100-101
Iverson, G.L., 111, 115, 116, 129

Jail/prison inmates, 219-221
    malingering and, 3-4, 6, 8, 10-11
    populations of, 6, 187, 189
Janata, J.W., 12
Johnston, D., 109
Johnston, J.D., 146
Journal for Clinical and Experimental Hypnosis, 136
Juveniles, 162. *See also* Adolescents; Children

Kasdan, M.L., 169
Keeler, Leonard, 152
Kelly, M.P., 110
Kennedy, J., 148
Kerensky, Alexander, 140
Kerr, K.L., 7
Kinder, B.N., 52
King, B.H., 6
Kinnument, T., 147
Kirsch, I., 146
Knight, S., 138, 144
Kooker, E.K., 111
Kosson, D.S., 187, 194
Krahn, L.E., 11
Kremer, T., 52
Krukowski, R.A., 131
Kumho Tire Co. v. Carmichael, 143
Kurtz, R., 93

Lacy, J.H., 6
Lanyon, R.I., 42
Larrabee, G.J., 73, 111-112, 114, 123-124, 129, 131-132
Larson, 151
Larson, L.H., 7, 63, 70, 78
Lees-Haley, P.R., 73, 128, 131, 132, 212
Legal systems, 140-143, 156-157
Lehman, R.A.W., 109
Lewak, R., 67
Lewis, J.L., 63, 112
Leyra v. Denno, 141
Li, H., 11
Lie(s)
    detection and polygraph, 151-158
    emotions and, 23-24
    pathological, 183
Liff, C.D., 5, 179
Linguistic Inquiry and Word Count software, 32
Lips, 28
Litigation, 5, 8
L+K index, 70

Loevinger, J., 44
Loss of consciousness (LOC), 120-
    121
Lu, P., 126
Lunde, Donald, 148
Lundy, 140
Lynn, S.J., 147

M Test, 89, 94-95, 96, 100-101,
    106
MACI. *See* Millon Adolescent
    Clinical Inventory
MACI Modifier Indices, 177-178
Malingered depression (Md) scale,
    75
Malingered neurocognitive
    dysfunction (MND), 115
  base rate of, 131
  classification criteria/system for,
    115-116, 118-122
  Criterion A, 119
  Criterion B, 119-120, 123-124
  Criterion C, 121-122, 124
  Criterion D, 122
  definite, 118
  definition of, 116
  diagnostic categories in, 118-
    122
  diagnostic tree for, 117
  possible, 119
  probable, 118, 124
Malingering, 38, 42. *See also*
    Deception
  adaptational/coping model for,
    9-11
  age/race/factors associated with,
    6-8
  in children, 161-182
  in clinical practice, 99
  construct specific tools for, 93-
    98
  criminological model for, 9-10
  definitions for, 2-4, 10
  detection of, 8, 74

Malingering *(Cont'd)*
  differentiation of, 4
  explanatory/theoretical models
    for, 9-11
  frequency of, 5
  hypnosis and, 143-151
  jail/prison detainees and, 3-4, 6,
    8, 10-11
  litigation and, 5, 8
  neurocognitive, 108-109, 133
  NRB and, 108-109
  personality and, 5-6, 44
  prevalence of, 4-6
  range of, 3-4
  Rogers on, 5, 9-10, 112
  screening for, 93-98
  -specific tests, 88-89
  strategies, 115
  test selection for, 98-101
  "totaling" and, 3
Malingering Index, 49
Malingering Probability Scale
    (MPS), 96, 100-101
Malingering Scale (MS), 96-97,
    100-101
Manipulators, 26-27
Mann, S., 26, 31
Marlowe-Crowne Social
    Desirability Scale
    (MCSDS), 106, 214-218
  development of, 102
  mean score on, 103
  Short Form C, 103
Marshall, W.L., 9
Marston, William Moulton, 151-
    152
Marten, N., 7
Martin, D.J., 147
Masculinity-Femininity, 59
The Mask of Sanity (Cleckley), 184
Mattingly, M.L., 111
Mayer, Ludwig, 140
McCann, J.T., 55, 162, 164, 172,
    177-178
McCrae, R.R., 66, 71

McFarlane, 169
McLearen, A.M., 98
MCMI-III. *See* Millon Clinical
    Multiaxial Inventory
MCSDS. *See* Marlowe-Crowne
    Social Desirability Scale
McVaugh, 179
Md. *See* Malingered depression
    scale
Mean Elevation (ME), 79, 217
Medications, 3, 4, 6, 8, 199, 204
Meloy, J.R., 199
Melton, G.B., 8
Memon, A., 32
Memory, 7. *See also* Rarely Missed
    Index of the Wechsler
    Memory Scale-III;
    Wechsler Memory Scale
CARB/short-term, 126-127, 133
of children, 166-167
Digit Memory Test and, 109
Hiscock Digit Memory Test and,
    110, 126
impaired, 121
impairment, identification of
        feigned remote, 129-130
loss, 33-34
Rey's 15-Item Memory Test
        and, 110, 126, 133, 212
RMT and, 110, 128
TOMM and, 127
WMT and, 111, 127, 212, 214
Men, 67, 187, 189
FD and, 11-12
young, 6, 7
Mental illness, severe, 6
Mercier, H., 195
Merckelbach, H., 130
Mesmer, Anton, 135
Meyer, R.G., 63-64, 66, 69, 73, 93,
        102, 138, 144, 204, 216
Meyers, J.E., 110, 129, 132
M-FAST. *See* Miller Forensic
    Assessment of Symptoms
    Test

Michie, C., 186
Michigan, 136
Micro-expressions, 28, 38
Miller Forensic Assessment of
    Symptoms Test (M-FAST),
    95-96, 100-101, 106
Millon Adolescent Clinical
    Inventory (MACI), 175,
    177-178
Millon Clinical Multiaxial
    Inventory (MCMI-III), 44-
    45, 88
Scale V, 45
Scale X (Disclosure), 45
Scale Y (Desirability), 45
Scale Z (Debasement), 45
Millis, S.R., 110, 116, 131
Minnesota Multiphasic Personality
    Inventory (MMPI), 41, 59,
    60, 68, 74, 76
Minnesota Multiphasic Personality
    Inventory-2 (MMPI-2), 41,
    43-44, 59-83, 192, 207-
    208, 212-218
"cannot say" scale and, 60-61
clinical scales of, 59-60, 133
Content Scales and Supple-
        mental Scales, 60
F scale in, 60, 63-66, 68, 82
Fb scale in, 63-66, 69, 82
items of, 72, 79-83
K scale in, 60, 62, 64, 66-68
L (Lie) scale in, 60, 61-62, 82
Psychopathic Deviate Scale,
        198
scale in, 60, 63-66, 68
test materials, 68
usage of, 46, 56, 63, 87-88
validity scales and, 60-80, 83
Minnesota Multiphasic Personality
    Inventory for Adolescents
    (MMPI-A), 174, 175-177

Minor, H.I., 6
Mittenberg, W., 111, 112
MMPI/MMPI-2. *See* Minnesota
Multiphasic Personality
Inventory
MMPI-A. *See* Minnesota
Multiphasic Personality
Inventory for Adolescents
MND. *See* Malingered
neurocognitive dysfunction
Moffit, T.E., 195
Moll, Albert, 139
Moreland, K., 55
Morey, L.C., 48
Morin, C., 7
Motivation, 204
of children, 168-169
for NRB, 1-2
Mouth, 26
Mp. *See* Positive Malingering scale
MPD. *See* Multiple Personality
Disorder
MPS. *See* Malingering Probability
Scale
MS. *See* Malingering Scale
Multiple Data Sources Model, 205-
206, 221
Multiple Personality Disorder
(MPD), 149
Muscles, 28

Nancy School, 139, 141
National Research Council, 152,
153, 154, 155
Negative Impression Management
Scale (NIM), 47
Negative Presentation Management
(NPM), 52
Negative Response Bias (NRB).
See also Malingering
base rate of, 111
in civil forensic settings, 109-
112
in criminal forensic settings, 112

Negative Response Bias *(Cont'd)*
definite, 120
detection methods for, 128
embedded indices of
neurocognitive, 128-129
freestanding indices of
neurocognitive, 125-128
general intellectual ability and,
125
identification of, 116
malingering and, 108-109
measures of, 132-133
motivations for, 1-2
types of, 13
NEO-PI-R, 44
administration of, 50-52
creation of, 51-52
usage of, 52, 57
Netter, B.E.C., 54
Neurocognitive dysfunction, 107-
133. *See also* Malingered
neurocognitive dysfunction
Neurocognitive malingering, 108-
109, 133
Neurocognitive performance
clinical strategies in, 113-114
identification of, 113-115
Neurocognitive test scores, 111
Neuropsychological evaluation case
example, 208-214
Newman, J.P., 187
Nicholas II, Tsar, 140
Nichols, D.S., 67, 70, 78
Nicholson, R.A., 62, 78
Nies, K.J., 113
NIM. *See* Negative Impression
Management Scale
North Dakota Supreme Court, 141
NPM. *See* Negative Presentation
Management
NRB. *See* Negative Response Bias
Nyenhuis, D.L., 111

O'Connor, M.K., 11
O'Connor, Sandra, 142
Oldershaw, L., 168-169
Orne, Martin T., 137, 145-146, 148-149
O-S index, 76
Otto, R.K., 8

Pankratz, L., 113
Paranoia, 59
Parents, 169
Patrick, C.J., 186, 200
Patton, C., 111, 112
Paulhus, D.L., 103, 104-105
Paulhus Deception Scales (PDS), 106, 214-218
    factors measured in, 104-105
    items on, 103-104
    Manual, 104
    usage of, 103-104
PCL. *See* Psychopathy Checklists
PCL-R. *See* Psychopathy Checklist-Revised
PCL: SV. *See* Psychopathy Checklist: Screening Version
PCL: YV. *See* Psychopathy Checklist: Youth Version
PCS. *See* Postconcussion syndrome
Pd. *See* Psychopathic Deviate
PDRT. *See* Portland Digit Recognition test
PDS. *See* Paulhus Deception Scales
Pennebaker, James, 32
Pensa, R., 69
Pentothal (thiopental), 140
People, of color, 6
People v. Ebanks, 141
People v. John Johnson, 140
People v. Royal, 140
People v. Stow, 60
People v. Worthington, 141

Perry, G., 52
Persistent postconcussive syndrome (PPCS), 110
Personality
    assessment, 52-53
    disorder, Cluster B, 6
    effects of, 7
    malingering and, 5-6, 44
Personality Assessment Laboratory (PAI). *See also specific indexes and scales,* 45-50
    usage of, 45-46, 49-50, 56, 88
    validity scales and, 46-47, 57
Personality Inventory for Children (PIC)
    Defensiveness (DEF) scale in, 178
    Frequency (F) scale in, 178
    K scale in, 178
    Lie (L) scale in, 178
    scales, 178
    Social Desirability (SD) scale in, 178
    usage of, 178, 179
Petrila, J., 8
PIC. *See* Personality Inventory for Children
PIM. *See* Positive Impression Management Scale
PMH. *See* Positive Mental Health
Polgar, Franz, 135
Police officers, 31
Polygraph
    effectiveness of, 153
    legal systems and, 156-157
    lie detection and, 151-158
    validity of, 153
Portland Digit Recognition test (PDRT), 110, 133
Positive Impression Management Scale (PIM), 47
Positive Malingering (Mp) scale, 76-77

Positive Mental Health (PMH), 78
Positive Presentation Management
    (PPM), 52
Postconcussion syndrome (PCS),
    110
Post-traumatic amnesia (PTA), 120
Posttraumatic Stress Disorder
    (PTSD), 35, 39, 54
Posture changes, 26
Powel, J., 109, 130
Poythress, N.G., 8, 198
PPCS. See Persistent
    postconcussive syndrome
PPI. See Psychopathic Personality
    Inventory
PPM. See Positive Presentation
    Management
Pritchard, D., 145
Probable response bias, 120
Projective test usage, 55-56
Psychasthenia, 59
Psychological dysfunction, 122
    exaggerated, 131-132
    fabricated, 131-132
Psychopathic Deviate (Pd), 59, 192
Psychopathic Personality Inventory
    (PPI), 192, 193
Psychopathology, 44, 164
Psychopathy, 7-8
    assessment of, 183-202, 185-
        196
    deception and, 196-202
    definition of, 184
    Factor 1 traits of, 200
    Factor 2 traits of, 200
    Rogers, on, 195, 197-198
Psychopathy Checklist-Revised
    (PCL-R), 183, 194, 195-
        196, 199, 200-202, 208
    clinical applications of, 188-190
    Clinical Interview Schedules,
        188
    items on, 185-186
    usage of, 187

Psychopathy Checklist: Screening
    Version (PCL: SV), 190-
        192
Psychopathy Checklist: Youth
    Version (PCL: YV), 193-
        195
Psychopathy Checklists (PCL),
    184, 200
Psychosis, 33, 38, 107
Psychotic disorders, 6
PTA. See Post-traumatic amnesia
PTSD. See Posttraumatic Stress
    Disorder
Pupil dilation, 29
Pusch, August, 141
Putnam, S.H., 110, 131

Quinn, K.M., 169

Random responding, 13, 51
Rarely Missed Index of the
    Wechsler Memory Scale-
    III, 128
Raskin, David, 154, 156-157
Rasputin, Father Gregory, 139-140
Rassin, E., 130
Raven's Standard Progressive
    Matrices (SPM), 179-180
Raw scores, 60
Razani, J., 126
RDS. See Reliable Digit Span
"Real-stimulating" model, 145-146
Recognition Memory Test (RMT),
    110, 128
Rector, N.A., 62
Rehnquist, William, 142
Reid, John, 152
Reiser, Martin, 142
Reliable Digit Span (RDS), 110,
    128, 133
Resnick, P.J., 7, 33-34
Response style, 8

Rey Dot Counting Test, 110
Rey 15-Item Memory Test, 110,
        126, 133, 212
Rey Word Recognition List, 110
Reynolds, S.K., 7
Reznikoff, M., 55
Ricker, J.H., 110
RMT. *See* Recognition Memory
        Test
Rock v. Arkansas, 142
Rock, Vickie, 142
Rogers, R., 5, 9, 48, 62, 69, 76, 91,
        164, 173, 176-177, 179,
        187, 198
    on malingering, 5, 9-10, 112
    on psychological testing, 48,
        173, 176-177
    on psychopathy, 195, 197-198
Rohling, M.L., 111
Rorschach
    empirical studies on, 54-55
    as psychological assessment
        tool, 53-54, 57
    responses, 54
Ross, S.R., 131
Rush, Benjamin, 135-136
Russian Romanov monarchy, 139-
        140
Rutherford, M.J., 189

S. *See* Superlative Self-assessment
        scale
Sadness, 28
Salazar, X., 126
Salekin, R.T., 76, 105, 187
Salpetriere School, 139
Sarfaty, S.D., 109
Scalia, A., 142
SCEH. *See* Society for Clinical and
        Experimental Hypnosis
Scheffer, Edward, 156
Schinka, J.A., 52, 72

Schizophrenia, 6, 34, 94
    detection of, 54
    as measurement, 60
Schlottmann, R.S., 76
Schmidt, M., 109
Schneck, Jerome, 136
Schneider, B., 69
Schretlen, D.J., 53
Schwartz, S.M., 7
SCL-90. *See* Symptom Checklist-
        90-Revised
Scott, A.B., 76
SCR. *See* Electrodermal skin
        response
Sd. *See* Social Desirability Scale
SDE. *See* Self-Deceptive
        Enhancement
SDS-17. *See* Social Desirability
        Scale-17
Seeman, M.V., 62
Self-Deceptive Enhancement
        (SDE), 13-14, 103, 216
Self-monitoring, 206
Self-Report, 124, 131-132, 147,
        157, 169, 192
Self-Report Psychopathy Scale-
        Revised, 193
Self-Report Psychopathy Scale-II
        (SRP-II), 192, 195
SEM. *See* Standard error of
        measurement
SES. *See* Socioeconomic status
Sewell, K.W., 9, 48, 76, 173, 176-
        177, 187
Sex offenders, 9
Sherman, E.M.S., 115, 116, 129
Shipley Institute of Living Scale,
        125
SHT. *See* Single Hallucination Test
Sierles, F.S., 7
Silva, C.E., 146
Simcox, A.M., 63, 112

Simon, B., 146
SIMS. *See* Structured Inventory of
  Malingered
  Symptomatology
Simulation
  anecdotal signs of, 145
  assessment models for, 145-146
Single Hallucination Test (SHT),
  149
Sinnett, E.R., 64
SIRS. *See* Structured Interview of
  Reported Symptoms
Sletten, I.W., 63-64
Slick, D.J., 115, 116, 129
Slobogin, C., 8
Smiles, 29
Smith, C.A., 111
Smith, G.P., 94
Smith, G.T., 7, 63, 70, 78
Smith, H.H., 109
Smith, Pascal B., 140
Smith, S.R., 102
Smith, S.S., 187
Social Desirability (Sd) Scale, 62,
  70, 77-78
Social Desirability Scale-17 (SDS-
  17), 105
Social Introversion, 60
Socialization (So) scale, 192
Socially desirable responding, 13-
  14, 102-106. *See also*
  Marlowe-Crowne Social
  Desirability Scale; Paulhus
  Deception Scales; Social
  Desirability Scale-17
Society for Clinical and
  Experimental Hypnosis
  (SCEH), 136
Socioeconomic status (SES), 62,
  66, 214, 216
Socioeconomic Status (Ss) scale,
  78
Somatoform disorders, 2, 114

Source Amnesia, 150
Specialty Guidelines for Forensic
  Psychologists (Committee
  on Ethical Guidelines for
  Forensic Psychologists),
  164, 181-182
Speech
  content of, 32-33
  pauses in, 24
  quality of, 32
  quantity of, 32
SPM. *See* Raven's Standard
  Progressive Matrices
Spoken cues, 31-36
Squelched expressions, 28, 38
SRP-II. *See* Self-Report
  Psychopathy Scale-II
Ss. *See* Socioeconomic Status scale
Stafford, K.P., 127
Standard error of measurement
  (SEM), 189
State v. Hurd, 142
State v. Pusch, 141
Stein, L.A.R., 176
Stevens, Justice, 156
Stober, J., 102
Storm, J., 72
Strachan, 187
Strong, D.R., 72
Structured Interview of Reported
  Symptoms (SIRS), 43, 48,
  53, 207-208
  Absurd/Improbable Symptoms
  in, 90
  administration of, 91
  for adolescents/children, 173-
  174
  Blatant Symptoms in, 90
  costs associated with, 99
  development of, 89-90
  false symptoms/symptoms and,
  90-91
  interpretation of, 91-92

Structured Interview of Reported
    Symptoms *(Cont'd)*
    items on, 90-91
    Observed v. Reported
        Symptoms in, 90
    Rare Symptoms in, 90
    research on, 92-93
    screening of, 97
    Selectivity of Symptoms in, 90
    Severity of Symptoms in, 90
    strengths of, 99, 105
    studies on, 87-89, 100-101
    Subtle Symptoms in, 90
    Symptom Combinations in, 90
    usage of, 112
Structured Inventory of Malingered
    Symptomatology (SIMS),
    97, 100-101, 174
Studien uber hysterie (Breuer &
    Freud), 135
Stutts, J.T., 169
Substance, 6
Subtle/obvious scales, 76
Superlative Self-assessment (S)
    scale, 77-78
Surreptitious observer design, 146
SVT. *See* Symptom Validity Testing
Swallowing, 27
Sweating, 27
Sweet, J.J., 107, 113
Symptom Checklist-90-Revised
    (SCL-90), 71
Symptom coaching, 169, 172
Symptom reports, 33-35
Symptom Validity Testing (SVT),
    123

Tabern, 140
Tardieau, 138-139
TAT. *See* Thematic Apperception
    Test
Tears, 29

Tehachapi Malingering Scale
    (TMS)
    -AC, 98, 100-101
    development of, 97-98
Teichner, G., 127
Terror, 28
Terry, S., 6
Test of Memory Malingering
    (TOMM), 127
Test of Nonverbal Intelligence, 125
Test-taking Defensiveness (Tt)
    scale, 77
Thelen study, 169
Thematic Apperception Test (TAT),
    55
Thinking, 25, 26
Thiopental. *See* Pentothal
Thomas, Clarence, 156
TMS. *See* Tehachapi Malingering
    Scale
Tombaugh, T.N., 127
Tomicic, T.L., 8
TOMM. *See* Test of Memory
    Malingering
Toupin, J., 195
Trilby (du Maurier), 138
True Response Inconsistency scale
    (TRIN), 70, 71-72, 175
Trueblood, W., 109
Truthfulness, 22
T-scores, 60, 64
Tt. *See* Test-taking Defensiveness
    scale

Ulstad, K.L., 48
United States (U.S.)
    Court of Appeals for the District
        of Columbia, 129
    hypnosis in, 136, 140-143
    legal systems, 140-143
University of Vienna, 135
University of Wisconsin, 136

U.S. *See* United States
U.S. Air Force Court of Criminal
    Appeals, 156
U.S. Congress' Office of
    Technology Assessment,
    155
U.S. Supreme Court, 142, 156, 157
U.S. v. Galbreth, 156
U.S. v. Scheffer, 156

Validity Indicator Profile (VIP), 89,
    125, 133
Vallabhajosula, B., 126, 128
van Gorp, W., 126, 128
Variable Response Inconsistency
    Scale (VRIN), 65, 70-71,
    81, 175, 193, 216
Veteran's Administration, 189
Victoria Symptom Validity Test
    (VSVT), 98, 126
  comparison of, 100-101
  cross-validation of, 111
Viglione, D.J., Jr., 54
Violence, 6
VIP. *See* Validity Indicator Profile
Vogt, A.T., 109
Voice cues, 24, 30, 38
Volbrecht, M., 110, 129, 132
Volwiler, 140
Vrij, A., 26, 31
VRIN. *See* Variable Response
    Inconsistency Scale
VSVT. *See* Victoria Symptom
    Validity Test

Wagner, M.T., 127
WAIS-III. *See* Wechsler Adult
    Intelligence Scale-Third
    Edition
Walters, G.D., 5
Walters, G.L., 74, 76
Waner-Chacon, K., 126
Wang, E.W., 48

Ward, R., 9
Wasyliw, O.E., 56
Watkins, John G., 148-149
Watkins, M.M., 198
Waud, S.P., 10
Wayne County General Hospital,
    136
Weaver, C.M., 63-64, 66, 69, 73
Webb, J.T., 67
Wechsler Adult Intelligence Scale-
    Third Edition (WAIS-III),
    87, 88, 133, 210
Wechsler Memory Scale
    -III Working Memory Index,
    210
    -Revised, 128
Wechsler Scales, 128
Wetter, M.W., 7, 63, 70, 78
White, 142
Whites, 187
Wiggins, J.S., 70, 77
Williams, C.L., 69, 176
Williamson, 187
Wisconsin Card Sorting Test, 123,
    128
WMT. *See* Word Memory Test
Women, 11-12, 67, 187
Wong, S., 189
Word Association Test, 55
Word Memory Test (WMT), 111,
    127, 212, 214
Words, 31
World's Fair of 1889, 139

Yaeger, H., 32
Yale University, 136
Young, P.C., 137
Young, R., 32
Youngjohn, J.R., 110

Zamansky, H.S., 147
Zapf, P.A., 98
Zani v. State, 142

If You Found This Book Useful . . .

You might want to know more about our other titles.

If you would like to receive our latest catalog, please return this form:

Name: _____
(Please Print)

Address: _____

Address: _____

City/State/Zip: _____
This is ☐ home ☐ office

Telephone: (_____)_____

E-mail: _____

Fax: (_____) _____

I am a:

☐   Psychologist   ☐   Mental Health Counselor
☐   Psychiatrist   ☐   Marriage and Family Therapist
☐   Attorney   ☐   Not in Mental Health Field
☐   Clinical Social Worker ☐   Other: _____

◆   ◆   ◆

Professional Resource Press
P.O. Box 15560
Sarasota, FL 34277-1560

Telephone: 800-443-3364
FAX: 941-343-9201
E-mail: orders@prpress.com
Website: http://www.prpress.com

Add A Colleague To Our Mailing List . . .

If you would like us to send our latest catalog to one of your colleagues, please return this form:

Name: _____
(Please Print)

Address: _____

Address: _____

City/State/Zip: _____
This is ❒ home ❒ office

Telephone: (_____)_____

E-mail: _____

Fax: (_____) _____

This person is a:

❒ Psychologist   ❒ Mental Health Counselor
❒ Psychiatrist   ❒ Marriage and Family Therapist
❒ Attorney   ❒ Not in Mental Health Field
❒ Clinical Social Worker   ❒ Other: _____

Name of person completing this form: _____

◆   ◆   ◆

Professional Resource Press
P.O. Box 15560
Sarasota, FL 34277-1560

Telephone: 800-443-3364
FAX: 941-343-9201
E-mail: orders@prpress.com
Website: http://www.prpress.com